Conrad Without Borders

Conrad Without Borders

Transcultural and Transtextual Perspectives

Edited by
Brendan Kavanagh, Grażyna Maria Teresa Branny,
and Agnieszka Adamowicz-Pośpiech

BLOOMSBURY ACADEMIC
LONDON • NEW YORK • OXFORD • NEW DELHI • SYDNEY

BLOOMSBURY ACADEMIC
Bloomsbury Publishing Plc
50 Bedford Square, London, WC1B 3DP, UK
1385 Broadway, New York, NY 10018, USA
29 Earlsfort Terrace, Dublin 2, Ireland

BLOOMSBURY, BLOOMSBURY ACADEMIC and the Diana logo are
trademarks of Bloomsbury Publishing Plc

First published in Great Britain 2023

Typeset by Newgen KnowledgeWorks Pvt. Ltd., Chennai, India

To find out more about our authors and books visit www.bloomsbury.com
and sign up for our newsletters.

Contents

Figures

Abbreviations

References to Conrad's works in this volume are to *The Cambridge Edition of the Works of Joseph Conrad* where volumes are available. Otherwise, they are to Dent's *The Collected Edition of the Works of Joseph Conrad*, 22 volumes (London: J. M. Dent & Sons, 1946–55), identified as [D]. The standard abbreviations of the titles of Conrad's works as used in the volume are cited below. Citations in the text of Conrad's letters (*CL*) come from *The Collected Letters of Joseph Conrad*, edited by Laurence Davies et al., nine volumes (Cambridge: Cambridge University Press, 1983–2008). References to contemporary reviews (*CR*) are to *Contemporary Reviews*, edited by Allan H. Simmons, John G. Peters, and J. H. Stape, four volumes (Cambridge: Cambridge University Press, 2012).

AF	"Amy Foster"
CL	*The Collected Letters of Joseph Conrad*
CR	*Contemporary Reviews*
F	"Falk"
HD	"Heart of Darkness"
LE	*Last Essays*
LJ	*Lord Jim*
MS	*The Mirror of the Sea*
N	*Nostromo*
NLL	*Notes on Life and Letters*
NN	*The Nigger of the "Narcissus"*
OI	*An Outcast of the Islands*
OP	"An Outpost of Progress"
PR	*A Personal Record*
SA	*The Secret Agent*
SS	"The Secret Sharer"
SoS	*A Set of Six*
TH	*Tales of Hearsay*
TLS	*'Twixt Land and Sea*
T	"Typhoon"
TS	*Typhoon and Other Stories*

TU	*Tales of Unrest*
UWE	*Under Western Eyes*
V	*Victory*
WT	*Within the Tides*
Y	"Youth"
YS	*Youth: A Narrative, and Two Other Stories*

Acknowledgments

The editors and publisher gratefully acknowledge the permission granted to reproduce the copyright material in this book. The editors also extend their gratitude to Dr. Keith Carabine of Canterbury University, Prof. Jan Gordon of Tokyo University, and Prof. Gill J. Holland of Dartmoor College for the time, passion, and professionalism that they put into advising a number of our contributors. Our thanks for professional guidance and advice as well as moral support, likewise, go to our senior contributors, Prof. Laurence Davies, Prof. Jakob Lothe, Prof. Robert Hampson, Prof. Anne Luyat, and Prof. Stephen W. G. Brodsky.

Prof. Grażyna M. T. Branny would like to express her gratitude to the Consulate General of the Republic of Poland in New York City for a generous all-inclusive invitation to speak on-site in commemoration of the 160th anniversary of Conrad's birth as part of the Polish Government project "Conrad Year 2017." The Commemorative Address she delivered within the framework of the Conference of the Conrad Society of America at Fordham University on June 2, 2017, prefigured the overarching themes of this project. Dr. Brendan Kavanagh extends his gratitude to Prof. Jolanta Dudek and Prof. Andrzej Juszczyk of the Joseph Conrad Research Center at the Jagiellonian University in Kraków for hosting the project research in 2019–20. Dr. Kavanagh would also like to thank the Polish-US Fulbright Commission for funding his research in Poland from March through September 2019. He is similarly grateful to the Kosciuszko Foundation for sponsoring the second phase of the research from November 2019 through March 2020.

Finally, we would like to thank our proofreader, Dr. Aeddan Shaw of the Jagiellonian University in Kraków, for his rapid and efficient work on the volume. Special gratitude is due to Jesuit University Ignatianum in Kraków for funding the proofreading process. Last, but not least, we are extremely grateful to Prof. Ewa Kujawska-Lis of the University of Warmia and Mazury for her technical support in formatting the volume and to the remaining members of the foundation group of this project—which apart from the editors included Prof. Joanna Skolik of the University of Opole and Prof. Karol Samsel of the University of Warsaw—for their intellectual input and availability at all times.

Preface

The volume *Conrad Without Borders: Transcultural and Transtextual Perspectives* has emerged as a product of a collaborative effort of the volume's editors and the project's foundation group—members of the Polish Joseph Conrad Society at the Joseph Conrad Research Center of the Jagiellonian University in Kraków. The original inspiration for the volume came from the Commemorative Address by Grażyna M. T. Branny, commissioned by the Polish government and delivered at the Consulate General of the Republic of Poland in New York City to mark the 160th anniversary of Conrad's birth. Her address prefigured the overarching themes of this volume: Conrad's artistry and building transtextual and transcultural bridges in Conrad studies, which at that intitial stage referred primarily to Polish and Anglo-American Conradology—the former mostly given to the study of Conrad's Polish heritage at the expense of literary criticism proper and the latter often undervaluing this heritage, sometimes misinterpreting it, or underestimating its role for Conrad's aesthetics. The present transcultural and transdisciplinary aspects of the project were conceived by Brendan Kavanagh, who proposed the writing of the volume and developed a framework for an inclusive showcasing of border-crossing scholarship. A further expansion of the project, to accommodate transmediality, came from Agnieszka Adamowicz-Pośpiech and Brendan Kavanagh. The resulting volume, which comprises the work of sixteen contributors in all, has brought together Conrad scholarship from across the globe—from the East (with authors from Taiwan, China, and Japan) and West (contributors from the United Kingdom, France, and the United States of America); from the North (critics from Norway and Canada) and South (a scholar from India); and from Poland—Conrad's motherland—geographically located in the middle of the four directions—at the very heart of Europe. As the chapters of this transcultural and transtextual volume demonstrate, the meaning of Conrad's prose is "not inside like a kernel but outside, enveloping the tale which brought it out only as a glow brings out a haze, in the likeness of one of these misty halos that sometimes are made visible by the spectral illumination of moonshine" (HD 50).

Introduction

Brendan Kavanagh, Grażyna M. T. Branny, and
Agnieszka Adamowicz-Pośpiech

Conrad Without Borders aims to reassess Conrad's aesthetic and transcultural consciousness as well as build bridges in Conrad studies by bringing together previously disparate fields of Conrad scholarship. The book discusses Joseph Conrad's texts across aesthetic, geographical, and disciplinary boundaries, with the following objectives in mind:

1. To highlight a diverse range of Conrad's existing and emergent cultural affiliations, while speaking to urgent debates regarding transculturalism, transnationalism, translation, borders, geopolitics, and mediality.
2. To bridge the gap between Anglo-American and Polish forms of Conrad studies, yet situate such bridging within wider transcultural considerations.
3. To provide a more nuanced account of the influence of Polish historical, cultural, and literary contexts on the texture and artistry of Conrad's narratives, while bringing more textual analysis back to Conrad criticism.
4. To formulate a timely remapping of the passages of Conrad's narratives across cultural, national, and disciplinary borders at a geopolitical moment that has witnessed the recrudescence of national boundaries.
5. To place renewed emphasis on scholarly inclusion, by cooperating with Conrad scholars from a number of world areas.

The book's overarching concerns are first explained. Next, this introduction dwells on two of the original objectives of the book: a reassessment of Conrad's artistry and the texture of his oeuvres as compared to their content, and helping to bridge the gap between Anglo-American and Polish Conrad studies. Subsequently, the book's transcultural framework is explicated, within which a transnational networking of emergent border-crossing scholarship is generated. Finally, the content of each individual chapter and its relevance to the book's objectives are detailed, in order to identify implicit connections between chapters and the rationale behind the book's organization.

* * *

One of the principal intentions behind this book (apart from transtextuality and transculturalism) has been to bring out the essence of Conrad's artistic imagination in accordance with the writer's own expectations and directives voiced in his paratexts, with regard to the artistic texture of his writings and the precedence of form over content in his works. As pertinently highlighted by Jakob Lothe in his seminal study *Conrad's Narrative Method* (1991),

> Most Conrad criticism to date appears to have proceeded from the critical assumption ... that literary content precedes the form ... [M]y book focuses instead on Conrad's narrative method as a most significant constituent aspect of his fiction. It also includes comments on the intriguing interplay of form and content in Conrad, or more specifically of narrative method and the thematics this method helps to shape. (1991: 1–2)

The present study has precisely taken up the challenge of demonstrating the mechanics of that "intriguing interplay of form and content" in Conrad's oeuvres and how this creates the "thematics" of his fiction, especially on the level of language (Ewa Kujawska-Lis), artistic devices (Laurence Davies, Grażyna M. T. Branny), or narrative method (Jakob Lothe, Anne Luyat, Karol Samsel). As pointed out in Grażyna M. T. Branny's commemorative address "How Much Conrad in Conrad Criticism?" (2018):

> Given the level of artistry of Conrad's oeuvres and his insistence on the importance of art in his fiction, it may seem surprising that so many interpretations of Conrad's works appear to be quite literal, resplendent with geographical identification of his exotic locations, classification of his characters' psychological states, mindsets and moral attitudes, as well as cataloguing of his father figures, women, villains ... animals, etc. The explanation of this phenomenon should perhaps be sought for in the historical, geographical, and cultural tangibilities of his settings as well as his experience "'twixt land and sea" in the remotest corners of the globe. (2018: 42)

However, apart from those tangibilities of Conrad's own settings, the precedence of content over form in Conrad criticism, quite contrary to the writer's

recommendations, seems to be mostly a matter of ideological conditioning—
that is, subjecting Conrad's narrative to the dictates of current ideologies to the
exclusion of "close reading" and Conrad's aesthetics. Since Jakob Lothe's seminal
study, and with Laurence Davies, Robert Hampson, Allan Simmons, Jeremy
Hawthorn (1990), and Michael Greaney (2001), Conrad criticism returned to
textual analysis: more recently with critics like Katherine Baxter (2018), Nidesh
Lawtoo (2016), Yael Levin (2008), Julie Napolin (2020), and Tania Zulli (2019),
even if oftentimes, this critical shift is inevitably overshadowed by current
ideologies.

Conrad's own impatience with downplaying the artistry of his fiction at the
expense of its literal understanding was voiced by him in his April 24, 1922,
letter to Richard Curle:

> *Explicitness, my dear fellow, is fatal to the glamour of all artistic work, robbing it*
> *of all suggestiveness, destroying all illusion.* You seem to believe in literalness and
> explicitness, in facts and also in expression. Yet nothing is more clear than the
> utter insignificance of explicit statement and also its power to call attention away
> from things that matter in the region of art. (*CL7* 457; emphasis added)

The publishers' and editors' lack of understanding for the artistic aspect of
Conrad's works surfaced, not infrequently, in connection with their serialization
when they insisted on cuts—as, for instance, in the case of "A Smile of Fortune"
or "Freya of the Seven Isles." In his November 17, 1910, letter to his editors,
Beaumont (and then to Pinker), the writer complains about the prospective
alterations to "the inner texture" of "A Smile of Fortune," which distort his
"art of expression" (*CL9* 148). As a result, the tale was only restored back to its
original version in 2007. "Freya of the Seven Isles" was rejected by *Century*, an
American magazine, for lack of a more optimistic ending (Billy 1997: 265, n27).
In an August 4, 1911 letter to his editor Edward Garnett, Conrad replied in no
uncertain terms: "As to faking a 'sunny' ending to my story I would see all the
American Magazines and all the american [*sic*] Editors damned in heaps before
lifting my pen for the task" (*CL4* 469).

Neglect of Conrad's artistry has likewise been an uncommendable attribute
of Conrad studies in Poland, albeit for entirely different reasons—patriotic,
historical, and ideological rather than aesthetic. On account of Conrad's Polish
origins and the tragic fate of Poland at the hands of the three partitioning powers
of Russia, Prussia, and Austria, with the country wiped off the map of Europe
for eighty-five years at the time of the writer's birth and throughout all but the
final six years of his life (123 years in total), he has been mostly studied in Poland

with a view to the biographical, historical, cultural, ideological, or ethical aspects of his works. This is being remedied in this book by the three Polish authors mentioned above, who discuss the aesthetic aspects of Conrad's oeuvres within the transtextual, transcultural, and bridging framework of the present book.

At the other end of the bridging process undertaken by this book comes a wider recognition by Anglo-American critics of the significance of Conrad's Polish historical, cultural, and literary heritage for the artistic texture of his oeuvres, an issue that has, more often than not, been downplayed, undervalued, or misunderstood in Western scholarship to date, as stressed in his *Joseph Conrad's Polish Soul* (2016) by a Canadian scholar with Polish Borderland roots, like Conrad's own, G. W. Stephen Brodsky. He emphasizes the one-sidedness of some of the Western interpretations of Conrad: "Largely restricted in knowledge and sentiment to their own cultural tradition, Western critics found it mirrored in the Conrad canon against the dark background of a Polish cultural *terra incognita*. This neglect of Conrad's centuries-old heritage resulted in some grotesque interpretations." Therefore, G. W. Stephen Brodsky calls for an "overdue" need "for redress of a critical imbalance," with Polish Conrad scholarship filling the gaps, supplying missing links, and correcting some Western views on Conrad's writing (2016: 48–9). In this book, the latter call is addressed by Joanna Skolik with her interpretation of *Under Western Eyes* from the perspective of the Polish historical experience.

G. W. Stephen Brodsky's plea addressed to Western scholarship to resolve the issue of the insufficient awareness of the role and importance of the writer's Polish roots (2016: 47–8) is addressed in the present book by such notable Anglo-American critics as Jakob Lothe, Laurence Davies, Anne Luyat, Robert Hampson, and George Z. Gasyna in their transtextual and transcultural discussions of the influence of the historical and literary aspects of Conrad's Polish heritage on "the inner texture" of Conrad's writings. This is done with regard to Conrad's aesthetics by Jakob Lothe, Laurence Davies, and Anne Luyat, and his thematics by Robert Hampson and George Z. Gasyna, rather than—as has mostly been done to date—with respect to the tangible or factual details with Polish overtones in those to be found in Conrad's fiction (cf. Jean M. Szczypien's "*Sailing towards Poland*" *with Joseph Conrad*, 2017; Maya Jasanoff's *The Dawn Watch: Joseph Conrad in a Global World*, 2017). In doing so, Jakob Lothe, Laurence Davies, Anne Luyat, Robert Hampson, and George Z. Gasyna demonstrate how Conrad's Polish identity is in one way or another "inscribed and reinscribed into the content and form of his oeuvre" (Branny 2018: 48).

* * *

Past critical accounts of a transcultural Conrad have implemented a combination of approaches that could broadly be called anthropological and ethnographic (Griffith 1995; Armstrong 1996); postcolonial and linguistic (GoGwilt 2013; Zulli 2019); and Polish-cultural (Krajka 2018). The transcultural framework of the present book incorporates elements of such approaches, but departs from existing scholarship through a more intensive consideration of Conrad's transcultural form, which we define as Conrad's formal and narrative generation of implicit textual pathways for the articulation of *trans*-cultural perspectives. The collection therefore takes its cue from the influential writings of Robert Hampson, who aptly writes that Conrad's "foregrounding of writing, reading, and the production of narrative" "repeatedly confronts the issue that was to become so important in twentieth-century anthropology: how to describe another culture" (2000: 1). Robert Hampson's "historical formalism" (2012: 5) extends John Griffith's ethnographic discussion of Conrad's engagement with the "dilemma" "of bridging cultural divides," but also challenges Griffith's conclusion that "Conrad writes pessimistically of ethnocentricity as a natural, if undesirable condition of humanity" (Griffith 1995: 56, 17).

The contrast between Griffith's and Robert Hampson's works is illustrative because it informs the transcultural motivation of this book. According to Griffith, Conrad's narratives highlight "the incompatibility of ethical or cultural norms" (1995: 188); as an example, Griffith quotes Marlow's description of Jim's death in *Lord Jim*: "People had trusted [Jim] with their lives ... and yet they could never, as he had said, never be made to understand him" (409). Jim's death thus "occurs largely as a result of cultural misunderstanding" (Griffith 1995: 188); Griffith here echoes John Batchelor's argument that *Lord Jim* dramatizes "an unbridgeable gulf between the races" (Batchelor 1983: 143). But Griffith and Batchelor both tilt attention to the content, rather than form, of Conrad's text. As Robert Hampson insightfully points out, Marlow's narrative is formally composed of European and Malay gossip and stories, such as Jewel's and Sura's stories of Jim. Malay stories "circulate within the novel as part of a larger world of stories which exists beyond the limits of the novel" and "gesture towards" "consciousnesses that cannot be expressed through the circulation of European male discourses" (Hampson 2000: 133, 134, 143).[1] The very form of *Lord Jim* thus constitutes a latent pathway for the articulation of transcultural identification and passage.

The distinction between Griffith's and Robert Hampson's readings also draws out an apparent antinomy in Conrad's writings. On the one hand, the contents of Conrad's narratives often "dramatize a pervasive state of cultural solipsism" (Armstrong 1996: 22) and present seemingly unbridgeable divides between cultures and races. To quote the narrator of *An Outcast of the Islands* (1896), "Hate filled the world, filled the space between them—the hate of race, the hate of hopeless diversity, the hate of blood" (*OI* 359). On the other hand, Conrad's Preface to *The Nigger of the "Narcissus"* speaks to "the latent feeling of fellowship with all creation" and "the subtle but invincible conviction of solidarity that knits together the loneliness of innumerable hearts" (*NN* xii). In his 1895 Author's Note to *Almayer's Folly*, Conrad states, "And there is a bond between us and that humanity so far away. I am speaking here of men and women ... possessed of all refinements, of all sensibilities, of all wisdom" (vi–vii).

From Griffith's point of view, this antinomy is "irreconcilable" (1995: 187). But readers may remember here Conrad's oft-quoted August 1901 letter to the *New York Times "Saturday Review"*: "The only legitimate basis of creative work lies in the courageous recognition of all the irreconcilable antagonisms that make our life so enigmatic, so burdensome, so fascinating, so dangerous— so full of hope" (*CL2* 348). A "courageous recognition" of an apparent irreconcilability between different cultural norms, languages, and value systems energizes Conrad's engagements with the problematics of writing against the grain of cultural, national, and linguistic divisions. An apt example is Conrad's "Typhoon" (1902), which depicts Captain MacWhirr's decision to stop the fighting on board ship during "dirty weather" (21). In simply "do[ing] what's fair, for all" (88), MacWhirr actualizes an ethical obligation to recognize the worsening climatological plight of the Chinese "coolies" below deck, amid significant cultural and linguistic barriers to comprehension.

Furthermore, as Robert Hampson's reading of *Lord Jim* demonstrates, a tension between cultural heritage and transcultural identification is constitutive of the substance of Conrad's writings. To quote Benita Parry, Conrad's narrative forms "allude to a reality that lies beyond" the "epistemologically constrained field[s] of vision" of the fiction's narrators and characters (2005: 41, 50). The chapters of this book gather transcultural and transdisciplinary perspectives made possible by the rich potentiality of Conrad's narrative forms—which continually offer readers latent textual passageways for the crossing of cultural and disciplinary boundaries. In so doing, the contributors recognize Conrad's awareness of consciousnesses beyond "the circulation of European male discourses," to recall

Robert Hampson's phrasing, but also seek to bring out transcultural affiliations beyond the Malay (Narugopal Mukherjee, Gloria Kwok Kan Lee, Ewa Kujawska-Lis, G. W. Stephen Brodsky). This book's writers therefore draw on a conviction that Conrad's narratives speak to readers for whom cultural and disciplinary diversity is "so full of hope."

Building on Christopher GoGwilt's emphasis of Conrad's "translingual, transcultural medium of English" (2013: 5), this collection places renewed emphasis on Conrad's textures. However, the following chapters decisively shift critical consideration of a transcultural Conrad from a basis in ethnography and linguistics to a focus on the transtextual—or "all that sets" Conrad's texts "in a relationship, whether obvious or concealed, with other texts," to use Gérard Genette's oft-quoted phrasing (1997: 1). The tracing of transtextual connections—among Conrad's works and various media forms, world narratives, and philosophies—allows authors to make manifest certain transcultural valences that thus far have remained implicit within Conrad's writings. In crossing national and disciplinary boundaries, the contributors bridge existing gaps between schools of Conrad criticism from different corners of the world in order to provide fresh accounts of present-day critical, theoretical, and political issues—including counter-narrativity and strategies of resistance (George Z. Gasyna, Pei-Wen Clio Kao), postcolonialism, sovereignty and hybridity (G. W. Stephen Brodsky, George Z. Gasyna, Narugopal Mukherjee), and political violence and geopolitics (Gerard Kilroy, Narugopal Mukherjee).

The more political chapters certainly retain the anti-imperialist textual politics of Parry's and Edward Said's postcolonial versions of Conrad studies,[2] yet the book's overall approach also incorporates what Rob Nixon calls an interdisciplinarity of "edge effects"—whereby "interpenetrating fields proliferate at the borders between once separate disciplines, at times creating new dynamic combinations" (2011: 30). In their own ways, the contributors demonstrate how Conrad's narratives become corridors that connect various disciplines, including transmediality (Laurence Davies, Anne Luyat, Agnieszka Adamowicz-Pośpiech, Gloria Kwok Kan Lee), comparative literature (Karol Samsel, Grażyna M. T. Branny, Pei-Wen Clio Kao, G. W. Stephen Brodsky), history (Jakob Lothe, Laurence Davies, Anne Luyat, Robert Hampson, Joanna Skolik), media studies (Agnieszka Adamowicz-Pośpiech, Kazumichi Enokida), and philosophy (Jakob Lothe, Karol Samsel, Pei-Wen Clio Kao, Gloria Kwok Kan Lee, George Z. Gasyna). Writers thereby work outside of inherited definitions of the postcolonial in order to open up new perspectives of resistance toward forms of imperialism, autocracy, colonial hegemony, and state-sponsored terrorism. Because the book's framework aims to be inclusive, the book has incorporated a range of individual research concerns; for this very reason, the concluding section of this Introduction traces relations between chapters and explains how each chapter fits into the greater text.

The editors of this book also would like to acknowledge the importance of the *Conrad: Eastern and Western Perspectives* series edited by Wiesław Krajka.[3] The international authorship of Krajka's volumes has shed new light on Conrad's Polish heritage and the role of Polish historical and cultural contexts for his writings, while also opening up discussion of transcultural topics.[4] Following Krajka's work, the present collection seeks to extend the thought of Zdzisław Najder: "To understand what [Conrad's] work means … in terms of what is the full implied cultural context of his work (its linguistic resources, literary forms and symbols, themes and motifs, etc.) we have to learn something about his national and social background" (Najder 1964: 1). Amar Acheraïou has suggested that Najder thus "offer[s] an exclusive picture of Conrad," because he "tends to accord a lion's share to Conrad's Polish cultural and social background" (Acheraïou 2009: 43). Yet Najder rather points out that the reconsideration of Conrad's Polish cultural and literary heritage opens an important route into "the full implied cultural context of his work." The present book validates Najder's words since Conrad's own Polish heritage exists in constitutive tension with his transcultural sensibility. Robert Hampson's chapter, for example, shows how Conrad's wider oeuvre manifests such tension, by its discussion of "Prince Roman" (1910) alongside "The Warrior's Soul" (1916). Across the chapters of this book, a composite reinterpretation of Conrad's Polish heritage paves the way for wider discussion of political issues and concerns of importance to all present-day Conradians, particularly those interested in decolonizing Western European or Anglo-American conceptions of Conrad the writer.

* * *

Conrad Without Borders: Transcultural and Transtextual Perspectives falls into three major parts: "Transtextual and Transcultural Bridges," "Transmedial and Transnational Negotiations," and "Transtextual and Transcultural Politics." The book opens with a chapter on Conrad's narrative strategies, titled "Conrad's Triple Perspective: History, Memory, Fiction," in which Jakob Lothe draws on Gérard Genette's distinction between narrative voice and perspective to show how Conrad's narrative perspective blends his Polish cultural heritage with his transcultural experience as a sailor and a creative writer. With respect to

Conrad's Polishness, Jakob Lothe's areas of focus include Conrad's childhood exposure to Russian tzarist imperialism and his inheritance of an ethos of honor. Jakob Lothe demonstrates how these two concerns inflect Conrad's narratives of maritime journeys throughout imperial networks of global transit in "Heart of Darkness" (1899) and *Lord Jim* (1900), and thereby argues for the two texts' mutual supplementation and enrichment.

Chapter 2 in Part 1, "Conrad as a Reader of Adam Mickiewicz's *Grażyna*," expands the focus on narrative methods. Karol Samsel concentrates on Adam Mickiewicz's epic poem *Grażyna* (1823), the importance of which Conrad emphasized in his 1914 interview with the Polish journalist Marian Dąbrowski. Karol Samsel argues that the stylistics of Mickiewicz's narrative poem provide a source for a number of ideas, narrative techniques, and literary devices throughout Conrad's texts (especially *Lord Jim*, "Typhoon," *Chance*, and "The Secret Sharer"). Such techniques include the layering of multiple narrative perspectives, the dramatization of a heroine's virtual voicelessness, the primary narrator's delayed introduction, polyphonic and gapped narration, mirrorings of character, and consciousness of the textual medium in which these devices are employed. As emphasized by Karol Samsel, the reading of Mickiewicz's influence calls for a transcultural awareness, whereby overlapping texts (and models of national literatures) constitute intertwined threadings within a multicultural fabric (the dynamics of which bring us close to René Wellek's notion of *Weltliteratur*). Karol Samsel's essay is also the first of a number of chapters that address Conrad's transtextuality.

Chapter 3, titled "An Epistemological and Denegative Reinterpretation in the Faulknerian Context of Conrad's Malay Tale 'The Planter of Malata,'" centers on the narrative form, texture, and literary aesthetics of Conrad's 1914 tale from the volume *Within the Tides*. Grażyna M. T. Branny formulates a transtextual and transcultural connection between Conrad's narrative method in "The Planter of Malata" and the narrative method of denegation (assertion of presence by absence and vice versa) employed in William Faulkner's *Absalom, Absalom!* and *The Sound and the Fury*, putting forward a legitimate claim of Conrad's precursorship in its use. Through her identification of denegation in Conrad's tale, Grażyna M. T. Branny invalidates the generally accepted reading of the story's ending, offering an epistemological reinterpretation of "The Planter of Malata." The content of Grażyna M. T. Branny's chapter anticipates Pei-Wen Clio Kao's comparison of Conrad and Faulkner in the next chapter as well as George Z. Gasyna's and G. W. Stephen Brodsky's engagements with the postcolonial topics in Part 3 of the book.

Chapter 4, by Pei-Wen Clio Kao, titled "The Power 'not to': Agambenian Thought in Conrad's *Victory* and Faulkner's *Intruder in the Dust*," analyzes characters of peripheral social status in both novels in the context of Giorgio Agamben's philosophy of "inoperativity" and "im/potentiality." Through placing the figures of Ms. Schomberg and Lucas Beauchaump alongside one another, Pei-Wen Clio Kao shows that both Conrad and Faulkner undermine hierarchical structures of power and thereby "render the production of dialectical relations inoperative." Pei-Wen Clio Kao then explicates these characters' wielding of the power "not to" do—an ability to exist within topologies of liminal space, between action/inaction and humanity/inhumanity, in resistance to gendered and racialized hierarchies that attempt to pin down the marginalized and the oppressed. In this respect, Pei-Wen Clio Kao's chapter anticipates George Z. Gasyna's discussion of "dangerous subjects" and Gerard Kilroy's discussion of Winnie as a marginalized figure in Part 3.

Chapter 5, which is the last chapter in Part 1, titled "'*Ich bin nicht einer von euch*': Language as a Tool to Construct the Identities of Conrad's German-Speaking Characters," by Ewa Kujawska-Lis, applies a transcultural linguistics approach to Conrad's writing of German dialogue in *Lord Jim* (1900), "Falk" (1903), and *Victory* (1915), thereby showing how Conrad's narratives incorporate variegated German idiolects (or stylized versions of habitual speech). As Ewa Kujawska-Lis demonstrates, Conrad's writing of the English speech of German individuals employs dialectal variations. She also shows that Conrad adjusts the language of transtextual characters to their functions in particular novels (as in the character of Schomberg, who appears in both "Falk" and *Victory*). Ewa Kujawska-Lis's chapter adds to the ongoing critical conversation regarding the breadth of Conrad's linguistic and meta-linguistic awareness.

Part 2 of the book opens with Chapter 6, by Laurence Davies, titled, "Time, Place, Scale, and Decorum: Conrad and the Polish Romantic Drama," which discusses Conrad's literary inheritance from Polish Romantic drama. Laurence Davies pays specific attention to the importance of Adam Mickiewicz's *Forefathers' Eve* (1823), Juliusz Słowacki's *Kordian* (1833), and Zygmunt Krasiński's *The Undivine Comedy* (1835), all of which focus intensely on national solidarity, shared suffering, and a paradoxical blending of traditional values with wild experimentation. As Laurence Davies points out, Conrad's writing and these works share such attributes as a dynamic sense of scale, consciousness of immense natural agencies and processes, awareness of spectral and metaphysical forces, and evocation of the absurd and the satirical. Laurence Davies's text is significant because his discussion surveys Conrad's Polish Romantic heritage in a way that makes it accessible to non-Polish Conrad readership. Laurence Davies's chapter is one of the central chapters of the book, because it bridges the transtextual and transcultural Part 1 with the discussion of the transmedial and transnational in Part 2.

Anne Luyat's Chapter 7, titled "The 'Curve' of Time: Modes of Imaginative Inquiry in *Under Western Eyes*," considers Conrad's political novel alongside Juliusz Słowacki's dramatization of the inhuman conditions of Siberian coal mines and Russian tzarist labor camps in *Anhelli* (1838). Anne Luyat's essay accentuates *Under Western Eyes*'s use of the burlesque, or reverse comic mode, specifically with regard to the narrative's retelling of Peter Ivanovitch's dramatic escape from a tzarist prison camp. For Anne Luyat, Conrad's application of the burlesque is an implicit response to the problem of conveying the extent of Russian tzarist oppression in the Siberian camps. In support of this argument, Anne Luyat emphasizes the difficulty that Słowacki's *Anhelli* has presented to many Western European or Anglo-American readers (for whom the brutal reality of the Russian camps escapes comprehension). Anne Luyat concludes by highlighting the last entry of Razumov's journal, in which "words disintegrate into an indelible black smear of solitude, terror and pain," creating "a tragedy of silence that is not unlike Słowacki's *Anhelli*." For Anne Luyat, such a juxtaposition exposes a far more horrifying truth of tzarist oppression than might otherwise have been imagined by "the residents of the polite and well governed city of Geneva"—which aligns this chapter's theme and approach with critical consideration of the difference between truth and post-truth in the twenty-first-century world. Anne Luyat's chapter extends Laurence Davies's transtextual discussion of Conrad's prose hinging on Polish Romantic drama; more significantly, her text formulates an intricate interpretation of Conrad's communication of traumatic truths across cultural boundaries and barriers.

Chapter 8, by Agnieszka Adamowicz-Pośpiech, titled "Conrad's Afterlife: Adaptations of Conrad's Biography in Contemporary Polish Culture," discusses the process of incorporating the facts from Conrad's life into Polish culture. Agnieszka Adamowicz-Pośpiech examines current transformations of Conrad's biography and thereby traces the recent evolution of Conrad's status in Polish culture. In so doing, Agnieszka Adamowicz-Pośpiech discusses three types of reworkings of the writer's life and legacy: the retelling of the writer's life in order to produce literary works of lasting artistic merit (e.g., Andrzej Braun's short story "The North Sea"); theatrical adaptations of Conrad's biography (such as Villqist's drama *Conrad*); and forms of popular culture (including Łukasz Godlewski and Maciej Jasiński's comic book *The Thrilling Tales of Joseph Conrad*; the graphic installation of *Conrad: The Nostromo Passenger*; and the advertising film *Joseph Conrad: A Pole, a Catholic, and a Gentleman*). Her essay articulates a transtextual assessment of Conrad's absorption into contemporary Polish culture across various media forms.

Chapter 9, titled "Communication with Marconi's Electric Waves: Conrad and Wireless Telegraphy," using an intermedial approach, which considers the medial capacities of literary writing alongside those of alternative media, Kazumichi Enokida explores Conrad's responses to early-twentieth-century communicational environs of wireless signals, Marconi "installations," and "electric waves." Kazumichi Enokida first compares Conrad's discussions of wireless telegraphy to narrative interrogations of wireless communication in H. G. Wells's *The First Men in the Moon* (1901) and Rudyard Kipling's "Wireless" (1902). Through these comparisons, Kazumichi Enokida highlights Conrad's initial ambivalence toward the communicational possibilities of wireless telegraphy. Furthermore, Kazumichi Enokida explicates the complexity of Conrad's response to telegraphic media, through rereading Conrad's late essay "The Unlighted Coast" (1917). Kazumichi Enokida argues that Conrad, in his late para-textual writings, finally embraced the potentiality of wireless as a means of reimagining the workings of his own creative process. Kazumichi Enokida thereby shows how Conrad's later statements of his art reflect the historically contingent intermedial relations that developed between literature and wireless telegraphy circa 1917.

The final two essays in Part 2 investigate a transcultural reception of the translations of Conrad's works. A transtextual analysis of the 1930s Chinese translations of "Youth," *Lord Jim*, *The Nigger of the "Narcissus,"* and *"Typhoon" and Other Stories* forms the subject of Chapter 10, by Gloria Kwok Kan Lee, in which she demonstrates how Conrad's textuality was gradually given transcultural depth through the mediation of Conrad's Chinese translators. They effectively introduced into Conrad's texts certain transcultural voices, including those of the following: Chinese-speaking narrators and characters; Chinese biographers, reviewers, and critics; and the Chinese translators themselves, who in their prefaces and explanatory notes worked to configure transcultural relations between Conrad's texts and his Chinese readers. In particular, Gloria Kwok Kan Lee emphasizes the ways in which Conrad's sea tales attained Chinese cultural affiliations by means of the Chinese translators' expansion of Conrad's implied readership, during a decade when republican China awakened to an

English author of Polish origin. For Gloria Kwok Kan Lee, the transcultural breadth of Conrad's transtextuality (beyond Anglo-European boundaries) is best illustrated through consideration of the translation practice of various Chinese literary agents, whose translations and para-texts constructed an image of Joseph Conrad that has successfully taken root on Chinese soil (and remains to this day).

The subsequent Chapter 11 by Narugopal Mukherjee shows that Conrad's major works of "Heart of Darkness" (1899), *Lord Jim* (1900), *Nostromo* (1904), and *The Secret Agent* (1907) deal with issues that largely belong to our times—in particular, political violence, revolutionary politics, financial irregularities, and the marginalization of subaltern others. Narugopal Mukherjee explicates how Conrad's broader literary engagements with these concerns often foreground intricate depictions of non-Eurocentric identity crises brought about by colonial legacy and economic imperialism. By citing a number of Indian responses to Conrad, Narugopal Mukherjee demonstrates Conrad's importance for present-day Indian writers and critics interested in the re-diversification and reconstitution of Indian cultural hybridity amid various psychosocial impacts (of diasporic migration, postcolonial nationalism, and revolutionary terrorism). Following Gloria Kwok Kan Lee's account of Conrad's reception within modern China, Narugopal Mukherjee's chapter adds to the book's consideration of Conrad beyond European boundaries. But most importantly, Narugopal Mukherjee's chapter also marks the first critical study of Conrad's reception within present-day Indian literary cultures.

Part 3 opens with Chapter 12 by Robert Hampson, titled "Transcultural Negotiations: *A Personal Record*, 'Prince Roman', and 'The Warrior's Soul'," which covers relations between Conrad's writing and the contexts of his Polish historical, cultural, and political background through examining Conrad's attempt to "make Polish life enter English Literature" (*CL4* 138). The central part of the essay is a comparison of Conrad's 1912 account of the long career of Nicholas B. in *A Personal Record*—which maps Poland's tragic history from the defeat of Napoleon to the brutal suppression of the 1863 uprising—with the presentation of Prince Roman and his commitment to Polish independence in "Prince Roman" (1910). The final part of the chapter considers Conrad's return to the Napoleonic War in "The Warrior's Soul" (1916).

In Chapter 13, titled "Rereading *Under Western Eyes* from the Polish Perspective," Joanna Skolik challenges some of the previous Anglo-American interpretations of the manifestation of Conrad's Polishness in *Under Western Eyes* (1911). Joanna Skolik first interrogates certain Anglo-American misreadings that run against specific historical, ideological, or political realities; she then juxtaposes such misreadings with Polish critical accounts of the novel and reinterprets them in relation to Polish historical contexts. She reconsiders the post–Second World War reception of *Under Western Eyes* (which was banned in communist Poland for ideological reasons, with Russia casting a long shadow all along). Joanna Skolik thus shows how specific political and sociohistorical circumstances have affected Polish interpretation and reception of Conrad's narratives. Throughout her analyses, she also provides a nuanced reading of Conrad's polyvocal narrative strategies, which articulate political commentary underneath the guise of sarcasm and irony. Joanna Skolik's discussion follows up on Anne Luyat's and Robert Hampson's bridgings of textual analysis with consideration of Conrad's Polish historical, cultural, and literary legacies.

In Chapter 14, George Z. Gasyna's "The Dangerous Subject Is the Displaced Subject: Conrad's Short Fictions" explores "Heart of Darkness" (1899) and "Amy Foster" (1901), both of which operate at the intersection of colonial subjectivity and sociogeographic difference, set across different continents and amid variant imperial spheres, in which English is often a lingua franca of enunciation. George Z. Gasyna emphasizes how these texts' non-English and non-Western European characters often refuse to speak (and thereby decline to voice their subjectivity). Following the work of Gayatri Chakravorty Spivak, George Z. Gasyna argues that if there is no space from which these characters can freely speak, it is because they represent various types of subaltern and marginalized individuals. As George Z. Gasyna goes on to suggest, Conrad's subaltern figures who *do* speak do so haltingly, translating from their native tongue, so that the cultural context of their enunciations is always already mediated by distance. His chapter thus follows up on Pei-Wen Clio Kao's account of Conrad's portrayal of marginalized characters.

Through reading Salman Rushdie's narratives alongside Conrad's *The Nigger of the "Narcissus"* (1897) in Chapter 15, which is titled "'I Must Live Till I Die—Mustn't I?': The Hybrid Art of Joseph Conrad and Salman Rushdie," G. W. Stephen Brodsky formulates a transcultural exegesis of the words of Conrad's James Wait. As G. W. Stephen Brodsky shows, Rushdie's *Joseph Anton: A Memoir* (2012) echoes Wait's words, in response to the threat of imminent death following the *fatwa* (the death sentence for Rushdie's *The Satanic Verses* [1988]). G. W. Stephen Brodsky explicates links between Wait's words and a number of symbolic referents throughout Rushdie's novels after the *fatwa*—in particular, imagery of breathings in and out, windows, drownings, water surfaces and depths, and abysses. In so doing, G. W. Stephen Brodsky shows that Conrad's Polish-Franco-English sensibility resonates with the genius of Rushdie's cultural hybridity born of his Indo-Pakistani-English experience. G. W. Stephen Brodsky's comparison of Rushdie and Conrad further reveals that Conrad may be seen as a proleptic postcolonial writer shaped and informed by exilic life. Following Agnieszka Adamowicz-Pośpiech's account of Conrad's afterlife within present-day Polish culture and Gloria Kwok Kan Lee's study of the passage of Conradian narrative across cultural and national boundaries, G. W. Stephen Brodsky's chapter emphasizes the hybridity of Conrad's cultural legacy.

The book closes with Chapter 16, titled "Metropolitan Terror in *The Secret Agent*: Truth and Fiction in a Surreal Drama." In the final chapter of *Conrad Without Borders*, Gerard Kilroy considers Conrad's texturing of relations between terror, surreal drama, and irony in *The Secret Agent*. Gerard Kilroy first emphasizes the savagely ironic language of Conrad's text through drawing a comparison with the language of T. S. Eliot's *The Waste Land* (1922). In discussing the dramatic function of Conrad's irony, Gerard Kilroy explicates how Conrad articulates an unsparing and devastating indictment of Russian state-sponsored terrorism. Moreover, Gerard Kilroy reexamines *The Secret Agent*'s portrayal of terror in the context of the metaphysical thought of the *Narodnaya Volya* (known as the "Nihilists," the first indiscriminate terrorists, who sheltered in London but conducted their outrages abroad). In the latter half of his chapter, Gerard Kilroy addresses the domestic drama of Conrad's tale and considers how Winnie Verloc rises above a world of indolent men through avenging the blowing to bits of her brother Stevie. According to Gerard Kilroy, Winnie's human story "redeem[s] nature from the general curse," in constitutive tension with the greater text's ironic and surreal depiction of anarchists in London at the turn of the century. Gerard Kilroy's conclusion regarding Winnie thus extends Pei-Wen Clio Kao's reassessment of Conrad's marginalized characters.

Acknowledgments

The initial part of the introduction is based on Grażyna M. T. Branny's article "How Much Conrad in Conrad Criticism?: Conrad's Artistry, Ideological Mediatization and Identity. A Commemorative Address on the 160th Anniversary of the Writer's Birth," published in the *Yearbook of Conrad Studies*

(Poland) 13 (2018): 41–54. Courtesy of the Jagiellonian University Publishing House in Kraków, Poland.

Notes

1 More recently, GoGwilt has stressed how Conrad's formulation of a "translingual, transcultural medium of English" "underwrites" "the coordination of different cultural traditions and different racial, ethnic, or national identities into a shared genealogy of literary heritage" (2011: 5, 60, 10). Following GoGwilt, Baxter and Hampson have addressed Conrad's "existence within and between multiple languages" (2016: 8). Zulli has most recently examined Conrad's transnational "multilingualism" and how "Conrad's presentation of characters of different nationalities" "offer[s] the reader a diversity of perspectives" through "creating a polyphonic literary space able to challenge Eurocentric traditional views" (2019: 21–2).

2 See, for example, Said's oft-quoted comment that Conrad's "narrative forms" "encourag[e] us to sense the potential of a reality that seemed inaccessible to imperialism, just beyond its control" (1994: 29).

3 In 1992–2013 (vols. 1–22) the series appeared under the auspices of East European Monographs Boulder. Since 2019, its other publisher, apart from Maria Curie-Skłodowska University Press Lublin all along, has been Columbia University Press New York, which has been its distributor since 1992 (Krajka, email to Branny, December 5, 2021).

4 See, for example, Krajka (2018, 2020).

References

Acheraïou, Amar. 2009. *Joseph Conrad and the Reader: Questioning Modern Theories of Narrative and Readership.* London: Palgrave Macmillan.

Armstrong, Paul B. 1996. "*Heart of Darkness* and the Epistemology of Cultural Differences." In *Under Postcolonial Eyes: Joseph Conrad After Empire*, edited by Gail Fincham and Myrtle Hooper, 21–39. Rondebosch: University of Cape Town Press.

Batchelor, John. 1983. Lord Jim: *A Tale*. Oxford: Oxford University Press.

Baxter, Katherine Isobel. 2018. *Joseph Conrad and the Swan Song of Romance.* New York: Routledge.

Baxter, Katherine Isobel, and Robert Hampson, eds. 2016. *Conrad and Language.* Edinburgh: Edinburgh University Press.

Billy, Ted. 1997. *A Wilderness of Words: Closure and Disclosure in Conrad's Short Fiction.* Lubbock: Texas Tech University Press.

Branny, Grażyna M. T. 2018. "How Much Conrad in Conrad Criticism?: Conrad's Artistry, Ideological Mediatization and Identity. A Commemorative Address on the 160th Anniversary of the Writer's Birth." *Yearbook of Conrad Studies (Poland)* 13: 41–54.

Brodsky, G. W. Stephen. 2016. *Joseph Conrad's Polish Soul: Realms of Memory and Self*, edited by George Z. Gasyna. Eastern and Western Perspectives Series, vol. 27, edited by Wiesław Krajka. Lublin: Maria Curie-Skłodowska University Press.

Genette, Gérard. 1997. *Palimpsests: Literature in the Second Degree*. Lincoln: University of Nebraska Press.

GoGwilt, Christopher. [1995] 2013. *The Passages of Literature: Genealogies of Modernism in Conrad, Rhys, and Pramoedya*. Oxford: Oxford University Press.

Greaney, Michael. 2001. *Conrad, Language, and Narrative*. Cambridge: Cambridge University Press.

Griffith, John W. 1995. *Joseph Conrad and the Anthropological Dilemma: The Bewildered Traveller*. Oxford: Oxford University Press.

Hampson, Robert. 2000. *Cross-Cultural Encounters in Conrad's Malay Fiction*. London: Palgrave Macmillan.

Hampson, Robert. 2012. *Conrad's Secrets*. London: Palgrave Macmillan.

Hawthorn, Jeremy. 1990. *Narrative Technique and Ideological Commitment*. London: Edward Arnold.

Krajka, Wiesław, ed. 2018. *Joseph Conrad's Authorial Self: Polish and Other*. Conrad: Eastern and Western Perspectives Series, vol. 28. Lublin: Maria Curie-Skłodowska University Press.

Krajka, Wiesław, ed. 2020. *Various Dimensions of the Other in Joseph Conrad's Fiction*. Conrad: Eastern and Western Perspectives Series, vol. 29. Lublin: Maria Curie-Skłodowska University Press; New York: Columbia University Press.

Lawtoo, Nidesh. 2016. *Conrad's Shadow: Catastrophe, Mimesis, Theory*. East Lansing: Michigan State University Press.

Levin, Yael. 2008. *Tracing the Aesthetic Principle in Conrad's Novels*. New York: Palgrave Macmillan.

Lothe, Jakob. [1989] 1991. *Conrad's Narrative Method*. Oxford: Clarendon Press.

Najder, Zdzisław, ed. 1964. *Conrad's Polish Background: Letters to and from Polish Friends*. Translated by Halina Carroll. London: Oxford University Press.

Napolin, Julie Beth. 2020. *The Fact of Resonance: Modernist Acoustics and Narrative Form*. Fordham: Fordham University Press.

Nixon, Rob. 2011. *Slow Violence and the Environmentalism of the Poor*. Cambridge, MA: Harvard University Press.

Parry, Benita. 2005. "The Moment and Afterlife of *Heart of Darkness*." In *Conrad in the Twenty-First Century: Contemporary Approaches and Perspectives*, edited by Carola M. Kaplan, Peter Mallios, and Andrea White, 39–54. New York: Routledge.

Said, Edward. 1994. *Culture and Imperialism*. New York: Vintage.

Zulli, Tania. 2019. *Joseph Conrad: Language and Transnationalism*. Chieti: Sofanelli.

Part 1

Transtextual and
Transcultural Bridges

1

Conrad's Triple Perspective:
History, Memory, Fiction

Jakob Lothe
University of Oslo

I begin by quoting a passage from Conrad's Author's Note to *A Personal Record*:

> Amongst them I remember my mother, a more familiar figure than the others, dressed in the black of the national mourning worn in defiance of ferocious police regulations. I have also preserved from that particular time the awe of her mysterious gravity which, indeed, was by no means smileless. For I remember her smiles too. Perhaps for me she could always find a smile. She was young then, certainly not thirty yet. She died four years later in exile. (*PR* 8)

This excerpt (published in 1919, just five years before his own death) presents the reader with fragments of the writer's childhood memories. While the fragments of memory are striking—and, at least for me as one reader, moving—it is much less certain how helpful they are, or could be, when it comes to the task of reading and interpreting Conrad's narrative fiction. That fiction is, as Conrad scholars have shown, exceptionally complex structurally as well as thematically. This kind of fictional complexity—which includes, among other constituent elements, a significant ethical component—is certainly not reducible to, or explicable by referring to, autobiographical elements. Yet it does not follow that there are no links between Conrad's life and fiction. No literary narrative can emerge from a historical, cultural, or biographical vacuum; any writer of fiction needs to draw on his or her experience and memories. Conrad knew this better than most authors do. As he observes in his "Familiar Preface" to *A Personal Record* (1906), "One's literary life must turn frequently for sustenance to memories and seek discourse with the shades" (14).

Focusing on a passage from "Heart of Darkness," this chapter will discuss how Conrad's perspective is shaped, enriched, and complicated by the ways in which the fictional characters, narrators, and narratees interact—both in relation to each other and in relation to Conrad as implied author. The chapter will also consider some of the ways in which this kind of identification, complication, and diversification of the author's perspective is connected with, though not necessarily explained by, traces of the writer's life in the narrative fiction he created. While in one sense any author's perspective is double since there is a difference between the author's perspective at the time of writing and that of the "shades" of the past with whom he or she "seek[s] discourse," in Conrad's case we can speak of a triple perspective since his past experience is unusually complex, constituted not only by his many years at sea, but also by his Polish childhood. Moreover, while Conrad's memories of his childhood are individual, there is also a sense in which they are collective and transcultural. In Conrad's memories of his Polish past, these aspects of memory are curiously intertwined.

* * *

A premise for the discussion is that the thematics of Conrad's fiction depends on his presentation of narrative; implied in this premise is the accompanying one that narrative aesthetics, thematics, and ethics are inseparable. These traces bear a certain resemblance to, and can thus be linked to, the word "sustenance" as Conrad uses it in "A Familiar Preface." A further premise is that these traces, which are difficult to identify and whose critical value is equally hard to ascertain, should lead us back to the text under consideration rather than distracting our attention from it.

Before I give a working definition of the term "perspective," I want to highlight a second sentence from "A Familiar Preface":

> Having broken away from my origins under a storm of blame from every quarter which had the merest shadow of right to voice an opinion, removed by great distances from such natural affections as were still left to me and even estranged in a measure from them by the totally unintelligible character of the life which had seduced me so mysteriously from my allegiance I may safely say that through the blind force of circumstances the sea was to be all my world and the Merchant Service my only home for a long succession of years. (*PR* 13)

In *A Preface to Conrad*, Cedric Watts writes of Conrad as *homo duplex*, the double man (1993: 7). Watts is quoting from Conrad's use of the phrase in his letter to Kazimierz Waliszewski on December 5, 1903 (*CL3* 89). In the quoted passage from "A Familiar Preface," the radical break with Conrad's "origins"—a keyword linked to the lives and deaths of both his parents—is juxtaposed with "the sea," which for approximately twenty years became "all my world."

The juxtaposition of Conrad's Polish origins and his years at sea approximates to a contrast that is not just temporal but spatial as well, marked by "great distances." This kind of contrast is related to Watts's description of Conrad as a "double man." Watts uses the phrase *homo duplex* to indicate Conrad's thematic and ideological complexity, a complexity that, for him as for Albert Guerard, involves "a series of major inward conflicts" (Guerard 1979: 57–8) in Conrad's fiction.

Linking Watts's description of Conrad as *homo duplex* to the concept of perspective, and particularly narrative perspective, I find Conrad's perspective remarkably nuanced and multifaceted. While this point has been made by many critics, I want to stress the ways in which it applies to, and characterizes, not just Conrad's fiction, but also an autobiographical text such as *A Personal Record*. Moreover, the sentence from "A Familiar Preface" quoted above is written from Conrad's perspective as an established author in England; it is this third perspective that enables him to establish the contrast between the first and second perspectives—those of his Polish origins and his years at sea. I suggest that a possible way of coming to terms with Conrad's complexity and multivocality is to consider the ways in which his triple perspective manifests itself and functions in a revealing passage in "Heart of Darkness." Moreover, I posit that Conrad's triple perspective also emerges, albeit covertly, in his major fiction overall, making the narratives' aesthetic structure more innovative and their ethics more urgent.

In *Narrative Discourse* (1980, first published in French as *Discours du récit* in 1972), Gérard Genette argues that "point of view," a term often used in discussions of narrative and of the novel, is confusing because it fails to differentiate between two questions we should ask when reading and interpreting a narrative text: "Who speaks?" and "Who sees?" While the former question refers to the narrative's *voice*, the latter indicates its *perspective*. This helpful distinction, which has proved influential in narrative theory and analysis, can enable us to see, for example, how Conrad in *The Secret Agent* makes his third-person narrator, whose voice is relatively stable, link his perspective to the characters while at the same time establishing varying degrees of distance from them. Yet it remains somewhat unclear what Genette means by the two terms, and neither does he discuss the ways in which—both generally and specifically in Conrad, whose fiction Genette does not discuss—they are combined with and mutually reinforce each other.

This kind of mutual reinforcement plays a key role in Conrad's fictional exploration of variants of perspective. For Mieke Bal, storytelling is "the presentation in whatever medium of a focalized series of events" (2018: 37). While all constituent elements of her definition of storytelling prove relevant to the following discussion, I highlight the way in which the "series of events" are "focalized." In the passage from "Heart of Darkness" under consideration here, the events are focalized in different ways; the verb "focalize" indicates how different perspectives are established.

Moreover, "perspective," as I understand the term, is closely associated with Conrad's presentation of narrative identity and of memory. Emphasizing narrative's temporal dimension, Ernst van Alphen finds that "narrative can be seen as an existential response to the world and to the experience of that world" (2018: 68). Narrative, he observes, has functioned as "the medium of identity" (68). Referring to Paul Ricoeur's *Oneself as Another* (1990), Alphen calls this notion of identity "narrative identity" (Alphen 2018: 68). Although, as Alphen notes, ongoing historical and cultural changes challenge the notion of narrative identity, this challenge does not in itself make the notion less significant. Ricoeur's understanding of identity becomes more, not less, pertinent when seen in the light of the challenge that historical changes pose to narrative identity. As the above quotations from the Author's Note and "A Familiar Preface" suggest, such historical changes can include those experienced by Conrad.

Implicit in these comments on narrative and identity is a view of memory that links memory, including traumatic memory, closely to both. It appears impossible to come to terms with the concepts of narrative and identity without activating, implicitly or explicitly, aspects of memory. If, as Jens Brockmeier has persuasively argued, there are important links between memory and narrative (2015: 99), there is also a significant connection between identity and memory. If I cannot conceive of narrative divorced from memory, neither can I think of identity without remembering something of myself before the point or stage of my life where I am now.

Linking these definitions of narrative to my understanding of narrative perspective, I suggest that Conrad's narrative perspective is further diversified through variations of temporal, spatial, and attitudinal (including cultural) distance.[1] When Conrad notes that he is "removed by great distances" from his "origins," he potentially invokes all three variants of distance. Moreover, he implicitly indicates how closely all of them are associated with aspects of narrative and narration.

These observations support Zdzisław Najder's important point that "Conrad's exceptionality as a writer was ... connected with the peculiarity of his biography" (1997: 189). In his indispensable biography of Conrad, Najder gives an illustrative example of this connection. The example concerns Conrad's discovery of Marlow—and "discovery," rather than just "creation," seems the appropriate word—who plays a key role as narrator and character both in "Heart of Darkness" and *Lord Jim*:

> Marlow, a model English gentleman, ex-officer of the merchant marine, was the embodiment of all that Conrad would wish to be if he were to be completely anglicized. And since that was not the case, and since he did not quite share his hero's point of view, there was no need to identify himself with Marlow, either emotionally or intellectually. Thanks to Marlow's duality, Conrad could feel solidarity with and a sense of belonging to England by proxy, at the same time maintaining a distance such as one has toward a creation of one's imagination—a distance visible especially in *Lord Jim*. (Najder 2007: 267)

"Distance," as Najder uses the word, is a variant on attitudinal distance—that is, a kind of distance that indicates the author's (or narrator's or character's) distinct and unique attitudes, priorities, and moral values. Marlow's opening words in "Heart of Darkness" provide an illustrative example: "'And this also,' said Marlow suddenly, 'has been one of the dark places of the earth'" (HD 45). Marlow's quiet remark not only exposes the relative naivety and limited insight of the frame narrator, but also prefigures the complex, somber implications of the story he is about to tell (Lothe 1989: 25). Anticipating his following reflection on the Romans' arrival in Britain "nineteen hundred years ago—the other day" (HD 46), Marlow's introductory comment also serves as a complex prolepsis of "darkness," the central metaphor in the narrative. Part of the narrative and thematic complexity of the darkness metaphor—which gradually, not least through patterns of repetition, grows into a powerful symbol—is suggested by the way in which Marlow's act of hindsight as he is reflecting on the Romans' arrival in Britain curiously foreshadows the thematic effects of the tale he is about to tell.

With a view to the argument of this chapter, it is significant that while Marlow's perspective is remarkably different from that of the frame narrator, it is also far from being identical to Conrad's. As Najder observes, Marlow is a narrative instrument designed by Conrad to present his narrative as effectively and convincingly as possible. Conrad as implied author is distanced from this "creation." Combining the functions of narrator and character, Marlow enables

Conrad to develop a complex thematics that, as presented in the narrative, is possessed of a significant ethical dimension. Marlow's perspective is limited to his experience as a sailor and as a British citizen. Conrad's triple perspective is different from and more nuanced than Marlow's because, as indicated already, it is colored not only by his experience at sea and that of being a British citizen and a writer in Britain, but also by memories of his Polish childhood. Conrad had experienced a form of voluntary exile in a way that Marlow had not.

The reader may counter that these memories are those of the historical Conrad, rather than those of Conrad as implied author. In one sense this is true—and one distinct quality of "Heart of Darkness" as a work of literature is that the narrative's significance is not dependent on the reader's knowledge of the author's biography. Still, if as a reader I am possessed of at least some information about the author's life, that knowledge will, as the following discussion suggests, do something to my reading of his or her narrative fiction.

As "Heart of Darkness" is an extraordinarily complex literary text, I briefly discuss just one passage:

> Now when I was a little chap I had a passion for maps. I would look for hours at South America, or Africa or Australia and lose myself in all the glories of exploration. At that time there were many blank spaces on the earth and when I saw one that looked particularly inviting on a map (but they all look that) I would put my finger on it and say: When I grow up I will go there. ... But there was one yet—the biggest—the most blank, so to speak—that I had a hankering after.
>
> True, by this time it was not a blank space any more. It had got filled since my boyhood with rivers and lakes and names. It had ceased to be a blank space of delightful mystery—a white patch for a boy to dream gloriously over. It had become a place of darkness. But there was in it one river especially, a mighty river you could see on the map, resembling an immense snake uncoiled, with its head in the sea, its body at rest curving afar over a vast country and its tail lost in the depths of the land. And as I looked at the map of it in a shop window it fascinated me like a snake would a bird—a silly little bird. (HD 48)

The voice we are hearing here is that of Marlow, who combines the functions of main character and main narrator in "Heart of Darkness." Marlow is addressing a small group of listeners (or narratees) aboard the *Nellie*; one of these is the anonymous frame narrator who, significantly, also combines two functions since he not only listens, but also framing and situating Marlow's story passes it on to the reader.

While Marlow's narrative voice is relatively stable, though by no means monotonous, the narrative perspective is rich and varied, as the quoted passage suggests. I am particularly struck by the way in which Marlow extends the narrative perspective by linking it to an act of memory. Marlow's memory of his fascination with maps as a boy partly explains why he became interested in the "blank spaces" of remote continents. Conrad's narrative presentation of Marlow's memory is an important part of Marlow's preamble: introducing his story, it furthers the narratees', and the reader's, interest in his story.

I link this observation to the following three points. First, as Marlow is not only the novella's main character but also Conrad's most important narrative instrument, Marlow's perspective is colored by, and in a way represents, Conrad's perspective. Yet as Najder points out, the two perspectives are not identical; while Marlow is "a model English gentleman," Conrad is not.[2] As an Englishman, Marlow presumably "had a passion for maps" when he was a child. Although neither the time nor place of the "passion" of the "little chap" is given, as a reader I am led to believe that, in the fictional universe of "Heart of Darkness," Marlow nurtured a passion for maps somewhere in England in the second half of the nineteenth century, perhaps around 1860. Significantly, this temporal and spatial location would apply to many of the novella's implied readers, particularly the readers of *Blackwood's Magazine* in which the serialized version of "Heart of Darkness" appeared in the spring of 1899. Many of these readers would be sympathetically inclined toward England's, and Europe's, efforts to map, and thus gain control over, the "blank spaces" of other continents.

This said, it is also significant that the time and place of Marlow's passion for maps is *not* specified: thus, it becomes interesting for, and linked to the memories of, many more readers who are introduced to, and reflect on, the passage at different points in time and in various places around the world. More general than that directed toward the (predominantly male) readers of *Blackwood's Magazine*, this kind of appeal is also more closely related to, and in a way prepares the reader for, the striking image of "one river … resembling an immense snake uncoiled." Again, it is important that Marlow does not give us the river's name—or, more precisely, that Conrad makes his narrator refrain from identifying the river.

Second, if Marlow's perspective is colored by Conrad's perspective, there is a strong sense in which, in "Heart of Darkness," Conrad's perspective is represented by Marlow. Marlow's perspective is essentially double. On the one hand, as an ex-officer of the British marine he contributes to the ongoing operation of the British Empire, which was utterly dependent on communication by sea. On the other hand, he is shocked by the brutality of European imperialism, a brutality condensed into the four words of Kurtz's "valuable post-scriptum": "Exterminate all the brutes!" (96, 95). As Marlow is the main character and the main narrator, and as the novella's thematics is indebted to, and in large part dependent on, Marlow's double perspective, it is extended to include Conrad too. Importantly, I can make this point without being possessed of the extratextual knowledge that Conrad visited the Congo in 1890.

Third, although Conrad makes Marlow share aspects of his own perspective, and although these aspects include a very considerable narrative skill that enables Marlow to captivate his audience, Conrad's perspective is more complex and multifaceted than that of his main narrator. One important reason is that, as communicated by Marlow, Conrad's perspective draws on, and is constituted by, fragments of experience and of memory that are complex and multilayered temporally as well as spatially.

David Carr has observed that as "narrative requires narration, ... what is essential to the story-teller's position ... is the advantage of ... hindsight" (1986: 60). Linking Carr's notion of hindsight to my concept of narrative distance, I note that the combination of temporal and spatial distance forms an important part of the basis for Marlow's narrative. One important reason is that, as Carr puts it, hindsight bears within it a "freedom from the constraint of the present assured by occupying a position after, above, or outside the events narrated" (Carr 1986: 60; cf. Freeman 2010: 175).

If this kind of freedom applies to Marlow, and in a way it does, it is more directly applicable to Conrad. By "Conrad" I primarily mean Conrad as implied author—that is, the image of Conrad that, whether I think of this mental process or not, I form and revise during the act of reading "Heart of Darkness." That the formation of this kind of image is not dependent on the reader's knowledge of the author's biography is an essential part of literature's generosity and inclusiveness. It is also a constituent element of narrative fiction.

Yet when I mention Conrad's experience, and when I link that experience to fragments of memory, I activate aspects of Conrad as historical author. Conrad's perspective is shaped not just by his Congo experience, but also by the memory of his fascination with maps when he was a child in Poland. Thus, as a reader of this passage, I am presented with, and gain access to, a triple perspective: the double one of Conrad as implied author and that of Conrad as historical author.

To put this another way, I suggest that some knowledge of the author's biography may be of interest, even helpful, with a view to the task of reading and interpreting this passage from "Heart of Darkness"—and, with specifications and qualifications that may vary from narrative to narrative, Conrad's fiction overall. I reiterate that I am not certain how, or in what way, biographical information can improve my understanding of Conrad. There is also a danger that discussion of autobiographical elements can distract attention from my attempt to come to terms with the structural, thematic, and ethical complexity of Conrad's literary discourse—that is, with Conrad as implied author. In some cases, though, elements of Conrad's life can improve our understanding of his literary discourse. Consider this passage from *A Personal Record*:

> It was in 1868, when nine years old or thereabouts, that while looking at a map of Africa of the time and putting my finger on the blank space then representing the unsolved mystery of that continent, I said to myself with an absolute assurance and an amazing audacity which are no longer in my character now:
>
> "When I grow up I will go *there*."
>
> And of course I thought no more about it till after a quarter of a century or so an opportunity offered to go there—as if the sin of childish audacity were to be visited on my mature head. Yes. I did go there: *There* being the region of Stanley Falls which in '68 was the blankest of blank spaces on the earth's figured surface. (26; emphasis in original)

The point I want to make about this passage is not that, since it bears a striking resemblance to that just quoted from "Heart of Darkness," it shows how closely Marlow is related to Conrad as historical author. Rather, my point is that while the two passages resemble each other, there are two notable differences between them. Significantly, one of these is spatial, the other temporal.

As regards the narrative presentation of space, Africa is mentioned in both passages. And yet, while Marlow links Africa to other continents in "Heart of Darkness," in *A Personal Record*, Conrad identifies the place in Africa that he went to. Thus, while in "Heart of Darkness" the presentation of space takes the form of a generalizing movement, in *A Personal Record*, Conrad records his memory of his trip to "the region of Stanley Falls." I am not suggesting that the role of memory is greater in the former narrative segment than in the latter. But I would argue that Marlow's act of remembering is different: as it is less specific and more inclusive, Conrad as implied author makes his narrator remember in a way that I as a reader can more easily relate to my own childhood memories. Thus, I am manipulated into a position resembling that of the frame narrator as narratee. Reading the passage from *A Personal Record* can also activate aspects of my own memory, but here the Polish context makes me as historical reader, as well as Conrad's implied reader, more aware of the difference between the

space of my own childhood and Conrad's. Demonstrating how various aspects
of space interact and cumulatively enrich each other, both passages under
consideration here are illustrative of Franco Moretti's observation that "space is
not the 'outside' of narrative, … but an internal force, that shapes it from within"
(1998: 70).

This last point also applies to the presentation of time in the two passages.
While that from *A Personal Record* mentions the year 1868 twice, Marlow does
not link the event to a particular year. This kind of temporal elasticity does not
mean that the plot, characters, and thematics of "Heart of Darkness" are not
situated historically; on the contrary, the novella is inseparable from the historical
process of European imperialism and the conquest of Africa in the second part
of the nineteenth century. Yet Conrad's refusal to specify the time of the plot
furthers his presentation of a fictional narrative that represents history indirectly,
but with a wider and more lasting relevance than a documentary narrative
could have done. Just a page after the passage from *A Personal Record* under
consideration here, Conrad asks: "And what is a novel if not a conviction of our
fellow men's existence, strong enough to take upon itself a form of imagined life
clearer than reality and whose accumulated verisimilitude of selected episodes
puts to shame the pride of documentary history?" (27–8). One implication of
this elegant defense of narrative fiction is that its "accumulated verisimilitude of
selected episodes" is, and perhaps needs to be, general and unspecific. It would
appear consistent with this understanding of fiction that when Marlow, for once,
uses the word "year," he refers to an extended time period: "I was thinking of
very old times, when the Romans first came here, nineteen hundred years ago—
the other day" (HD 46).

By contrast, the year 1868, whose significance is enhanced when Conrad
repeats it in *A Personal Record*, links his memory of his fascination with maps
directly and explicitly to one particular year of his childhood in Poland. This
childhood was, and is, very different from that of the reader—and not just for me
as a reader of *A Personal Record* in Norway in 2022, but also for Conrad's implied
readers in England at the time when this piece of autobiographical writing was
serialized in 1908–9 in the *English Review* under the title "Some Reminiscences"
(and also when it was published in book form in 1912).

While this kind of difference consists of various elements, including language,
I want to highlight the last word of the quotation from the Author's Note at
the beginning of this chapter. Conrad's mother died "in exile"; Conrad lived,
wrote, and died in a kind of voluntary exile. I am certainly not arguing that their
experiences of exile were identical. But I am suggesting that Conrad's experience

of exile was particularly painful because of his mother's early death—a huge loss for which he held the Russian authorities responsible.

As I have noted in an earlier essay on Joyce and Conrad, exile is a difficult topic to discuss because it is not just a critical term but also a concept which purports to illuminate, in one sense even represent, a particular kind of human experience. As Edward W. Said puts it in his collection of essays titled *Reflections on Exile*, "exile is strangely compelling to think about but terrible to experience" (2001: 73; cf. Lothe 2003). Said's observation is interestingly related to Anglo-French author Christine Brooke-Rose's reflections on exile, both in its present sense of living elsewhere and in its etymological sense of "springing forth"—that is, as both sorrow and renewal. Brooke-Rose distinguishes between

> *Involuntary exile*, usually political or punitive ("Isaiah," Ovid, Dante, Thibault, Charles d'Orleans, Byron, Mickiewicz … Kundera, Solzhenitsyn, etc.) [and] *Voluntary exile*, which is usually called expatriation and occurs for many more personal reasons: social, economic, sexual (e.g. Radclyffe Hall and the lesbian group in Paris in the twenties), or simple preference (Beerbohm retired in Rapallo, Ezra Pound choosing Italy). (1998: 11; emphasis in original)

Linking Conrad and his family to this bipartite distinction, it would seem obvious that his parents experienced involuntary exile. Whether Conrad experienced voluntary exile when he decided to leave Poland, going first to France and then eventually settling in England, is less clear. He probably had, to use Brooke-Rose's phrase, "personal reasons" to leave Poland; moreover, when it comes to the choice of England, there was evidently also an element of "preference"—and it meant a lot to him to obtain British citizenship in 1886. And yet, when, after trial by a military tribunal in 1862, Conrad's parents were sentenced to exile and escorted to Vologda, 480 kilometers north of Moscow, they took their 4-year-old son with them (Knowles and Moore 2000: 393–5). Thus, in common with his parents, he also experienced involuntary exile. And he could see for himself what it did to his mother, who died just three years later.

I am not suggesting that the example of Conrad makes Brooke-Rose's distinction between two variants of exile invalid; on the contrary, it helpfully illustrates how complex, and in some ways contradictory, Conrad's experience of exile was. Conrad's childhood experience of involuntary exile left a mark on him that would color his experience of exile after he had left his native land in 1874, thus making a "standing jump out of his racial surroundings and associations" (*PR* 108). Moreover, when, as an author in voluntary exile in England, he felt compelled to turn "for sustenance to memories and seek discourse with the shades" (*PR* 14), these shades would necessarily be imbued with elements of involuntary exile.

Enriching his perspective as a sailor in the British merchant fleet and as an author of fiction in Britain, Conrad's memories—his "discourse with the shades"—constitute a third perspective that, combined with and filtered through the first two, is remarkably complex. It includes individual memories, several of which must have been traumatic. A striking example is his father's funeral in Cracow on May 23, 1869. The funeral of Apollo Korzeniowski turned into a patriotic demonstration, with 11-year-old Conrad at the head of a procession of several thousand people who followed the coffin in silence (Najder 2007: 35). Yet these individual memories are colored by collective memories of Polish patriotism and of Poland as a nation partitioned and suppressed by neighboring powers, Russia in particular. Combined with "his knowledge of various cultural traditions and conceptual frameworks" (Najder 1997: 168), this unique combination of perspectives enables Conrad "to look at the described events from different angles" (Najder 1997: 168)—whether these events are factual or fictional. Najder goes on to note that Conrad's "European multiculturalism was ineluctably linked to his condition as an exile" (1997: 168). Conrad's multiculturalism blends into a kind of transculturalism that, as I have attempted to show, emerges through, and is characterized by, the combination of three narrative perspectives. Although, but also because, they are cognizant of cultural and historical differences, transcultural authors may seek to negotiate and move beyond these differences. Richard Slimbach has observed that "transculturalism is rooted in the quest to define and discuss shared interests and common values across cultural and national borders" (2005: 206). Not only as implied but also as historical author, Conrad was engaged in such a quest.

This concluding point about the significance of Conrad's memories and their relevance for his narrative fiction blends into a concluding comment on "Heart of Darkness." The novella is a work of fiction in which characters and narrators invented by Conrad are engaged in imagined events and actions that refer to historical reality indirectly. Yet fiction's indirect presentation of history, including the elements of violence of which historical decisions and processes are possessed, can be strikingly effective. If Conrad's scathing critique of Belgian, and by implication European, imperialism in "Heart of Darkness" draws on his trip to the Congo in 1890, it is also inspired, or perhaps rather infiltrated, by shades of his Polish childhood. In contrast to most European authors writing at the turn of the twentieth century, Conrad had not only observed the Belgians' systematic use of violence against Black Africans in the Congo, but as a child he had himself been the victim of imperialist suppression. Thus, in one sense there is a link between the "black shadows of disease and starvation" (HD 58) that Marlow encounters in "Heart of Darkness" and the shades of Conrad's memory of his mother's death in exile. Conrad's unique combination of experience and literary imagination contributes decisively to his triple perspective.

Notes

1 The emphasis I put on these variations signals that my use of perspective is inspired not just by Genette, Bal, and Alphen, but also by Hubert Damisch and Mieke Bal's discussions of the significant yet problematic status of perspective in the history of art (Damisch 1991; Bal 2021).

2 As Jeremy Hawthorn has pointed out to me in conversation, although Marlow may be a model Englishman, he is not a typical one—just as the text of "Heart of Darkness" makes clear that he is not a typical sailor-tale-teller. I thank Hawthorn for his helpful comments on an earlier version of this chapter.

References

Alphen, Ernst van. 2018. "The Decline of Narrative and the Rise of the Archive." In *Storytelling and Ethics: Literature, Visual Arts and the Power of Narrative*, edited by Hanna Meretoja and Colin Davis, 68–83. London: Routledge.

Bal, Mieke. 2018. "Is There an Ethics to Story-Telling?" In *Storytelling and Ethics: Literature, Visual Arts and the Power of Narrative*, edited by Hanna Meretoja and Colin Davis, 37–54. London: Routledge.

Bal, Mieke. 2021. "Munch Bringing Thinking Home." In *Nordic Travels*, edited by Janicke S. Kaasa, Jakob Lothe, and Ulrike Spring, 25–48. Oslo: Novus Press.

Brockmeier, Jens. 2015. *Beyond the Archive: Narrative, Memory, and the Autobiographical Process*. New York: Oxford University Press.

Brooke-Rose, Christine. 1998. "Exsul." In *Exile and Creativity: Signposts, Travelers, Outsiders, Backward Glances*, edited by Susan Rubin Suleiman, 9–24. Durham, NC: Duke University Press.

Carr, David. 1986. *Time, Narrative, and History*. Bloomington: Indiana University Press.

Damisch, Hubert. 1991. *The Origin of Perspective*. Cambridge, MA: MIT Press.

Freeman, Mark. 2010. *Hindsight: The Promise and Peril of Looking Backward*. Oxford: Oxford University Press.

Genette, Gérard. 1980. *Narrative Discourse: An Essay on Method*. Oxford: Blackwell.

Guerard, Albert. 1979. *Conrad the Novelist*. Cambridge, MA: Harvard University Press.

Knowles, Owen, and Gene Moore, eds. 2000. *Oxford Reader's Companion to Conrad.*
    Oxford: Oxford University Press.

Lothe, Jakob. 1989. *Conrad's Narrative Method.* Oxford: Clarendon Press.

Lothe, Jakob. 2003. "Involuntary and/or Voluntary Exile: Joyce Compared with
    Conrad." In *Literary Sinews: Essays in Honour of Bjørn Tysdahl*, edited by Jakob
    Lothe, Tore Rem, and Juan Christian Pellicer, 225–36. Oslo: Novus Press.

Moretti, Franco. 1998. *Atlas of the European Novel: 1800–1900.* London: Verso.

Najder, Zdzisław. 1997. *Conrad in Perspective: Essays on Art and Fidelity.*
    Cambridge: Cambridge University Press.

Najder, Zdzisław. 2007. *Joseph Conrad: A Life.* Rochester: Camden House.

Ricoeur, Paul. 1990. *Oneself as Another.* Chicago: University of Chicago Press.

Said, Edward W. 2001. *Reflections on Exile and Other Literary and Cultural Essays.*
    London: Granta.

Slimbach, Richard. 2005. "Transcultural Journey." *Frontiers: The Interdisciplinary
    Journal of Study Abroad* 11, no. 1: 205–30. doi.org/10.36366/frontiers.v11i1.159.

Watts, Cedric. 1993. *A Preface to Conrad.* London: Longman.

2

Conrad as a Reader of
Adam Mickiewicz's *Grażyna*

Karol Samsel
Warsaw University

Introduction: *Grażyna* as Conrad's "Inspirational" Reading

"My father used to read *Pan Tadeusz* to me aloud, and made me read it to him aloud. Not once, not twice. I preferred *Konrad Wallenrod* and *Grażyna*," Joseph Conrad confessed to Marian Dąbrowski in a special interview published in the *Tygodnik Ilustrowany* (*Illustrated Weekly*) of April 18, 1914 (Dąbrowska 1974: 44). This prominent interview confirms numerous hypotheses connected with tracing Polish intertextuality in Conrad's texts and provides a good foundation for constructing a thesis about the extensive stylistic inspiration of Adam Mickiewicz—known to Conrad thoroughly, partly by heart—on his works. In his book *Conrad and His Contemporaries*, Józef Hieronim Retinger makes a digression concerning Conrad's style, recollecting this directly experienced scene:

> There is one feature in Conrad's art that is unique in English literature. Writers in this country when depicting Nature, the landscape and its phenomena, usually portray them in a static manner and seize the passing moments as if they were frozen in immobility. They give successive pictures as if a cinematographic ribbon were cut into separate stills. Wordsworth is a typical example of an author who, when describing events in Nature, renders them in successive immobile landscape paintings. Conrad, on the other hand, puts movement into his words, and catches Nature in the act of changing from one mood into another. When I commented on that to him and observed that this is a typically Polish verbal procedure, he made no reply for a moment, then handed me a faded volume out

of his library, saying: "Here is the reason." The book was *Pan Tadeusz*. (Retinger 1943: 112–13)

Conrad's direct comment on the influence of Polish Romantic literature on his own writing legitimizes an investigation of the matter, all the more so since he does not mention *Pan Tadeusz* alone in his interview quoted above.

In Polish Conrad studies, Dąbrowski's interview with Conrad has become one of the most frequently quoted texts pertaining to the writer's literary heritage related to the country of his origin. It has equally strongly resounded in the literary analyses of his works in Polish criticism. Nowadays, however, it should be acknowledged that the Conradians' interest in the latter two titles of one of the three greatest Polish Romantic poets, Adam Mickiewicz, has not at all been balanced. This is because the philological attention given to the influence of *Konrad Wallenrod* on Conrad's writings has not been accompanied by an equally intensive reflection (albeit equally justified) on how the writer may have read *Grażyna* and—which will be my main interest here—particularly on how *Grażyna* may have become an "inspirational reading"[1] for him.

From Being Stereotyped to Blazing the Trail: Studies in the Reception of *Grażyna* in Poland

The imbalance mentioned above may have been occasioned by an unfair stereotyping of *Grażyna* in Polish criticism, which considered it to be a failure, as if, "corrected" by Mickiewicz in *Konrad Wallenrod* in both the formal and thematic senses. Although renowned Polish Conradians have rarely spoken directly about *Grażyna's* structural weaknesses, they have also been caught up in this "prejudiced" way of thinking. The effects of such reasoning seem to have had greater consequences than originally assumed. The most important result was an involuntary reduction of the significance of the "*Grażyna* element" in Conrad's writing, not only quantitatively but also qualitatively, which reduced the potential impact of the poem on Conrad's writing to single, more or less clear and convincing thematic borrowings. This was, among others, the case of Wit Tarnawski's remarks on the references to *Grażyna* in *Lord Jim* and *Victory*, when he stopped at stating that, actually, "it is hard to explain this [Conrad's] fascination with this early, still imperfect, work of the poet [Mickiewicz]" (1972: 207–8).[2]

Although the reference to *Grażyna* suggested by Tarnawski in the context of *Victory* still stands, he was not the first to make this observation. As early as 1932, while deliberating on the Polish sources for Conrad's works, Julian Krzyżanowski remarked that "the end of *Victory*, with Lena dying from a bullet intended for her husband, clearly resembles the death of Litawor and Grażyna, and is probably genetically related to Mickiewicz's poem" (1932: 247).[3]

Unfortunately, such associations (rather superficial, albeit convincing) do not bring us any closer to a proper reflection on Mickiewicz's *Grażyna* as an "inspirational" reading for Joseph Conrad, as I have allowed myself to call it. All in all, we still remain at the point marked by Krzyżanowski, despite the eighty years that have elapsed since then. A certain justification can be found in the fact that a breakthrough in the assessment of *Grażyna* in Polish studies also came late (1996), and only with a seminal essay on the subject by Rolf Fieguth, titled "Kilka uwag o stylu *Grażyny*" (A Few Remarks on the Style of *Grażyna*). First of all, the scholar dismisses the fundamental illusion of the poem, that of a heroic hybrid stylization in the Homeric-Eddaic-Walter Scott style. Next, he identifies the *genus proximum* of the poem as a *transgenus* "novella with elements of drama" (Fieguth 1996: 134): "The poem contains numerous 'Homeric' accents; but it is not them that characterise the narration—it cannot be so also because Mickiewicz does not create a slow-pace epic of space, but rather a 'quick-pace' novella in verse, quick despite several slow-downs" (133).

The traditional argument claiming heroic stylization for *Grażyna*, which seems rather naïve from this perspective, led to a rejection of another (fundamental here) argument about its pioneering nature. Fieguth points to a deadlock created thereby, by citing the case of an innovative ending of the poem in the form of "Editor's Epilogue" and "editorial fiction" contained therein (1996: 129, 130), as well as "Historical Notes" added to the work, which some of the critics "neglect, throwing in a few words about the unnecessary homage by a young poet to the Walter Scott fad" (128). It is such simplifications in the criticism of *Grażyna*, accumulated over time, that led Fieguth to his strategy of reading the poem as a dramatized polyphonic novella. To emphasize this critical perspective, Fieguth deliberately repeats himself: "*Grażyna* is not an attempt to create some folk epic in a mythical prehistoric style, after the manner of *Kalevala*; on the contrary, it is a compact 'novella in verse,' its form nothing but rigorous and style nothing but rough" (132).

Rolf Fieguth's Interpretation of *Grażyna* versus Conrad's Approach to the Polish Romantic Tradition

What may Conrad have actually adopted from Mickiewicz's *Grażyna* for his own writing? Let the preliminary answer make a meaningful distinction between those who think that it was not much more than a final plot twist—a view shared by such notable Polish scholars as Juliusz Kleiner, Wacław Borowy, Wacław Kubacki, or Maria Janion (Fieguth 1996: 128)—and those who see Conrad's debt to Mickiewicz's poem in the entire spectrum of narrative techniques—a view not only taken by Rolf Fieguth, but also Marian Maciejewski before him (Maciejewski 1970: 88–184). These two interpretative hypotheses lead us to two entirely different strategic approaches to Conrad's Polish literary heritage: as an heir to the Polish Romantic and post-Romantic traditions, in general, and a reader of Mickiewicz, in particular. The former casts an image of Conrad as a diligent writer and disciple, who reads between the lines for what seems invisible at first sight and who "senses" the seams of the characteristic syncretic narrations of Polish Romanticism; the latter casts his image of a collector of motifs, themes, tricks, poetic figures, and plot strategies that he later smartly puts together for his own narrative purposes. To my mind, *Grażyna* is one of the few texts of the era that renders the latter (and more promising at that) model of Conrad's strategy probable.

Nothing seems to be more convincing as regards the scale of the pioneering nature of *Grażyna* than some of Fieguth's sweeping associations (even though they may occasionally appear extravagant, especially that the critic is not only extremely knowledgeable, but also, generally, daring in his comparisons). In his already cited text, Fieguth suggests the Russian stream prose of the nineteenth century (and the twentieth) as a *tertium comparationis* for the young Mickiewicz as the author of *Grażyna*, who was still in the process of learning to master epic poetry writing. The greatest surprise here comes with the association that Fieguth makes between the two above-mentioned narrative "additions" to *Grażyna* and the Notes to Vladimir Nabokov's *The Pale Fire*, even though, unfortunately, the critic fails to elaborate on the issue more extensively:

> The two additions to the poem [*Grażyna*], "Editor's Epilogue" in verse and "Historical Notes," among others, constitute a dramatization of the dispute over the poem's historical truth. … This staged polemics includes elements of Romantic irony, as well as Romantic humour; for today's reader those are clearly evocative of Vladimir Nabokov's *The Pale Fire*. (Fieguth 1996: 137)

This is not the end of surprises, although the next association seems more understandable. Once more referring to the ending of *Grażyna*, Fieguth argues that "the prose of 'Historical Notes' is a display of typical historical journalism of the nineteenth century, which, in its polyphonic engagement, anticipates the essays of another great Slav, Fyodor Dostoevsky" (136). Finally, the study ends in a spectacular (although for an entirely different reason) analogy drawn between Mickiewicz's *Grażyna*, with both "additions" evoking Dostoevskyan polyphony, and the poem's artistic counterpart in the form of the paintings of Siegfried Angermüller, where blurred vision of detail enhances cohesion and correspondence of the whole:

> While returning to the main thesis of the significant aesthetic value of the two polyphonic epilogues for this apparently monophonic poem [*Grażyna*], I would like to illustrate it with a rather risky comparison. There is an artist in Heidelberg, Siegfried Angermüller, who paints large, heavy structures, as if vast abstract iron gates, which, at the bottom of the picture become gradually blurred into vapoury mists, opening in them, only to re-emerge from those vapours at the top. [By analogy] in relation to the poem itself, "Editor's Epilogue" and "Historical Notes" create, as if, a sphere of such blurred potentiality, or alternativeness, from which the poem as such emerges, or into which it is absorbed. (140)

How much of this was Conrad aware of? How much of *Grażyna*'s pioneering value, the way Fieguth describes it in so many aspects, was he able to put his finger on? As a writer himself, Conrad could hardly have remained blind to Mickiewicz's innovative narration. Familiar with a writer's workshop, Conrad must have also been aware of the quality of his own national literary heritage (particularly after his visit to Poland in 1914). In other words, he was in possession of the requisite competences to evaluate it *ex post*; furthermore, he was particularly predisposed to do so from the perspective of a budding modernist. Therefore, in the latter part of this study, I will juxtapose the pioneering elements of *Grażyna*'s style with parallel elements of Conrad's own.

Doubling in *Grażyna*

The notorious aberrations of style observable in *Grażyna*, where nothing in the plot seems to stick together, make this historical poem "melt" into a modern mystery novella before our very eyes. What seems of utmost importance to specialists in Conrad studies is contained in the "twisted" narration of the poem and the semi-indirect speech applied therein. The narration itself is conducted by Rymwid, Litawor's most loyal servant and counselor as well as Grażyna's confidant, who, in his double role, seems to resemble Conrad's Marlow: "The duke calls him the other self," says Mickiewicz's outer narrator when speaking of Rymwid before the latter takes over in recounting the story.[4] *Grażyna* ends with a statement of uncertainty as to what actually passed at the Novgorod castle on the night of its defence against the attack by the Teutonic Knights. One can safely assume that such an ambiguous ending must have been "programed" from the very beginning of the poem, considering the fact that, at the request of Litawor himself, Rymwid withholds information about the heroic act of a woman knight, as indicated by the words of Grażyna's husband in his conversation with his counselor, particularly that both of them understand each other without words perfectly well, as doubles:

> I dislike airing plans of an unformed kind
> Before the eyes of various strangers,
> For intentions hatched in a murky mind
> Exposed prematurely can be quite dangerous.
> It is better to make the accomplished deed
> A thunderbolt ere lightning flashes forth.

> (Mickiewicz 1989: 79)

Clearly, what Litawor means here is his strategy of stealthy military activities against the Teutonic Knights. However, from the hermeneutic position, and in view of *Grażyna*'s ambiguous mode of narration, one may take the duke's words as performing a double function, by, literally, referring to Litawor's political strategies and, figuratively, to the narrative confusion occasioned by the two "additions" to the poem in the form of "Editor's Epilogue" and "Historical Notes."

The doubling of Litawor and Rymwid is mirrored in the doubling of Grażyna and Litawor: "Upon returning she fools every squire/By accepting homage meant for the duke/From the duped servants without a rebuke" (Mickiewicz 1989: 86). This is significant mainly because of Rymwid being, on the one hand, an important element of the triangle of doubling, and, on the other hand, his being "an odd man out" in that triangle. Being Litawor's alter ego, Rymwid is simultaneously Grażyna's confidant, so there is a risk of his testimony to her not being quite so impartial. Incidentally, a similar risk of partiality, or bias, characterizes Marlow's narrations in relation to Jim and Kurtz, as repeatedly marked by Ian Watt (1984: 173–6, 349–79).

Narration Modeling in *Grażyna*: Mickiewicz's
Rymwid versus Conrad's Marlow

In view of the above, Grażyna's appearance only halfway through the poem (around line 500, of 1089 lines in total), despite the fact that the poem is named after her, can hardly be ignored. Apart from her initial conversation with Rymwid (which only partly reveals her as the main heroine), we do not hear her voice during any of the conversations at the castle. The duchess of Lida must remain voiceless to prevent betraying herself not only during the battle itself, but also in her rather grotesque nonverbal command of Litawor's army.

The heroine's double absence—physical and verbal—evokes associations with Conrad's Flora de Barral in *Chance*, whose figure also comes to the fore only halfway through the novel, herself otherwise remaining silent, and thus mesmerizing Marlow with her reticence. As marked by Bruce Harkness, in her absence, the information about Flora comes from the narrators and focus reporters:

> As we get a portion of the story, coming through as many as five narrator-lenses, each lens is somehow distorting, untrue, in its picturing of Flora; but with Marlow's juxtaposition of the many lenses, we at last see her in the true light. ... The lenses in *Chance* are not only multiple in the sense that Marlow learns part of Flora's story from one person, then later learns more from another, but they are also multiple in a simultaneous sense. (1974: 562–3)

As mentioned before, Rymwid acts in a similar capacity in *Grażyna*. He doses information and averts attention from the events (and particularly from the conversations at the castle, which are crucial to the fate of the couple and the entire Duchy of Novgorod) with romantic descriptions like "Their armor emits a glistening ray,/The hoofbeats pound and then slowly abate,/The horses faintly whinny or neigh" (Mickiewicz 1989: 89). It is thus hard to avoid a sensation that Rymwid's hearing is selective: the more attentive the Lithuanian counselor is to the sounds of the night, and the horses' hooves, the more he wishes to hide away the content of human conversations. The narrator can be a true virtuoso in this respect, similarly to Conrad in his modernist impressionistic style. Overwhelmed with this discrete but subtle dissonance, we take no heed of what is missing in the narrative—that is, lack of confirmed information about Grażyna's conversation with Litawor about her going to battle in his stead and her dismissive send-off exchange with the Teutonic envoy Ditrich Halstark von Kniprode. What is more, the heroine does not seem to remember what she has been doing just then, and when Rymwid reminds her, only slivers emerge compared to what the reader would like to know, thus leaving them puzzled about Rymwid's sudden passage from euphoria to panic.

The only fragment of *Grażyna* that could justify Rymwid's abrupt cutting off of the narrative and depriving the reader of a direct access to the actual events are lines 760–6 (below), where he attributes Grażyna's actions to madness. If we were to take his suppositions at face value, the Lithuanians' worship of Grażyna's sacrificial act would amount to a worship of madness. Hence, similarly to Marlow in relation to Jim, Rymwid acts in the interest of Grażyna not "speaking … incoherently," which is also why after her initial "Yes," the narrative switches into free indirect discourse for a spell, to cover that up in a meta-narrative trick:

> "Yes," says the duchess, her pale face averted,
> Visibly agitated and most disconcerted,
> Speaking almost incoherently:
> "Now I remember, what you say is true …
> How could the facts escape me so quickly!
> I'm off—no, let us wait—or, I know what to do"
>
> (Mickiewicz 1989: 92)

Mickiewicz's Experiment with Free Indirect Discourse

If we were to agree with Bernard Cerquiglini that "the concept of free indirect discourse derives principally from the concept of modernity as a certain vision accommodating contradictions and lack of acuity" (1990: 337), we should consider *Grażyna* to be the first Polish work that, from the perspective of the first half of the nineteenth century, could be defined as an epic in the modern sense of the word, and so, hailing literary modernism:[5]

> This is because Litawor is no longer a man of the former mythical and ritual tribal community; he is a modern individualist, and thus, as a ruler, he is ruthless as regards his people, his enemies, and himself. I believe that, in the stylistic dimension, this modern individualism of the protagonist finds its reflection in the phenomena of discrete polyphony, and, particularly, free indirect discourse. (Fieguth 1996: 136; after Maciejewski 1970)

Secondly, one of the most interesting "narrative knots" (as Maciejewski calls them) involving "rhetorical free direct discourse" and "anti-rhetorical free indirect discourse" in *Grażyna* comes in the fragment of the battle with

Figure 1 A monument of Grażyna and Litawor in Kraków's Planty by Alfred Daun (unveiled on July 7, 1886). Courtesy ©Weronika Branny.

the female knight in the picture (Fieguth 1996: 134).[6] Grażyna aestheticizes the battlefield to a specific end (as it turns out)—to evoke the *furor militans* in herself. Her "battle wrath" is linguistically rendered through the use of gentle, unmanly imagery, although the source of this female imagination lies in a male, that is Rymwid, continuing his discourse, and probably creating this moment of the battle *post factum* for the reader. As in the case of Marlow's narrative games and playing with gender in *Chance*, we have no real access to Grażyna's mind. What we view here is the female mind *als ob*—namely "as if" this access were an actual fact:

> They are as splendid as a dense forest
> Adorning a hilltop on a moonlit night
> When gales have stripped it of summer's best,
> And the dew hangs beads, luminous and bright,
> Then suddenly changes into pearly hoarfrost,
> The wayward stroller then, indeed, believes
> That trees are silver and crystal their leaves.
>
> (Mickiewicz 1989: 94)

"Typhoon" in the Light of *Grażyna*'s Pioneering Role

If *Grażyna* may have served as a generator of ideas as well as literary and structural concepts for Conrad over a longer period of time—for instance, in his Marlow narratives (*Lord Jim* and *Chance*, but possibly also "Heart of Darkness")—it might also be possible to select Conrad's "variant of *Grażyna*," which would mimic its entire structure as well as formal content while using the plot of a marine story. And this work would have to be "Typhoon."

Here, one would clearly be speaking about *dynamic experience*—that is a *progressive loss* of knowledge about the topic, rather than absence of knowledge. This is achieved by a narrative of deprivation rather than enrichment as the story operates *à rebours*. This *modus operandi* of Conrad's long short story is "disenchanting," "robbing," "stripping" the reader of the assumed knowledge about the world presented and its central topic, in which "Typhoon" matches *Grażyna* to an astounding degree.

Agnieszka Adamowicz-Pośpiech writes about "Typhoon" in language that could successfully be used to describe the "tricks" of Mickiewicz's Rymwid, who is telling the story in such a way as to turn void as much as possible from what remains to be told or what has already been told earlier. Finally, *Grażyna*'s readers find themselves in the same position as the readers of "Typhoon," who wish to know "what really happened during the central attack of the typhoon on the ship." Speaking on behalf of the latter, Adamowicz-Pośpiech writes, "while ending the novella, we know nothing about the eponymous event; in the book titled 'Typhoon,' there is no word about the actual hurricane: there is BEFORE and there is AFTER, but there is no DURING" (2016: 96–7).

Just like Grażyna's, MacWhirre's act remains concealed from us. We are informed about both via different "media": in *Grażyna*, through a manuscript by an unknown author (the author of the poem), a squire's report, a compilation of sources written by the "editor," and, oxymoronically, through Rymwid's silence. It is also unknown who "authorized" the poem. All we know is that it is not anyone from the location, but rather someone "who remained at the town of Novgorod at the time," a stranger, an "editor," who openly admits his own lack of knowledge about the legendary events. To boot, the manuscript was acquired in rather unclear circumstances:

> If you, dear reader, have read to the end, tantalized,
> Without succumbing to sleep, I am not surprised.
> For if loose ends of a tangled tale aren't tied,
> Curiosity will remain vexed and unsatisfied.
> *Why did the duke stay behind and send forth his wife?*
> *Why did his aid come too late in the midst of strife?*
> *Did the duchess decide on her own to take his place?*
> *Then why did Litawor enter the battle apace?*
> You'd look for answers to all these questions in vain.
> However, this much the story's author made plain:
> What he saw and heard (being present in town as a guest)
> He promptly wrote down but kept silent about the rest.
> Unable to find out the truth and bring it to light,
> He was loath to betray it by guesswork, by not being right.

> (Mickiewicz 1989: 103; emphasis added)

The micro-motif of a wandering manuscript, incidentally signaled in *Grażyna*, may bring associations with *The Manuscript Found in Saragossa* by Jan Potocki. Conrad's choice of Potocki, if any, could also be due to the fact that Potocki's book represents a modern approach to concentric prose, and thus differs from the Enlightenment version of one. To all appearances, Mickiewicz's *Grażyna* also represents the same post-Enlightenment model of a concentric story (Davies 1996: 6; Pacukiewicz 2010: 6–7).

According to the "editor," the deadlock that the author of the manuscript in *Grażyna* has found himself in has its source not so much in his own tricks as in his inability "*to find out the truth* and *to bring it to light*" (emphasis added). What comes as a surprise in this context are the colloquialisms popping up out of the blue in the report of the "editor." Mickiewicz's playing with stylistic registers in a spontaneous speculation over the nature of the fiction shaped by the narrator may have been "inspirational" for Conrad in *Lord Jim* or *Chance* (Marlow) as well as "The Inn of the Two Witches."

As Agnieszka Adamowicz-Pośpiech explains, what "holds the story together" in "Typhoon" are fragments of letters by Captain Tom MacWhirr, First Engineer Salomon Rout, and First Mate Jukes, with which "the *Nan-Shan*'s voyage begins and ends" (2016: 87), although, similarly to the situation in *Grażyna*, this seems to be a purely rhetorical device for the story to come full circle. Likewise, the frameworks of both "Typhoon" and *Grażyna* are molded out of the analogical texture of questions and doubts pertaining to the nature of the event that passed in the blink of an eye: one night's tragedy, in the case of Mickiewicz's poem, and the miraculous overnight survival of the *Nan-Shan*, in the case of Conrad's story.

Moreover, it is more likely than not that Conrad's "epistolary report fiction" in "Typhoon" has its prototype in Mickiewicz's "editorial fiction" in *Grażyna*. Hence, "Typhoon" may indeed be seen as a foil to Mickiewicz's poem. Further, common points between the two texts include not so much the selectiveness of the information available to the reader as rather its deliberate fragmentation, tearing up whole reports (already lacking coherence) into remnants of accounts. This is characteristic of Conrad's tale principally with respect to MacWhirre's wife, who reads her husband's correspondence, as detailed by Adamowicz-Pośpiech (2016: 90). If we were to nuance the two approaches, for a change, Conrad focuses on the circulation of the comment on the events, whereas Mickiewicz, on the mechanism of turning those events into a myth, a legend, and public worship.

Jukes's letter could then be seen as having its equivalent in the oral account of Grażyna's squire, most fundamental to the poem's "editor," who records it in writing as the only available "live" report from the tragic night of the battle:

> By luck, one other man knew the secret as well:
> The duchess' alert groom then employed by the court,
> *Less reluctant to speak, being a simple sort.*
> I took notes as he spoke because I saw that his words
> Agree indeed with all that the author records.
> That they are reliable I truthfully cannot attest;
> Therefore, if accused of falsehood, I will not protest.
> But I add nothing and am repeating verbatim
> Merely that which I heard directly from him.
>
> (Mickiewicz 1989: 103; emphasis added)

"The Secret Sharer" in the Light of *Grażyna's* Pioneering Role

Because of the limited space available in this book, this study only covers a small selection of *Grażyna's* contexts that may have been potentially important to Conrad. The most significant of them, involving doubling in two different configurations, which may have inspired Conrad in his creation of Marlow, has already been mentioned as the triangle of Grażyna, Litawor, and Rymwid and dual doubles (Litawor and Grażyna), the latter deriving from Plato's androgenic myth of the *Symposium*. As such, the similarity between Grażyna and Litawor relates to their physiognomies and involves mirroring. The Duchess is reported to be left-handed, while the Duke is right-handed; the Duchess lives in "the castle's left side" (Mickiewicz 1989: 85), while the Duke in the opposite (right) one. Grażyna's left-handedness is only hypothetical, but cannot be ruled out, judging by the witness accounts coming from the battlefield: "And, strangely, fastens his sword at his right,/But though all witness the fault with a shiver,/ No one dares to correct the master tonight" (Mickiewicz 1989: 83). This is a fascinating moment in the poem, which is later echoed in the squire's account recorded in "Editor's Epilogue." Grażyna's mistake (or left-handedness) can also lead to another conclusion about the ending of the poem. The squire, who knows about the entire masquerade *ex post*, can conclude (from what he has seen) that Grażyna, dressed up as Litawor, went to the battle deliberately unarmed—most probably wishing to sacrifice herself to pay for her husband's betrayal of their people to the Teutonic Knights Order rather than to fight the enemy: "His horse had been saddled; as she prepared to mount,/I saw no sword on her left; therefore I thought/That, in the dark, she had lost it or simply forgot" (Mickiewicz 1989: 104).

Mishaps, ambiguities, delusions, and games of illusions observable in *Grażyna* also lie at the core of Conrad's workshop as a mature writer. They also constitute a key element of his literary "approach" of "cognitive impressionism" (Peters 2001: 123–58). The doubles of Mickiewicz's type seem to revive in "The Secret Sharer": "Like him in face and in body's outline,/She, like her husband, has a stout heart"; "Not merely in body and soul his treasure,/She also shares his thoughts and authority" (Mickiewicz 1989: 86). A similar sort of mental (but also emotional) communication can be observed between the Captain of the *Sephora* and Leggatt: "He appealed to me as if our experiences had been as identical as our clothes"; "My sleeping suit was just right for his size"; "I saw it all going on as though I were myself inside that other sleeping suit" (SS 1230–1). The motif of dressing up in the other's clothes is also present in Mickiewicz, although even without it, "As by a low, level forest, the pair/Resembles two poplars, handsome and tall" (Mickiewicz 1989: 85).

> Needles, spindles, any female pastime
> She spurns in favor of a manly art.
> Often hunting astride a Samogitian steed,
> Dressed in a rough bearskin cuirass,
> White claws of a lynx clasping her head,
> She romps amid hunting riflemen's mass.
> To her husband's delight, in this attire,
> Upon returning she foods every squire
> By accepting homage meant for the duke
> From the duped servants without a rebuke.
>
> (Mickiewicz 1989: 86)

Similarly, in Conrad, "anybody bold enough to open it [the door] stealthily would have been treated to the uncanny sight of a double captain busy talking in whispers with his other self" (SS 1233):

> It occurred to me that if old "Bless my soul—you don't say so" were to put his head up the companion and catch sight of us, he would think he was seeing double, or imagine himself come upon a scene of weird witchcraft; the strange captain having a quiet confabulation by the wheel with his own gray ghost. (SS 1232)

Conclusion

This holistic attempt to trace a possibly "inspirational" role of *Grażyna* for some of Conrad's texts—as may follow from Conrad's 1914 interview for Marian Dąbrowski, which testifies to the writer's intense childhood exposure also to other epic poems in verse by Mickiewicz (*Pan Tadeusz, Konrad Wallenrod*)—shows that Conrad may have turned to Mickiewicz for motifs and modern narrative devices that Fieguth associates with the poetic novella in the Dostoyevskyan and Nabokovian styles, which surface in *Grażyna*'s pioneering narrative form. In this context, rather than pointing to specific parallels between Conrad's texts and *Grażyna*, or the other two texts by Mickiewicz mentioned in Conrad's Polish interview, it is far more important to underscore his ability to creatively rewrite *Grażyna's* "editor's fiction" in the "epistolary fiction" of "Typhoon"; Mickiewicz's doubling of characters in the said poem in the *doppelganger* strategy of "The Secret Sharer"; and diverse narratorial accounts and silences in *Grażyna* in the narrative strategies of *Lord Jim*, "Heart of Darkness," or *Chance*. The present analysis may only be pointing out the tip of the iceberg—namely, the covert existence of a "global" intertextuality of Polish Romanticism in Conrad's prose, mirroring the hidden aspect of Conrad's artistry coupled with transtextuality and transculturalism—to be as yet brought from the hypothetical to a functional level in Conrad studies.

Notes

1 The plot of Mickiewicz's poem takes place in the fourteenth century within Novgorod Castle in Lithuania during the course of one night. Litawor, the duke of the castle, welcomes messengers from the Order of Teutonic Knights, with whom he is bound by a secret alliance. The Order is to help him regain Lida, a Lithuanian land and dowry of his wife, Grażyna, but claimed by the Lithuanian ruler Witołd. Litawor is contacted about the awaiting messengers by Rymwid, his faithful servant, who attempts to discourage the duke from entering into the controversial alliance. Unable to succeed, he addresses Grażyna about the problematic allies, and she engages in another conversation with her husband in his private chambers. Neither Rymwid nor the reader witnesses the conversation, but they can see its consequences: the duchess's servant sends the Teutonic messengers away, which is perceived as a breach of the alliance, provoking a Teutonic attack on Litawor's castle. Not only on her husband's behalf, but also dressed as him (as she very much resembled her husband), Grażyna goes into battle and receives a lethal blow from the hand of the Teutonic *Komtur* Dmitrich von Kniprode. On the day after the battle, when the duchess's body is about to be ritually burnt on a pyre, Litawor follows her into the fire to be burnt alive together with his wife. The story is told *ex post* from several perspectives, which surface in Rymwid's reconstructed narration in verse called the "Editor's Epilogue" (based on the recovered manuscript of the story) and "Historical Notes" in prose, perhaps written from the authorial point of view.
2 All translations from the works of Polish critics by Justyna Piątkowska.
3 Krzyżanowski extended his remark in a separate article published two years later, titled "O tragedii na Samburanie" (1963: 333–7).
4 Fieguth goes even further in suggesting a Conrad–Mickiewicz parallel (quite a risky one, however) in this doubling game, by putting forward the idea of the polyhedronic relations involved therein: Conrad–Marlow–Jim/Kurtz versus Mickiewicz–Rymwid–Litawor/Grażyna (1996: 135).

5 In this respect, *Grażyna* leaves behind both Mickiewicz's own later creation of *Pan Tadeusz* and Juliusz Słowacki's much praised *Beniowski*, in containing at least a few cases of free indirect discourse, which are absolutely unique for Polish Romanticism and were catalogued by Rolf Fieguth and Marian Maciejewski.

6 Fieguth explains the "rhetorical 'free direct discourse'" in *Grażyna* as "the direct speech of the protagonist, which was clearly engineered by the narrator" and "anti-rhetorical 'free indirect discourse'" as "equally a result of interference between the speech of the narrator and that of the protagonist" (1996: 134).

References

Adamowicz-Pośpiech, Agnieszka. 2016. *Podróże z Conradem. Szkice* [Travels with Conrad. Sketches]. Kraków: Universitas.

Cerquiglini, Bernard. 1990. "Mowa pozornie zależna i nowoczesność" [Free Indirect Discourse and Modernity]. *Pamiętnik Literacki* 4: 337–48.

Dąbrowska, Maria. 1974. *Szkice o Conradzie* [Conrad Sketches], edited by E. Korzeniewska. Warszawa: Państwowy Instytut Wydawniczy.

Davies, Laurence. 1996. "Conrad and Potocki: A Speculation." In *Conrad and Poland*, edited by A. S. Kurczaba, 179–94. Lublin: UMCS and Boulder.

Fieguth, Rolf. 1996. "Kilka uwag o stylu *Grażyny*" [A Few Remarks on the Style of *Grażyna*]. *Pamiętnik Literacki* 1: 127–40.

Harkness, Bruce. 1974. "Epigraf *Gry losu*" [The Epigraph of *Chance*]. Translated by M. Ronikier. In *Conrad w oczach krytyki światowej* [Conrad in the Eyes of World Critics], edited by Zdzisław Najder, 557–75. Warszawa: Państwowy Instytut Wydawniczy.

Krzyżanowski, Julian. 1932. "U źródeł publicystyki Josepha Conrada" [At the Roots of Conrad's Political Essays]. *Ruch Literacki* 8: 243–8.

Krzyżanowski, Julian. 1963. "O tragedii na Samburanie" [On the Tragedy on Samburan]. In *Wspomnienia i studia o Conradzie* [Memories and Studies on Conrad], edited by B. Kocówna, 333–7. Warszawa: Państwowy Instytut Wydawniczy.

Maciejewski, Marian. 1970. *Narodziny powieści poetyckiej w Polsce* [The Birth of Poetic Novel in Poland]. Wrocław: Zakład Narodowy imienia Ossolińskich—Wydawnictwo Polskiej Akademii Nauk.

Mickiewicz, Adam. 1989. *Grażyna: A Lithuanian Tale*. In *Konrad Wallenrod* and *Grażyna*. Translated by I. Suboczewski. New York: University Press of America.

Pacukiewicz, Marek. 2010. "Conrad i Potocki—dwa 'rękopisy'" [Conrad and Potocki: Two "Manuscripts"]. *Pamiętnik Literacki* 3: 5–22.

Peters, John. 2001. *Conrad and Impressionism*. Cambridge: Cambridge University Press.

Retinger, Józef Hieronim. 1943. *Conrad and His Contemporaries. Souvenirs.* New York: Roy Publishers.

Tarnawski, Wit. 1972. *Conrad. Człowiek—pisarz—Polak* [Conrad: Man, Writer, Pole]. London: Polska Fundacja Kulturalna.

Watt, Ian. 1984. *Conrad w wieku dziewiętnastym* [*Conrad in the Nineteenth Century* (1979)]. Translated by M. Boduszyńska-Borowikowa. Gdańsk: Wydawnictwo Morskie.

3

An Epistemological and Denegative Reinterpretation in the Faulknerian Context of Conrad's Malay Tale "The Planter of Malata"

Grażyna Maria Teresa Branny
Jesuit University Ignatianum, Kraków

Conrad's so-called weaker short fiction, including "The Planter of Malata," has been notoriously undervalued, if not altogether downgraded, by his critics for its apparent "strangeness," melodrama, and even incongruity. This critical tendency seems to have been a consequence of the content of Conrad's tales being taken too much at face value and given precedence over their form and expression. Indeed, it is only a convergence of all three of these factors that fully reveals the extent of the writer's artistic achievement, especially with regard to modernist narrative techniques, in some of his underrated short stories, including "The Planter of Malata."

The aesthetic, transtextual, and transcultural approach to Conrad's 1914 tale adopted in this chapter reveals its full artistic dimension. With its multiple voices and truths as well as denegative narration, "The Planter of Malata"—like some of Conrad's other tales[1]—appears to anticipate William Faulkner's use of denegation in his greatest novels, notably *The Sound and the Fury* ([1929] 1954 and *Absalom, Absalom!* ([1936] 1972). Defined by François Pitavy in relation to Faulkner's oeuvres, denegation as a modernist narrative technique involves asserting presence by absence (or vice versa), making a fact the more present for its absence or for the absence of the apparent reasons for that presence, thus affirming the truth of the matter by its apparent negation.[2] Although it is Faulkner who has generally been deemed the precursor of denegation to date, it transpires that Conrad may have been the first to set the pace by experimenting with this oxymoronic narrative technique, and thus the modernist relativity of truth, more than a decade before Faulkner.

Indeed, the whole of Conrad's volume of *Within the Tides*, which is home to "The Planter of Malata," revolves around the idea of truth as opposed to facts, an issue of prime concern in Faulkner's *Requiem for a Nun* ([1951] 1953) written almost four decades later. The multiplicity of "truths" surfacing in "The Planter of Malata"—none of which proves valid in the end—brings to mind the multiple "truths" of Faulkner's narrators in *Absalom, Absalom!* each of whom provides his own "way of looking at a blackbird"—that is, the story of the Sutpen progeny's triangular love centered in Charles Bon, which, incidentally, bears a striking resemblance to the tragic love trio in "The Planter of Malata," with the ghostly presence of Arthur vel Walter at its center.

That said, "The Planter of Malata," which has so far been perceived as opening the phase of "Conrad's artistic 'decline'" (Erdinast-Vulcan 1999: 155) and dubbed Conrad's "interesting and problematic failure" (Knowles 1979: 177–84), or else charged with "excessive sentimentality" (McLauchlan 1986: 178, n11), may in fact be perceived as Conrad's modernist exercise in epistemological truth, with denegation at its core. As such, it may have provided William Faulkner with a number of ideas for the construction of his narratives in *Absalom, Absalom!* and *The Sound and the Fury* as well as elsewhere in his fiction, although the American modernist never directly acknowledged his literary debt to Conrad, claiming instead that a writer "is so busy stealing and using it that he himself probably never knows where he gets what he uses" (Faulkner, qtd. in Jeliffe 1956: 72).[3]

* * *

Set partly in Sydney and partly on a fictional island of Malata, Conrad's story apparently capitalizes on his Malaysian period of twenty years before and memories of a friend, captain Carlos Marris's 1909 visit to his house in England (Hampson 2000: 11–12). The story is considered one of Conrad's bleakest, if not the bleakest of all his tales (Kehler 1976: 161), chiefly on account of its tragic ending involving an apparent suicide of its main protagonist. As indicated by Ted Billy, notwithstanding all its scrutiny with regard to "artistic strategy," "The Planter of Malata" has "rarely" been "considered … exclusively on its own terms" (1997: 150). It has been particularly analyzed in relation to *Victory* (Johnson 1989: 177–204) and perceived as its miniature, or considered in the context of the writer's biography as a follow-up on his 1910 breakdown (Meyer 1967: 222). It has also been seen as "generally schizophrenic" and an expression of Conrad's own preoccupations, if not "obsessions" (Erdinast-Vulcan 1999: 155), related to, as pointed out by Bernard Meyer, the writer's rejection by Eugénie Renouf during his sojourn in Mauritius, and, as such, is "ample material for a psychological analysis" (Erdinast-Vulcan 1999: 155).

Judged upon its artistic merit, it has been marked for its "melodramatic imagery and rhetoric" (Billy 1997: 150), "extreme romanticism" (Baines 1986: 470), and "black and white simplicity," "platitudes," and "easy formulas" (Meyer 1967: 222). Treated straightforwardly, as a tragic love story, it has been stereotyped as "a crude juxtaposition of masculine integrity versus feminine falsehood" in accordance with "the underlying assumptions of Conrad's work through most of his writing life" (Erdinast-Vulcan 1999: 157). Or, quite the contrary, it has been seen as "a satire on the romantic idealization of womanhood, a burlesque of the estranged loner, and a *reductio ad absurdum* of the doppelgänger theme" (Billy 1997: 150), with its final and generally unappreciated "ironic twist" exploding its melodramatic content (163).

The critical readings of the short story that approximate to my own tend to perceive it as a representation of "a quest for knowledge," which Kehler calls "quasi-allegorical" (qtd. in Billy 1997: 255, n.1), while Billy refers to as a "parody" (1997: 150). In view of the Author's Note added to *Within the Tides* seven years after the volume's publication, where Conrad specifically names truth rather than knowledge as an object of his interest in both "The Planter of Malata" and the volume as a whole, in my approach to this Conrad tale, I follow the writer's specific recommendations and treat truth as an overriding category in relation to facts. A similar distinction between the two categories is made by William Faulkner in his *Requiem for a Nun*, where he sees the fact of Nancy Mannigoe's murder of Temple's little daughter as standing in no relation to the overriding truth of the salvation of Temple's soul thereby. An analogical distinction between truth and facts, or truth and knowledge, provides insight into Conrad's use of denegation in the story's ending, which features the Planter's apparent suicide.

In the Author's Note to *Within the Tides*, Conrad delineates his aim in his fiction as "that conscientious rendering of truth in thought and fact" (*WT* 6), wherein seems to lie the key to the difference between a quest for knowledge (as seen by Kehler) and a quest for truth as Conrad's basic premise in "The Planter of Malata," as seen here. While the former defines the story's thematics, the latter delineates its aesthetics and as such remains of primary relevance for the ensuing argument. The other case of Conrad harping on about truth in the Author's Note relates truth to art and life. Notably, the characters of the story are described by the author as "made to give themselves away" (through passions) rather than "disclosing themselves" (through speech). The former kind of exposition identified by the writer as "neither art nor life … Not yet truth!" (7) is perceived by him as forming an opposition to the latter, which Conrad identifies as art. Simultaneously, "the whole truth" is seen by the author as tantamount to "all its necessary and sympathetic reservations and qualifications which give it its form, its just proportions, its semblance of human fellowship," with the main difficulty, according to the author, lying in translating "passions into speech," the issue bearing directly on the modernist inability to communicate (8).

Hence, on a personal level, Conrad's tragic protagonists in "The Planter of Malata" seem to owe their failure to discover the truth to the breakdown of communication between them caused by a lack of nuanced empathy on either side—and not just on Felicia's own. This lack of the "necessary and sympathetic reservations and qualifications" on both sides is coupled with an inability to meet halfway: in her admitting to her budding love for Renouard and him controlling his blinding jealousy over Arthur's ghostly presence in Felicia's life. On the general level, however, the failure of communication in the tale seems to be related to something larger than personal relations—namely, to the basic irrecoverableness of truth, the phenomenon to which both the fates of the two protagonists and the scope of vision of the remaining characters as well as the tale's narrative perspectives appear to testify.

The most glaring example of that is the scene of Renouard's departure from the Dunsters' party when he overhears the inmates of the party expressing their divergent impressions of his persona: "old Dunster uttering oracularly—'… the leading man here some day … Like me'"; Professor Moorsom replying, "He never counted the cost they say. Not even of lives"; Mrs. Dunster adding, "Don't let yourself be shocked by the tales you may hear of him, my dear. Most of it is envy"; and finally, Miss Moorsom concluding, "Oh! I am not easily deceived. I think I may say I have an instinct for truth." Hearing all that makes the Planter leave the house "with his heart full of dread" (*WT* 42), and justifiably so, considering that none of those opinions proves true in the end, not even Miss Moorsom's about her own abilities to detect the truth. This inability of the characters to know the truth of the matter proves most ironic in the story's denegative ending—incidentally, unrecognized as such to date by Conrad's critics, none of whom has ever questioned the validity of the characters' supposition as to Renouard's death in general and his death by suicide in particular, despite a lack of textual evidence to substantiate either.

To the more discerning, further consideration of the Author's Note to *Within the Tides* reveals more than meets the eye, and definitely more than met the eye of one of Conrad's critics, who described the Note as an "elaborate and peculiar apologia for the story" upon recognizing "its weaknesses and yet refus[ing] to let go of it" by way of "a direct reply to critical charges ... a muffled, not quite coherent, attempt at an artistic manifesto" (Erdinast-Vulcan 1999: 165). However, the same critic marks a striking similarity in phrasing between the fragment of the Author's Note pertaining to "The Planter of Malata" and the writer's comment on *Romance* twenty years earlier, with Conrad's intentions in the story described as "mainly aesthetic" (*WT* 10) and in the novel as "purely aesthetic" (Najder 1964: 236). While pointing to the inferiority of both texts, Daphna Erdinast-Vulcan fails to recognize the connection between them in both appearing to be examples of Conrad's artistic experimentations. In the tale in question, those experimentations would be encoded in Renouard's planting and manufacturing experiment with an artificial "Arghan" silk plant, the economic vogue of the day (cf. Lane 2007), and in *Romance* they would relate to "something which was very much in vogue with the public"—as Conrad wrote in his 1903 letter to Kazimierz Waliszewski (Najder 1964: 236)—apparently referring to his modernist techniques later capitalized on by William Faulkner and T. S. Eliot (cf. Renner 1998).

Moreover, Conrad's repeated revisions of "The Planter of Malata," coupled with the story's opening position in the *Within the Tides* collection as well as the amount of space it is afforded in the Author's Note (practically to the exclusion of all other tales in the volume), find their reflection in its description by the author as "a nearly successful attempt at doing a very difficult thing which I would have liked to have made as perfect as it lay in my power." Ending on a somewhat playful note—"Perhaps a little mistrust of my own powers would not have been altogether out of place in this connection" (*WT* 7)—the writer expresses general distrust of explicitness, which he later voices in his 1922 letter to Richard Curle in the following way: "Nothing is more clear than the utter insignificance of explicit statement and also its power to call attention away from things that matter in the region of art" (*CL7* 457). Without being explicit, then, about what precisely he is doing in "The Planter of Malata" aesthetically, Conrad seems to be implying that it is of paramount importance for art.

In view of the aesthetic approach to "The Planter of Malata" adopted in this chapter, which sees the story as dramatizing Conrad's modernist quest for truth rather than his characters' quest for knowledge, the shift in the tale's narrative perspective, which Daphna Erdinast-Vulcan perceives as a major reason for the disruption of the story's "initial framing strategy" (1999: 162)—and thus a proof of its "artistic failure"—should be seen as an asset rather than a flaw. For it is precisely in the story's shifts between the personal, authorial, and omniscient narrations, on the one hand, and between reported speech and psychological realism passages, on the other hand, that lies, what Jakob Lothe calls, "the narrative sophistication" of Conrad's fiction (1989: 303). In "The Planter of Malata" it surfaces in an interplay of professional and intellectual vanities on the part of the Editor and Professor Moorsom; the hidden agenda of discretion and reticence about personal feelings, enmities, and jealousies on the part of Renouard; and half-baked truths, society's clichés, and personal misconceptions on the part of Felicia Moorsom—all this leading to personal disillusionments on the level of the plot and paradoxical ironies on the thematic level. This chapter subscribes to Lothe's opinion that "the narrative sophistication of [Conrad's] fiction" lies in the "thematic implications" of the writer's "narrative devices or functions which at first seem redundant, obscure, even baffling" but come into their own in the process of close reading and/or rereading of a Conrad text (1989: 303–4).

* * *

Throughout his narrative in "The Planter of Malata," Conrad seems to be drawing a line between truth and facts by demonstrating how those who should be in possession of knowledge, either by virtue of their professions ("the all-knowing Editor," and Professor Moorsom, the physicist) or their access to facts (Felicia Moorsom and Renouard), fail to command the truth of the matter, even while claiming otherwise. For as Renouard exclaims at the rock: "Oh! If you could only understand the truth that is in me!" (*WT* 66), and Felicia echoes him in the same scene, "It's I who stand for truth here" (*WT* 66). The question therefore arises as to who, or what, appears to be at fault—the protagonists' egos and their lack of "sympathetic reservations" or the fundamental irrecoverableness of truth as such.

The first step that the narration of the story takes toward an assertion of the divergence between truth and facts, and thus toward the modernist relativity of truth, is to disclaim the very stereotypes it sets out to establish, by branding the three male members of the search party for Felicia's fiancé, and the tale's chief male authorities on the "truth" of the matter, as: Editor, a man of facts and expression; Planter, a man of action and "force" (*WT* 41); and Professor, a man of thought and knowledge. As the story progresses, despite their claims to the contrary, none of the three male authorities proves to be the bearer of truth—neither the newsmonger, nor the scientist, nor even the explorer endowed in the story with such accessories of enlightenment as, first, a lantern and then a lamp, the latter appropriately seen by Kehler as the epitome of the Jungian self, overshadowing the truth rather than illuminating it (1976: 156–7). Nor can either of the two female members of the search party—Felicia Moorsom or her elderly aunt and sister to Professor Moorsom—claim ownership of the truth for themselves, the former given to pretense and appearances ("Foam and Froth") and the latter to nothing but convention. To uphold appearances, toward the end of the story, Felicia sacrifices the last vestiges of her claims to truth by choosing to disclose to the search party nothing but the bare fact of Arthur's eventual demise while keeping to herself the truth about Renouard's role and motivation in withholding this truth from everyone but himself.

Hence, the story's substance for the most part consists of the "hidden agendas" (Hawthorn 2003: 129) of truth commented on by its personal narrators (the Editor and the Planter) and the agendas implicit in omniscient, authorial, and psychological realism narrations. The resultant effect is tantamount to the multiple voice narration of modernist fiction later found in the novels of William Faulkner. Coupled with the hidden and implicit agendas, "multiple voice" narration is one ensuing from the story's closest relationship—the male friendship between the Editor and the Planter, of whom the former is given to pleasing and publicity and the latter to privacy and skepticism, both alternately misreading each other.

The interaction between Renouard and the Editor, with one correcting the narrative perspective of the other, especially after the arrival of the guilt-ridden Felicia Moorsom in search of her wronged fiancé, anticipates the relationship between Quentin and Shreve in Faulkner's *Absalom, Absalom!* and *The Sound and the Fury*. Just as to Renouard, "Malata was himself. He and Malata were one" (*WT* 53), so was the plantation South to Quentin, even though his was a love-hate relationship, which he vehemently denied in front of Shreve: "I dont hate it … I dont hate it … *I dont!*" (Faulkner 1972: 378; emphasis in original). Just as the Editor is putting things into proportion for Renouard in speculating about the nature of the love bond between Arthur and Felicia, so does Shreve do the same *per proxy* for the obsessed Quentin twenty years later, in their mutual reconstruction of the story of alleged love between Charles Bon and Judith Sutpen, the authenticity of the actual affection in both cases appearing highly suspect in the process. Even the Editor's narrative, described by Renouard as "robbed as it was of all glamour by the prosaic personality of the narrator" (*WT* 27) appears to be a prototype of Shreve's matter-of-fact narration in *Absalom, Absalom!* Likewise, the Editor's speculation about "the great love at the root of it. Ah! Love!" (*WT* 26), conducted on the level of modality in his wild guessing as to Arthur's whereabouts—"he *may have* lit out into the Western Pacific" (*WT* 29; emphasis added) or "*may* be passing at this very moment under this very window" (*WT* 29; emphasis added)—appears to preclude the contingencies of Faulkner's convoluted style, full of qualifying phrases, conditional clauses, perfect infinitives, and modalities, in Rosa Coldfield's narrative in *Absalom, Absalom!*

Moreover, the suspicions raised against Renouard toward the end of Conrad's story about his possible murder of Felicia's fiancé anticipate the speculations concerning Henry Sutpen's murder of his half-brother Charles Bon in Faulkner's novel, sick jealousy at stake in both cases. Even Faulkner's phrasing in the famous passage where Henry envies any man's intimacy with his sister is vaguely evocative of Conrad's phrasing in Renouard saying to himself in a fit of "a misty creeping jealousy ... that another man would have found long before the happy release of madness, his wits burnt to cinders in that radiance. But no such luck for him" (*WT* 27–36).

Likewise, more than one critic remarks on the obviously intended identification in Conrad's story between Arthur and Renouard, where they not infrequently merge into one and the same pronoun (Erdinast-Vulcan 1999: 159) "as alter-egos" (Billy 1997: 154), just as do Quentin and Henry, Quentin and Shreve, and Henry and Charles Bon: "not two but four of them riding the two horses through the dark" to Sutpen's Hundred (Faulkner 1972: 334). Another curious analogy between Conrad's tale and Faulkner's novel concerns Renouard and Felicia's synecdochal representation as the heads of two goddesses—Pallas and Minerva—merged into one and then merging with the image of Arthur looking at Renouard from the mirror in the latter's dream, where both Renouard's and Felicia's heads turn into dust. The analogy is possibly exploited in Faulkner's creation of the incestuous relationship between Henry and Judith, and Judith and Charles Bon, where Quentin merges with Henry as at once a narrator of his story, his fellow Southerner, and brother to a sister (Caddy), whom he loves incestuously to the point of committing suicide by drowning in *The Sound and the Fury* (1929).

The analogies between "The Planter of Malata" and *Absalom, Absalom!* likewise extend to both authors' presentations of their heroines' misconceptions about their fiancés' alleged affections for them. In Conrad's tale, Felicia Moorsom believes about Arthur—who really hates her after being rejected by her on the basis of false corruption charges raised against him—that "He will come back to claim me; and I'll marry him" (*WT* 29). In *Absalom, Absalom!* Judith Sutpen expects Charles Bon to send for her on the basis of the only letter from him from the front, in which he states, "I have waited long enough" (Faulkner 1972: 132), which in fact refers to his father's acknowledgment of himself as half-caste rather than his intended marriage to Judith. Moreover, just as Miss Moorsom intends to marry her fiancé out of a sheer and impassioned sense of duty in order to rectify the wrong she has done to him and exclusively out of a moral debt she thinks she owes him, Judith receives the news of Charles Bon's death dispassionately and keeps going about her daily business as usual.

The plot and narrative parallels between Conrad's tale and Faulkner's novels are rich in other, as much puzzling as dazzling, detail, coupled with analogical phrasing in both texts abundant enough to fill in a separate study and bring Faulkner to the pillory for his unacknowledged debt to Conrad.

* * *

As the action of "The Planter of Malata" unfolds, the secret feelings, motivations, and agendas of the characters become slowly unveiled through the story's narrative complexity until nothing is the same as what it appeared to be at the start. Thus Renouard turns out to be an introvert rather than a socialite, a man of passions, such as morbid love and obsessive jealousy, rather than a man of action, especially that it is in inaction that his life apparently ends, and his single-mindedness is more a matter of love and personal reticence than cruelty. The Editor "of the principal newspaper in a great colonial city" (*WT* 13), "the place where everything is known about everybody—including even a great deal of nobodies" (*WT* 15), ironically, ends up literally in the dark— "under the mysterious silence" and "a black cloud hung listlessly over the high rock" (*WT* 73), speculating about his friend's alleged death by drowning upon coming across a heap of his clothing on the shore. Stripped of her patent for truth, and a noble if pathetic chance to provide her fiancé with a destiny that she had deprived him of in the first place, Felicia Moorsom shapes her own by deliberately depriving herself of the love of the only man who was ever in love with her and whose feelings she realizes she begins to reciprocate, even if against her own will and better judgment. Mercilessly castigating his daughter for being given to the two F's of "Froth and Foam," while himself having fallen prey to two other ones, "Finance and Fashions," Professor Moorsom secretly expresses his relief at the failure of his daughter's resolve to marry Arthur, upon learning about the latter's demise.

By way of hard facts, "The Planter of Malata" revolves around two of those: the discovery of Arthur's innocence, prior to the action of the story, and Arthur's death—of which, however, the information is deliberately withheld from the search party by Renouard, who thus hopes to prolong Felicia's stay on the island. The third "fact," of Renouard's apparent suicide by drowning, on which the story closes, is hardly tantamount to the truth of the matter as remaining unconfirmed either in life—in Renouard's body never recovered—or in art—in a lack of textual evidence. Hence Renouard's actual suicide, let alone demise, remains in the sphere of sheer speculation and conjecture, all the more so given that the final scene of the tale does not feature any supposition of suicide. In fact, the sensational news of Renouard's death is blown out of proportion through the agency of his best friend and the principal newsmonger of the story, who, incidentally, erred about his friend a few times before. Even so, as often transpires in the present-day era of post-truth and fake news, the information about the Planter's death by suicide is taken for granted by the search party and Conrad critics alike.

It is Conrad's use of denegation in asserting presence by absence and absence by presence in three scenes of the tale that does the trick here. Two of those scenes, occurring earlier in the story, harp on about suicide. The first one features Renouard contemplating "never go[ing] back [to the Dunster house] any more" (*WT* 42) upon discovering the "thirteen ways of looking at" himself, none of which appears to be true. Conrad places this scene in the context of a legend about the suicide of the governor general of the Dutch East Indies, only to allow Renouard to profess his resolve not to succumb to frustration despite the circumstances:

> Nothing easier! Yet, in the end, this young man, almost ill-famed for his ruthless daring, the inflexible leader of two tragically successful expeditions, shrank from an act of savage energy, and began, instead to hunt for excuses … No! It was not for him to run away like an incurable who cuts his throat. (*WT* 43)

The second scene where the idea of suicide appears in the tale is one of the strenuous swims in the bay that Renouard takes to both the apprehension and admiration of his plantation boy. And it is partly in the similarity between the phrasing of this passage and the final scene of the tale that the key to the conjecture about the Planter's suicide seems to lie.

In both scenes, Renouard is seen swimming "beyond the confines of life": in the former, "looking at a star" (*WT* 56) and in the latter, with "his eyes fixed on a star!" (*WT* 73), the idea of suicide appearing solely in the earlier scene and not in the least as an actual option but, quite the contrary, as a potential, and rather odious, conjecture to be concocted by the search party in case of his prolonged absence, an option which he therefore immediately dismisses as dishonorable and cowardly: "But the thought: 'They will think I dared not face them and committed suicide,' caused a revolt of his mind which carried him on. He returned on board" (56). Notwithstanding the above, it is not only the issue of the suicide of the main protagonist, but even of his accidental drowning that should be completely ruled out as a possibility here, contrary to the suggestions of the sensation-seeking Editor, precisely because Renouard's stamina was successfully tested in the earlier swim scene.

Conrad construes the idea of suicide in all three scenes in a denegative way—asserting presence by absence and absence by presence—evidently to demonstrate both the relativity of truth and the truth's divergence from facts. After introducing the notion of suicide in the first two scenes, while at the same time making it quite clear that Renouard is too honorable a man to succumb to the temptation, the writer removes the idea of suicide from the final scene of the story altogether, while simultaneously retaining the aura of demise through the sheer fact of the Planter's sudden disappearance, and yet suspending the resolution of the story for a lack of hard evidence. This makes the protagonist's suicide, misleadingly, the more present for its absence in the final passage of the tale, where no actual hint of it is dropped, but only various conjectures about Renouard's disappearance, including his demise, are raised.

To further substantiate the non-suicide, and even the non-death, option in the tale's resolution, it is useful to read closely the two swim scenes for their phrasing. Predictably, considering Conrad's use of denegation, it is the first one that sounds more dramatic, even though Renouard is presented here as returning from his strenuous plunge unscathed and, additionally, prompted by an apprehension that he might be viewed as a coward were he not to return on time. The scene sounds dramatic not only for the presence in it of the idea of suicide, but also because of the threefold repetition of the phrase "beyond the confines of life" in three different configurations: as an impression ("it seemed to him that he must have swum beyond the confines of life"), comment on the actual action ("It was easy to swim like this beyond the confines of life") and a hindsight ("he had been beyond the confines of life") (56).

The presence of all these dramatizing factors in a passage where suicide is mentioned but the protagonist clearly does not intend to commit it, makes the final scene of the tale, where it is not mentioned and Renouard simply vanishes into thin air, appear unconvincing as a case of suicide, also for a lack of hard evidence. Moreover, in the final episode, the phrase "beyond the confines of life" is part of a speculative and impersonal generalization unmarked by any visible drama and phrased like a rhetorical question rather than as a statement of fact: "For to whom could it have occurred that a man would set out *calmly* to swim beyond the confines of life—with *a steady* stroke—his eyes fixed on a star!" (73; emphasis added).

What *is* then the significance of Renouard's sudden disappearance? The calm vision of his "steady stroke" suggests a deliberate resolve directed toward a specific goal (his gaze "fixed on a star"), of "an explorer" who "has been there before," as Renouard has, and is thus unafraid to experiment and "never count[s] the cost" (42). His dismantling of the experimental silk plantation prior to the alleged suicide, the plantation apparently set up with the cultivation of the more economical artificial silk plant in mind (Lane 2007: 278–81), as well as his dismissal of the boy servants and all plantation workers, point to a conscious, long-term, and deliberate plan rather than an off-the-cuff decision. Apparently disillusioned with the world of the four Fs—not just Felicia's "Froth and Foam," but also her father's and his own worlds of "Finance and Fashion," of which the said silk plant had been an inseparable factor—he may have realized that he was no better than the father and the daughter in pandering to the four Fs. Besides, the very phrase "beyond the confines of life" seems to be opening new vistas rather than closing all perspectives as suicide would, in perfect agreement with the significance of Renouard's name, which as critics imply, suggests "renewal" (Billy 1997: 155).

This brings us to the issue of foreshadowing the non-suicide option in the story. The protagonist's rebirth seems to be symbolically implied by Renouard's nightmarish dream of the two goddesses' heads (Minerva's and Pallas's)—associated in the story with Renouard and Felicia, respectively—turning to dust. The "daemonic" aspect of his dream is associated by the protagonist with "one of those experiences which throw a man out of conformity with the established order of his kind and make him a creature of obscure suggestions" (34). The very choice of words here—*conformity, established order,* and *obscure suggestions*—seems to both foreshadow and explain Renouard's sudden disappearance at the close of the tale by naming the rationale behind what can be dubbed as his renewal rather than demise.

Thus, in the end, the protagonist seems to emerge as a nonconformist to the established order of the world of the four Fs that he visibly disagrees with all along, the obscurity of the suggestions apparently referring to the modernist and epistemological irrecoverableness of truth and Renouard's final nonconformist choices, which brings us back to Jakob Lothe's idea of Conrad's "redundant, obscure, even baffling narrative devices," which may in the long run have specific "thematic implications." Here, it is the modernist device of denegation that performs this thematic role of asserting the presence of new vistas for Renouard (the *truth* of the non-suicide version) by the absence of the evidence to the contrary (the *fact* of his suicide). The merely apparent presence of suicide in the story seems, therefore, to have been designed solely for the purpose of diverting the attention of reader and critic alike from the truth of the matter—which is irrecoverable anyway—in the trickster-like fashion only to be found in the later fictions of such great American masters as William Faulkner and Toni Morrison.

To conclude, "The Planter of Malata"—and, for that matter, the whole volume of *Within the Tides* to which it belongs—revolves around the modernist issue of the relativity of truth as well as truth's multiplicities. Using denegation, Conrad sidetracks his readers and critics alike into mistaking the protagonist's final act of defying the established order of things for suicide. Hence, upon an aesthetic, transtextual, and transcultural consideration, "The Planter of Malata," which has so far been interpreted as a "troubled romance" and found fault with, proves to be the writer's conscious modernist exercise in epistemological truth, multiple narrative perspectives, and denegation. The presence of the latter in this early 1914 tale clearly testifies to Conrad's precursorship in the use of denegation and Faulkner's unacknowledged debt to the Polish–English master—and, as demonstrated here, in more than one sense, too.

Acknowledgments

A version of this essay was presented at the 46th Annual International Conference of The Joseph Conrad Society (UK), St. Mary's University, Twickenham, July 2019.

Notes

1 For an extensive discussion of the use of denegation in "Freya of the Seven Isles," "A Smile of Fortune," and "The Tale," see my articles (respectively): "The Unfathomability of Conrad's Shallow Waters in 'Freya of the Seven Isles': An Intertextual Reading of Conrad's Story" (Branny 2015); "What 'A Smile of Fortune' Has to Hide: An Intertextual and Comparative Reconsideration of the Texture and Theme of Conrad's Tale" Branny 2019; and "An Intertextual and Denegative Reassessment of 'The Tale'" (Branny, forthcoming).

2 As defined by Pitavy, denegation is a psychological term referring to the speaker. In calling Sutpen a "nothusband" in Faulkner's *Absalom, Absalom!* Rosa Coldfield does

not mean that he did not ever become her spouse but that he was "the more present for being perceived as the negative of a husband" (1989: 29).

3 For a wider discussion of the issue, see Grażyna M. T. Branny, *A Conflict of Values: Alienation and Commitment in the Novels of Joseph Conrad and William Faulkner* (1997), 17–32.

References

Baines, Jocelyn. [1960] 1986. *Joseph Conrad: A Critical Biography.* Harmondsworth: Penguin Books.

Billy, Ted. 1997. *A Wilderness of Words: Closure and Disclosure in Conrad's Short Fiction.* Lubbock: Texas Tech University Press.

Branny, Grażyna. 1997. *A Conflict of Values: Alienation and Commitment in the Novels of Joseph Conrad and William Faulkner.* Kraków: Wydawnictwo "Sponsor."

Branny, Grażyna M. T. 2015. "The Unfathomability of Conrad's Shallow Waters in 'Freya of the Seven Isles': An Intertextual Reading of Conrad's Story." *Yearbook of Conrad Studies (Poland)* 10: 127–50.

Branny, Grażyna M. T. 2019. "What 'A Smile of Fortune' Has to Hide: An Intertextual and Comparative Reconsideration of the Texture and Theme of Conrad's Tale." *Yearbook of Conrad Studies (Poland)* 14: 7–33.

Branny, Grażyna M. T. Forthcoming. "An Intertextual and Denegative Reassessment of 'The Tale.'" *Yearbook of Conrad Studies (Poland)* 15.

Erdinast-Vulcan, Daphna. 1999. *The Strange Short Fiction of Joseph Conrad: Writing, Culture and Subjectivity.* Oxford: Oxford University Press.

Faulkner, William. [1951] 1953. *Requiem for a Nun.* Harmondsworth: Penguin Books.

Faulkner, William. [1929] 1954. *The Sound and the Fury.* New York: Random House.

Faulkner, William. [1936] 1972. *Absalom, Absalom!* New York: Random House.

Hampson, Robert. 2000. *Cross-Cultural Encounters in Joseph Conrad's Malay Fiction.* Basingstoke, Hampshire: Palgrave.

Hawthorn, Jeremy. 2003. "Conrad and the Erotic: 'A Smile of Fortune' and 'The Planter of Malata.'" *The Conradian* 28, no. 2: 111–41.

Jeliffe, Robert A., ed. 1956. *Faulkner at Nagano.* Tokyo: Kenkyusha.

Johnson, Bruce. 1989. *Conrad's Models of Mind.* Ann Arbor: University of Michigan Press.

Kehler, Joel R. 1976. "'The Planter of Malata': Renouard's Sinking Star of Knowledge." *Conradiana* 8, no. 2: 148–62.

Knowles, Owen. 1979. "Conrad and Mérimée: The Legend of Venus in 'The Planter of Malata.'" *Conradiana* 11: 177–84.

Lane, A. 2007. "Joseph Conrad's 'The Planter of Malata': Timing and the Forgotten Adventure of the Silk Plant 'Arghan.'" *Textile* 5, no. 3: 276–99.

Lothe, Jacob. [1989]1991. *Conrad's Narrative Method.* Oxford: Oxford University Press.

McLauchlan, Juliet. 1986. "Conrad's Heart of Emptiness: 'The Planter of Malata.'" *Conradiana* 18, no. 3: 180–92.

Meyer, Bernard C. 1967. *Joseph Conrad: A Psychoanalytic Biography*. Princeton, NJ: Princeton University Press.

Najder, Zdzisław. 1964. *Conrad's Polish Background*. London: Oxford University Press.

Pitavy, François L. 1989. "Some Remarks on Negation and Denegation in William Faulkner's *Absalom, Absalom!*" In *Faulkner's Discourse: An International Symposium*, edited by Lothar Hönninghausen, 25–32. Tübingen: Max Niemeyer Verlag.

Renner, Stanley. 1998. "'The Planer of Malata,' the Love Song of Geoffrey Renouard, and the Question of Conrad's Artistic Integrity." *Conradiana* 30, no. 1: 3–23.

4

The Power "not to": Agambenian Thought in Conrad's *Victory* and Faulkner's *Intruder in the Dust*

Pei-Wen Clio Kao
National Ilan University

According to Joseph Blotner's biography of William Faulkner, the American modernist master viewed Conrad as "one of the writers ... he had loved at eighteen" (1991: 688). Those literary influences surfaced throughout Faulkner's writing career in various forms, starting with his Nobel Prize address (1949), where he draws heavily on Conrad's "Preface to *The Nigger of the 'Narcissus.'*" In his address, Faulkner says that the material worth writing about constituted "a life's work in the agony and sweat of the human spirit" (1965: 119). It seems that in representing humanity's "spirit capable of compassion and sacrifice and endurance" (120), Faulkner specifically pays attention to the invisible and the voiceless, such as working-class laborers, innocent women and children, and ethnic minorities. Similarly, for Conrad, the value of human solidarity embraced by the artist is always mirrored in the "disregarded multitude of the bewildered, the simple, and the voiceless," as observed by him in "Preface to *The Nigger of the 'Narcissus'*" (*NN* 6).

Given the case of his Anglo-American successor Faulkner, it has proved that Conrad's influence goes beyond the confines of Polish and English literature. With a view to connecting the two writers' visions of the artist's responsibility to represent the human spirit of solidarity and resilience in the face of pain and suffering, this chapter attempts to analyze the characters of peripheral social status in Conrad's *Victory* (1915) and Faulkner's *Intruder in the Dust* (1948) in the context of the philosophical thought of the contemporary theorist Giorgio Agamben. This demonstrates the transcultural and transtextual features of Conrad's legacy in terms of not only language style, but also thematic conceptions. I shall focus on the marginalized but decent female figure Mrs. Schomberg in *Victory* and the scapegoated, but noble, racial Other Lucas Beauchamp in *Intruder in the Dust*, in order to spell out their enduring and prevailing powers as human beings despite their social marginalization and exclusion. Both Conrad's Mrs. Schomberg and Faulkner's Lucas are not typical protagonists, the former being a snubbed wife of a lower-middle-class white in the colonial East, and the latter a lower-middle-class mulatto fathered by a white plantation owner in the American South. Hence, they hover on the verge of the binary divide between life/non-life, white/Black, and rescuer/rescued.

Giorgio Agamben's philosophical thought as a prolific contemporary philosopher of ethics, political theory, and law, is mainly based on Walter Benjamin's theorization of history as a "dialectical image" or "dialectics at a standstill" ([1982] 2002: 462), which is a philosophical attempt at subverting the Western tradition of binarism by disrupting the hierarchical opposition ingrained in our thoughts and everyday practices. What underpins the whole of Agamben's oeuvre is a project "to render the production of dialectical relations inoperative, attempting to explore and deactivate them in order to make them unworkable" (Murray 2010: 34). Inspired by Agamben's undialectical thought and his determination to undermine the hierarchical structure of power, this chapter will apply his concepts of "inoperativity" and "im/potentiality" to rethink the issues of human relationships and judicial justice as represented in *Victory* and *Intruder in the Dust*.

Agamben's philosophical thought runs against the dialectical forms of Western metaphysics, whose aim, or telos, is progress toward a desired end of modernity. As "undialectical," Agamben's philosophy distrusts all forms of hierarchy that divide the world into two opposing parties. Thus, his thought is grounded in an attempt to "undo" or make "inoperative" the hierarchical forms of Western metaphysics bolstering the history of humankind and its relation to the world. Unlike Marx and Hegel, who see a fulfilled future of history in dialectical thinking, Agamben draws on Walter Benjamin's idea of "dialectics at a standstill" to (Tiedemann 2002: 942) imagine a "coming community" where the binary structure is undermined or made "inoperative." Broadly speaking, the emphasis on a "standstill" brings into focus the status of the "interval," or the "in-between," of the opposing forms, be they language, judicial systems, or world history in general.

The Agambenian Concepts of "Inoperativity" and "Im/potentiality"

In his short book *The Open: Man and Animal* (2002), Agamben seeks to subvert the traditional Western metaphysics based on "the anthropological machine," which is a "device for producing the recognition of the human" (26). The "man/animal distinction" featuring in the anthropological machine is employed extensively by Western thought to distinguish humanity from the Other in order to consolidate mankind's central role in a binary hierarchy:

> Homo is a constitutively "anthropomorphous" animal … who must recognize himself in a non-man in order to be human (27) … The humanist discovery of man is the discovery that he lacks himself, the discovery of his irremediable lack of *dignitas* (30) … What would thus be obtained, however, is neither an animal life nor a human life but only a life that is separated and excluded from itself—only a *bare life*. (27–38; emphases in original)

It is this anti-binary perspective that underpins the works of Giorgio Agamben, who attempts to overthrow the anthropocentric tradition of Western thought based on the binary hierarchy involving a human being and nonhuman Otherness. Agamben traces his "bare life" to Walter Benjamin's idea of "dialectical at a standstill" in which the status of "in-betweenness," or "interval," carries the weight of subversion and new possibility (Agamben 2002: 81–4). The "anthropological machine" is therefore "stopped" or "at a standstill," so what consequently follows is a "reciprocal suspension" of the two sides of the hierarchical order (83). Thus, the point is to defuse the "machine" rather than reverse the hierarchy between the human and the animal. And it is in this kind of liminal space that the "machine" is rendered "inoperative" and "deactivated." Agamben's notion of "inoperativity" is associated with ideas of "unworking, inertia, lack of work" (Murray 2010: 45). This leads to the "possibilities of undoing," a potential that has been produced by the tension between action and inaction (46). Agamben's literary example of Herman Melville's novella "Bartleby, the Scrivener" underscores the "ability to disrupt the function of power by refusing to either obey or reject it" (Murray 2010: 49), which is an alternative way to dismantle the binary hierarchy of power relations, thus rendering them inoperative.

Following Aristotle's distinction between two kinds of potentiality, Agamben elaborates on the power of potentiality based on "knowledge" or "ability" (1999: 179). The Aristotelian doctrine of potentiality "dictates the human power and agency" that "transforms every potentiality in itself into an impotentiality"

(Agamben 1999: 245). It is potentiality that bears the "potential to not-do, potential not to pass into actuality" (180). For Agamben, the greatness of humanity lies in its "potential not to act, *potential for darkness*" (181; emphasis in original). Drawing on this kind of thought, the "potentiality for darkness" is also the "potentiality for light"—henceforth the paradox of human power and agency: "To be potential means: to be one's own lack, *to be in relation to one's own incapacity*. Beings that exist in the mode of potentiality *are capable of their own impotentiality*, and only in this way do they become potential" (1999: 182; emphases in original). Agamben takes human freedom as a prime example of the power of "im/potentiality"; it is both the freedom to do and the freedom to refuse to do. The famous literary embodiment of Agamben's thought of "im/potentiality" can be found in the figure of Melville's Bartleby, who "neither accepts nor refuses, stepping forward and stepping backward at the same time" (Agamben 1999: 255). Bartleby's "dictum"—"I would prefer not to"—has become a "possibility suspended between occurrence and nonoccurrence, between capacity to be and the capacity not to be" (266).

In the light of Agamben's philosophical thought of "inoperativity" and "im/potentiality," my reading of Conrad's and Faulkner's works is focused on the marginalized Mrs. Schomberg and the oppressed mulatto figure of Lucas Beauchamp. Their seemingly marginal and subordinate status will turn out to be their power "not to," a defiance of the dominant white-male thought based on binary hierarchy. In being herself, that is, an inactive and bullied wife, Mrs. Schomberg will unwittingly help rescue Lena, the beleaguered maiden in distress. As for Lucas Beauchamp, in his determination to keep silent and inactive in defending his own innocence against a biased judicial system and a lynching mob, he enlists other marginalized people of the Southern community to clear his name and teach the white-dominated community a moral lesson about racial equality.

The "Im/potentiality" of the "Inoperative" Wife: Mrs. Schomberg in *Victory*

In most critical interpretations of *Victory*, the marginalized Mrs. Schomberg, this seemingly lifeless woman, is mainly categorized by Conrad scholars as redundant. By contrast, Ellen Burton Harrington takes more feminist interest in this figure, expressing doubt about Mrs. Schomberg's motive in helping Lena, while maintaining that Conrad, the writer, "leaves the possibility open that her [Mrs. Schomberg's] assistance is also tinged with compassion" (2015: 15). Harrington's open-ended conclusion has inspired me to take a more sympathetic approach to Mrs. Schomberg's seemingly wooden figure in the novel.

According to Harrington, Conrad employs the "dummy" figure of Mrs. Schomberg to indict the "dehumanizing effects of the dominating male desire" (2015: 16). Apart from indictment of male domination and commodification of women, as Harrington claims, Mrs. Schomberg is also a "mouthpiece" to "critique the [Victorian and patriarchal] ideal of marriage itself" (21). In contrast to Harrington's argument about Mrs. Schomberg's "demoralization" and "dehumanization" that have induced her with "no impetus to escape on her own behalf" (22), I would argue that it is precisely those "dehumanized" and "dummy-like" features of Mrs. Schomberg that empower her.

In my analysis of Mrs. Schomberg's case and character in the light of Agamben's philosophical thought, the concern about this peripheral figure's "inaction," or "inoperation," is quite different from Conrad's definition of "detachment" in his representation of Heyst in the Author's Note to *Victory* (x). As Yael Levin observes in comparing Conrad with Henry James, "while both begin by espousing disinterest—prompting the Schopenhaurian-inspired maxim that 'he who forms a tie is lost'—both end with the suspicion that such a principle is inherently flawed" (2013: 3). In other words, in Levin's interpretation, in this moral allegory of humanity, Conrad is advocating connection over inaction, attachment over detachment. By contrast, in my rereading of *Victory* based on Agamben's philosophy, I shall attempt to tease out the "im/potentiality" of mankind in its entrapment between action (endurance, perseverance) and inaction (detachment, aloofness) as exemplified in the much ignored and marginalized figure of Mrs. Schomberg.

Mrs. Schomberg is constantly described by Conrad as an "enthroned idol" made of "wood," whose "silence" and "immobility" are accentuated throughout Davidson's account (*V* 39). Her image of inaction is set in high relief against her subsequent action to help Lena. Furthermore, Mrs. Schomberg is referred to as lifeless: "automaton, a very plain dummy, with an arrangement for bowing the head and smiling stupidly now and then" (40). She seems to be deprived of humanity to become a "mechanism" that overthrows the binary dynamics of Western thought, bordering on action/inaction and humanity/inhumanity, making the "anthropological machine" "inoperative." In her situation as an observant bystander, she is entrusted by Heyst with the role of a go-between in the plan of Lena's flight: "Mrs. Schomberg's immobility gave her an appearance of listening intently" (41). It is Mrs. Schomberg's passage from inaction to action that creates her potentiality to protect the girl, to fulfill the love between Heyst and Lena, and to make their redemptive victory possible. Mrs. Schomberg occupies the borderline space between action/inaction and humanity/inhumanity—that is, a third, liminal, space that enables her to assert her power to resist the hierarchical structure that attempts to pin down the marginalized and the oppressed like herself. Her power "not to" has been transformed into a subversive force to confront "the anthropological machine['s]" epistemological violence. She has become the triggering force of the subsequent events in the novel. In the narrator's, or the implied author's, point of view, "she's more resourceful than one would give her credit for" (55). In other words, her power "not to do" is her true power to make the potentiality of victory for the hero and heroine of Conrad's novel possible. In her appearance of "looking so helpless, so inane" (59), Mrs. Schomberg is transforming her concealing into revealing, her inaction into action, all that made possible by her power "not to do." Thus Davidson seems to be right in his assessment of Mrs. Schomberg's character:

> He believed, now, that the woman had been *putting it on* for years. She never even winked. It was immense! The insight he had obtained almost frightened him; he couldn't get over his wonder at knowing more of the real Mrs. Schomberg than anybody in the Islands, including Schomberg himself. She was *a miracle of dissimulation*. No wonder Heyst got the girl away from under two men's noses; if he had her to help with the job! (59; emphases added)

Mrs. Schomberg's seeming imbecility, indifference, and stupidity are only a "mask" to be put on at will, which testifies to her power and potentiality "not to": she concealed "her tortures of abject humiliation and terror under her stupid, set, everlasting grin, which, having been provided for her by nature, was an excellent mask inasmuch as nothing—not even death itself, perhaps— could tear [it] away" (95–6). At best, Mrs. Schomberg's potentiality "not to" is devised to resist the chauvinistic and masochistic Schomberg, to rescue Lena and Heyst, and most importantly, to defend her own position as a dignified human being. As Heyst observes, Mrs. Schomberg "was engaged in the task of defending her position in life," which is "a very respectable task" (56). With her miraculous force of "dissimulation," she wields her power "not to" to defend her position as a human who deserves to be treated with respect. It is at the point of defending her sense of human dignity that her power "not to" and her force of "im/potentiality" are best linked to Lucas's case in the context of the postbellum American South.

The Silent "Im/potentiality" of a Southern Mulatto: Lucas Beauchamp in *Intruder in the Dust*

Throughout the novel, the silent Lucas Beauchamp is described as "intractable and composed" (Faulkner 1994: 7), "with an air solitary independent" (8). Although consistently referred to as a "Negro," or "nigger" by Chick, the white boy, in his thoughts, and called "Sambo" in the white lawyer's harangues, Lucas displays pride and agency in his power "not to," which eventually explodes the bigotry and supremacy of the Old South. His in-betweenness as a mulatto descendant of the white planter McCaslin is both literal and metaphorical, in the sense that he embodies the dismantling of the "anthropological machine" in Western metaphysics based on the binary oppositions of white/Black, good/evil, and light/dark. His silent, inscrutable, and composed manner carries the potential of "not to," which unwittingly undermines the power relations and racial hierarchy of the South and also for Chick Mallison, the young white boy, who "could never give up now [Lucas] who had debased not merely his manhood but his whole race too" (21). Under Lucas's influence, the boy's stereotyped and prejudiced ideas against racial Otherness at the beginning of the story give way to a youthful quest for moral conscience and sense of racial justice.

Lucas does not believe in the power of the legal system based on racial presumptions to clear his name of the allegations of murder of a white man. In other words, he does not trust the typical white Southern male adult, like Gavin Stevens, to execute justice in his favor. Instead, he has two children and an old spinster to act for him of their own accord, in which they represent the agency of minority figures in this racist white male-dominated power structure of the South. Old Ephriam's advice and exhortation to the young Chick about the "im/potentiality" of women and children to address difficult and sensitive issues ironically demonstrates the power of the minority figures in Faulkner's novel:

> Young folks and womens, they aint cluttered. They can listen. But a middle-year man … they cant listen. They aint got time. They're too busy with facks … If you ever needs to get anything done outside the common run, dont waste yo time on the menfolks; get the womens and children to working at it. (70)

In his mission to find out the true murderer and clear Lucas's name, Chick undergoes an awakening of his ethical conscience in acquiring an awareness of racial violence and injustice perpetrated by the white Southern society:

> It seemed to him now that he was responsible for having brought into the light and glare of day something shocking and shameful out of the whole white foundation of the county which he himself must partake of too since he was bred of it, which otherwise might have flared and blazed merely out of Beat Four and then vanished back into its darkness or at least invisibility with the fading embres of Lucas' crucifixion. (135)

Lucas's inactivity and "im/potentiality," then, trigger the conscience of the whole white community, propelling it to grow up and acquire a true sense of justice: "Lucas Beauchamp once the slave of any white man within range of whose notice he happened to come, now tyrant over the whole county's white conscience" (194). Hence, not only Chick Mallison, but also the whole white Southern community are taught a lesson of expiation for their past sins and injustice toward the racial Other.

Both Lucas Beauchamp and Mrs. Schomberg are trying to "defend their own positions" as dignified human beings: the former against the segregating and discriminating American South, the latter against the dominant patriarchal tradition. Lucas turns down Chick Malison's payment for the favor he rendered him once in saving his life, for he refuses to be demeaned as a racial Other serving the white boy as his master. What Lucas desires is human recognition and acceptance of simple kindness and hospitality between fellow human beings. According to Faulkner's Nobel Prize address, a good writer should commit himself to representing "the human heart in conflict with itself" (Faulkner 1965: 119). To a large degree, Faulkner's Nobel Prize observation could be applied to *Intruder in the Dust*, for the two texts were published only one year apart. The "human heart in conflict with itself" could refer to the two protagonists of the novel as both Chick and Lucas are struggling against the socio-cultural constructs of the Southern society that have deprived them of "love and honor and pity and pride and compassion and sacrifice" (1965: 120). Lucas is confronting two forces that have put his "heart in conflict with itself." On the one hand, he wields the power of his individual conception of himself as a human being with self-pride and dignity, who, in his being neither white nor Black, reaches beyond the confines of racial hierarchy, social ideology, and cultural stereotype. On the other hand, the society's dominant force attempts to pin him down as the Other, an inferior, and a member of a racial minority group. This stereotyping is vitiated by

Lucas's strong individual will "not" to conform to the whole sociocultural construct of the segregated South. Lucas's power "not to" prevails over the society's ideology and survives the conflict at the heart of the Southerners, including Chick Malison. For the young white boy also reaches beyond the confines of his sociocultural background, with its ingrained ideas of racist ideology and white supremacy. He must remain at odds with his community, or even the whole South, to make the social change possible in rescuing Lucas's life. Both Lucas's and Chick's individual subjectivities take the lead in changing cultural stereotypes and constructs. With his power "not to," Lucas has the "im/potentiality" to subvert the workings of racial identity by starting with an innate belief and proceeding toward a change of the external sociocultural construct, rather than the reverse.

Chick also experiences the "human heart in conflict with itself": he would like to recognize Lucas as a fellow human being, but the "condition" of the segregated Southern society will not let him do this. In Chick's consciousness, the smells of Lucas's household

> were really not the odor of a race nor even actually of poverty but perhaps of a condition: an idea: a belief: an acceptance, a passive acceptance by them themselves of the idea that being Negroes they were not supposed to have facilities to wash properly often or even to wash bath often even without the facilities to do it with; that in fact it was a little to be preferred that they did not. (Faulkner 1994: 11)

Lucas's mixed blood makes him straddle two worlds, white and Black, and his image forever reminds Chick of his grandfather with his recognition of the common heritage of all fellow human beings. In such recognition, Lucas always carries

> a gold toothpick such as his own grandfather had used: and the hat was a worn handmade beaver such as his grandfather had paid thirty and forty dollars apiece for, not set but raked slightly above the face pigmented like a Negro's but with a nose high in the bridge and even looked a little and what looked out through it or from behind it not black nor white either, not arrogant at all and not even scornful: just intolerable inflexible and composed. (12)

Under the historical conditions of the Jim Crow Law, Lucas is forced to behave in a way that is acceptable to the hierarchical and segregated Southern society: Chick is aware that *"we got to make him be a nigger first. He's got to admit he's a nigger. Then maybe we will accept him as he seems to intend to be accepted"*

(18; emphases in original). In the scenario where Lucas is provoked by white folks in the local grocery store, he wields the power "not to" fight back and "not to" argue, but still with the full "im/potentiality" to subvert white supremacy: "But still Lucas didn't move, quite calm, not even scornful, not even contemptuous, not even very alert" (20). Throughout the story, Lucas insists on behaving like a noble aristocrat rather than an enslaved Negro, which suggests his attempt to defend his position as a dignified human being. He has to silently confront the segregated Southern society that tries hard to make him succumb to the unjust racial hierarchy, thus depriving him of his human dignity, his rights, and a sense of well-being. In Faulkner's novel, we witness how the working of "altering ideology involves an intricate negotiation between the individual, history, and culture" (Schreiber 2004: 248). It is Lucas's power "not to" that plunges the whole community into a process of re-education and revival. The following passage about Chick's inner struggle on the horns of the dilemma could best serve as a footnote to Faulkner's Nobel Prize address centered on the "human heart in conflict with itself":

> A provincial Mississippian, a child who when the sun set this same day had appeared to be—and even himself believed, provided he had thought about it at all—still a swaddled unwitting infant in the long tradition of his native land—or for that matter a witless foetus itself struggling. (Faulkner 1994: 70)

Hence, Chick is torn between the racist history of his native land and his racial awareness newly awakened by Lucas's case.

Arguing against other critics' dismissal of Lucas's silence in *Intruder in the Dust* as a form of incapacitation in the face of racial violence, Alan Nadel invokes Cleanth Brooks's interpretation to elaborate on the significance of Lucas's "passivity" being transformed into a "positive force" (Brooks, qtd. in Nadel 2012: 201). What Lucas aims at, at the end of his silent drama, is not a (material) return of his favor from Chick, but "an assertion of humanity" (Nadel 2012: 200). Nadel trenchantly argues for the importance of Lucas's silence, which is rendered "not as a form of submission but as a form of transcendence that places Lucas above the law" (203). Akin to Nadel's line of argument, my reading of the novel is grounded in the power of Lucas's silence, which is a form of "im/potentiality," which, in the light of the Agambenian thought, empowers Lucas to subvert the Southern status quo.

Indeed, with his silence meant to clear his name and assert his humanity, Lucas Beauchamp sets in motion a series of acts that threaten to undermine Chick's belief in white supremacy, bringing him an opportunity of racial awakening.

In Erik Dussere's view, Lucas's trump is contextualized in the background and tradition of Southern honor focused on an "overpowering debt, with its emphasis on money and property, responsibility and reparation" (2001: 37). This sense of honor is closely knit with the notion of debt, but it is distinct from the Northern debt grounded in the economics of "industrial capitalism" (37). Furthermore, this debt of honor is inextricably bound to the history of slavery, with the white Southerners' moral debt to Blacks linked to their sense of guilt over slavery and need for expiation. Dussere argues, though, that in the Southern context, such debt is reduced to "a game of mastery and submission," with the two parties competing over the value of gift exchange (2001: 45), for, in giving a gift which is impossible to return, the gift giver is merely asserting his mastery and superiority. The novel shows us the drama of gift giving and debt unpaid, with Lucas's favor in saving Chick's life as its centerpiece, unpaid and unpayable by the white boy, whose endeavors to do so in pecuniary terms are undercut by the mulatto's insistence on refusing to accept the payback. Simultaneously, Chick's assistance in Lucas's acquittal comes up against Lucas's insistence on his own payback. All this demonstrates Lucas's attempt to debunk the code of Southern honor to include the Other in an equal human exchange of give-and-take.

Richard C. Moreland discusses the difficulty of contextualizing Faulkner's novels, and sees *Intruder in the Dust* as a case in point by demonstrating the (multiple) possible reading strategies for twenty-first-century readers witnessing the era of decolonization in the departure from the European–US world power. In my understanding, Moreland is not trying to negate a reading of Faulkner based on the historical context; rather, he emphasizes the importance of transcending the fixed context to "[make] learning and change possible" (1997: 67). Regarding the heterogeneous times and places of contemporary readers, I suggest we interpret *Intruder in the Dust* from the vantage point of the modern decolonizing era, beyond the fixation on the Jim Crow period of the post-Reconstruction South. Inspired by Moreland's ideas to "de-contextualize" Faulkner, my interpretation of *Intruder in the Dust* is aimed at rereading this text from the perspective of modernity as exemplified in Giorgio Agamben's contemporary philosophy of "im/potentiality."

Rachel Watson's article about the "hard" evidence based on scientific truth also illuminates the importance of transcending the sociocultural confines to reach over to the universal human truths of racial progress and universal equality. Chick's "moment of human recognition" (Watson 2009: 95) is triggered by Lucas's insistence on silence and resorting to concrete forensic evidence to exonerate himself, clear his name, and reclaim his own dignified humanity. In her words, "Lucas lets the forensic evidence do his talking" (97). By creating a silent and inactive Black figure in this ideology-ridden novel, Faulkner demonstrates how the "forensic hermeneutics" might transform the "racialized body" into the "racially transcendent, or 'universal,' human individual" (97).

Esther Sánchez-Padro points out that in writing this detective narrative, Faulkner exhorts the readers to "examine, and indeed reject, the white southern legal system's presumption of black male criminality" (2009: 123). While the narrative consciousness is that of the young white boy Chick Mallison, the real mystery to be solved is the mind of the old mulatto Lucas Beauchamp. In his attempt to unfold the mystery of the murder, Chick is also prying into the "mind of [the] black man whose individual subjectivity resists being categorized, contained, and understood by whites" (Sánchez-Padro 2009: 123). Lucas's inactivity turns out to be the driving force behind Chick's moral journey, the white boy's search for his moral conscience and expiation for the white community. Sánchez-Padro argues that Lucas's "inscrutability," or his "opacity," as Glissant terms it (2000: 89), actually exhibits the power of his agency, "a form of resistance to [a] justice system that contains no outlet through which he can be allowed to speak for himself" (Sánchez-Padro 2009: 124). In other words, with his "inscrutability," his "inaction," and "silence," Lucas attempts to transform the unequal and unjust status quo of the South, which shows his "im/ potentiality" to indict its white community. Lucas is an "intruder" in the sense that he disrupts the order of the Southern legal system based on racial prejudice (Sánchez-Padro 2009: 132). That Faulkner leaves the novel's last sentence to Lucas indeed demonstrates the power of the Black man's agency as well as his empowerment to speak for himself and become the voice of conscience for the white-dominated South.

The Power "not to": Inaction, Silence, and "Im/potentiality"

Faulkner is greatly influenced by Conrad's literary as well as social visions of the writer's responsibility as a spokesperson for the disadvantaged and the marginalized. Both novelists' emphasis on a writer's social accountability remains relevant in today's world, where racial, class, and gender equalities are sought after by people across the world. My methodological approach grounded in the thought of the continental European philosopher Giorgio Agamben testifies to the universal value of Conrad studies beyond the confines of Anglo-American literature.

Both Conrad and Faulkner are admirable modernist masters in their concern for the marginalized and voiceless figures in a society based on binary hierarchy. Their sympathy for the oppressed is expressed in their personal essays and speeches as well as works of fiction. In their novels discussed in this chapter, they leave room for a seemingly lifeless wife and a silent mulatto, respectively. They empower these characters not through a strong voice but through their power "not to."

For Agamben, there is always something unsaid included in the said, a caesura hung up between possibility and impossibility. This state of exception propels us to think beyond a fixed pattern of potentiality immanent in the disability: the power "not to." In the application of this idea to literary works, we as readers are encouraged to see the unseen, to hear the unheard, and to tease out the power "not to" embedded in the text. Marginal in their respective conditions, Mrs. Schomberg and Lucas Beauchamp wield power "not to" to defend their own positions as human beings and undermine the dominant structure of patriarchy and racism, respectively.

In Agamben's philosophy, what is "unsaid" in the works of art or literature indicates a possibility of "development" of the work itself (Durantaye 2009: 9). The unsaid and unsayable parts of the text, therefore, carry the weight of deconstructing and tearing apart the whole fabric of literary texture. In Conrad's *Victory*, the marginal character of Mrs. Schomberg serves as the unsaid possibility and "im/potentiality," whose underestimated help for the protagonists facilitates the final moral message of "victory" in the novel. In Faulkner's *Intruder in the Dust*, Lucas Beauchamp starts on the margin and then moves to the center of the narrative, triggering the consciousness of a white boy Chick Mallison to provide moral guidance for the Southern community.

Although Conrad's dummy-like figure of Mrs. Schomberg disappears, or is dismissed halfway through the narrative, she serves as the groundwork for the hero and heroine's moral victory. By contrast, in following the model set up by his modernist predecessor, Faulkner places the inscrutable mulatto at the heart of the novel's mystery, making him into a pillar of the Southern community's moral construction and consolidation. While the boy dominates the consciousness of the narrative, the old mulatto utters the last sentence of the narrative, and thus has the final say in the narrative's conscience. Hence, in both novels, the power "not to" of the peripheral figures remains "im/potential," thus making an "im/potential" impact on the readers of their times and beyond.

References

Agamben, Giorgio. 1999. *Potentialities: Collected Essays in Philosophy*, edited by Daniel Heller-Roazen. Stanford, CA: Stanford University Press.

Agamben, Giorgio. 2002. *The Open: Man and Animal*. Translated by Kevin Atell. Stanford, CA: Stanford University Press.

Benjamin, Walter. [1982] 2002. *The Arcade Project*. Translated by Howard Eiland and Kevin McLaughlin. Cambridge, MA: Harvard University Press.

Blotner, Joseph. 1991. *Faulkner: A Biography*. New York: Vintage Books.

Durantaye, Leland de la. 2009. *Giorgio Agamben: A Critical Introduction*. Stanford, CA: Stanford University Press.

Dussere, Erik. 2001. "The Debts of History: Southern Honor, Affirmative Action, and Faulkner's *Intruder in the Dust*." *Faulkner Journal* 19, no. 1: 37–58.

Faulkner, William. [1950] 1965. "Address Upon Receiving the Nobel Prize for Literature." In *Essays, Speeches and Public Letters*, edited by James B. Meriwether, 119–21. New York: Random House.

Faulkner, William. [1948] 1994. *Intruder in the Dust*. New York: Vintage International.

Glissant, Eduorad. 2000. *Faulkner: Mississippi*. Translated by Barbara B. Lewis and Thomas C. Spear. Chicago: University of Chicago Press.

Harrington, Ellen Burton. 2015. "The Case of Mrs. Schomberg in *Victory*." *The Conradian* 40, no. 2: 15–24.

Levin, Yael. 2013. "Masters of Disinterest: Everything You Always Wanted to Know about Conrad's *Victory* but Were Afraid to Ask James." *Conradiana* 45, no. 3: 1–19.

Moreland, Richard C. 1997. "Contextualizing Faulkner's *Intruder in the Dust*: Sherlock Holmes, Chick Mallison, Decolonization, and Change." *Faulkner Journal* 19, no. 1: 57–68.

Murray, Alex. 2010. *Giorgio Agamben*. New York: Routledge.

Nadel, Alan. 2012. "'We—He and Us—Should Confederate': Stylistic Inversion in *Intruder in the Dust* and Faulkner's Cold War Agenda." In *Fifty Years After Faulkner: Faulkner and Yoknapatawpha*, edited by Jay Watson and Ann J. Abadie, 200–11. Jackson: University Press of Mississippi.

Sánchez-Padro, Esther. 2009. "Critical Intruders: Unraveling Race and Mystery in *Intruder in the Dust*." In *Faulkner and Mystery*, edited by Annette Trefzer and Ann J. Abadie, 123–38. Jackson: University of Mississippi Press.

Schreiber, Evelyn Jaffe. 2004. "'The Sum of Your Ancestry': Cultural Context and *Intruder in the Dust*." In *A Gathering of Evidence: Essays on William Faulkner's* Intruder in the Dust, edited by Michael Gresset and Patrick Samway, 247–58. New York: Fordham University Press.

Tiedemann, Rolf. 2002. "Dialectics at a Standstill: Approaches to Passagen-Werk." In *The Arcades Project*, by Walter Benjamin, 929–45. Translated by Howard Eiland and Kevin McLaughlin. Cambridge: Harvard University Press.

Watson, Rachel. 2009. "'To Survive What Looked Out': The Forensic Trial and William Faulkner's *Intruder in the Dust*." In *Faulkner and Mystery*, edited by Annette Trefzer and Ann J. Abadie, 90–106. Jackson: University of Mississippi Press.

5

"*Ich Bin Nicht Einer Von Euch*": Language as a Tool to Construct the Identities of Conrad's German-Speaking Characters

Ewa Kujawska-Lis
University of Warmia and Mazury

Joseph Conrad's fictional worlds are extraordinarily multicultural and multilingual, reflecting his personal experiences throughout the world, subsequently filtered through his imagination. He populated his works with characters from various geographical and national backgrounds. In these culturally and ethnically heterogeneous worlds, the language is diversified, with English being only the matrix code employed by Conrad to construct distinct languages and their varieties for his characters. However, not all of the characters are provided with recognizable idiolects. Also, not all non-English characters speak their native languages; nor is their English always marked with traces of their mother tongues. Sometimes such characters actually are not given a chance to speak—they are only mentioned or their utterances are reconstructed by the narrator, as is the case with the French Lieutenant in *Lord Jim*, whose version of the events is retold in English by Marlow. However, in many novels, Conrad introduces linguistic heterogeneity to achieve various artistic and ideological effects. His artistry and superior linguistic awareness are evidenced in the manner in which he constructs non-English characters via language and develops some of them transtextually, simultaneously crafting their idiolects to stress that transformation. Adopting a sociolinguistic approach to analyze specific idiolects created by Conrad for his German-origin characters sheds light on ways in which the author differentiates them not only in the sense of their individualization, including their personality traits, ethics, professional conduct, education, and economic standing, but also in their transcultural experience in crossing national and linguistic boundaries. This experience exposes their bilingualism; yet Conrad goes further and skilfully illustrates how language reflects who they are and so adjusts their speech to their functions in particular novels.

Language and identity, as stressed by sociolinguists, are closely interwoven, and language not only expresses identities but also constructs them. Michael Halliday (2003: 81, 69) views language and grammar as serving two primary purposes—the transmission of knowledge/information (the "ideational" function of language) and the construction of relationships (the "relational" function of language). Language allows people not only to communicate, but also to establish personal and social relationships and hierarchies. Norman Fairclough posits the argument that language shapes the information that it expresses and the two are inseparable since discursive practices influence social practices: "The language activity which goes on in social contexts (as all language activity does) is not merely a reflection or expression of social processes and practices, it is a part of those processes and practices" (2001: 19). Hence, "language not only reflects and expresses relationships, ideas and information, but also actually plays a large part in constructing them" (Evans 2016: 3). If language is considered as a social practice, as indicated by Ruqaiya Hasan, it is inscribed with social relations, divisions, and hierarchies (2005). Thus, individuals speak from positions they occupy in society, and their utterances are shaped by the social structures they experience. Consequently, the language they use, including social registers, and standard versus nonstandard varieties, is correlated with their position and identity, or rather identities, as a person may assume various linguistic identities for various purposes.

Having functioned in multiple linguistic, cultural, and social environments, Conrad developed an extraordinary linguistic awareness, as is evident from his works. Conrad's fiction illustrates sociolinguistic tensions and the manner in which language contributes both to a person's identity and the perception of this person by others. Thanks to his traveling and to his work experience, he was not only accustomed to various national languages and their varieties, but also understood the ways in which language contributes to one's national identity and professional position. He consciously applied language in his works not only to create his characters (after all, in traditional fiction—a monomodal medium—language is the only code available for the construction of the world, although the visual aspect of the text organization may also contribute to the meaning), mark their position in various hierarchies, and endow them with individual traits, but also—in some cases—to develop them transtextually with their recurrence in different works. This application of language can be exemplified by Conrad's German-speaking characters and is the focus of this chapter.[1]

In *Lord Jim*, Conrad skilfully handles language to construct three distinctive characters of the same linguistic background: the *Patna* skipper, Schomberg, and Stein.[2] They differ ethically, professionally, and ideologically, and each of them speaks a different variant of English, which is additionally, in two cases (the skipper and Stein), stylized to sound as if spoken by a German. Their identities are shaped by the type of stylization selected, and their reception is further augmented by the narrators' attitudes toward them, be it the omniscient narrator's in the opening chapters or the intradiegetic narrators' (Marlow and Jim). The narrators' language reveals their attitudes, even in the absence of explicitly judgmental utterances.

The first description of the skipper includes the negatively loaded lexeme *renegade*: "a sort of renegade New South Wales German, very anxious to curse publicly his native country, but who, apparently on the strength of Bismarck's victorious policy, brutalized all those he was not afraid of" (*LJ* 17). This word, which denotes a person who deserts and betrays an organization, a country, or a set of principles or someone who rejects lawful or conventionalized behaviors, reappears later in "it was the renegade's trick" (22) and thus becomes attached to the skipper. This noun not only refers to a directly expressed betrayal of the homeland evident from the skipper's cursing of his country, but—more significantly—foreshadows his betrayal of professional principles. Initially, the person described remains anonymous, his German origin is stressed explicitly by the narrator and confirmed by himself in his first utterance, in which the mispronounced demonstrative pronoun *these* betrays his non-English nationality: " 'Look at *dese*[3] cattle,' said the German skipper" (17). Only later is the name of the skipper's ship provided, thus concretizing the character. Conrad employs the same descriptive technique to deal with the French lieutenant: in both cases, only the rank and the nationality are provided, the persons remaining unnamed otherwise. These two characters represent opposing forms of professional behavior and—by extension—ethical versus nonethical.

Conrad, who established his writing career in an acquired language and became an English citizen, must have felt some sort of allegiance to his newly adopted country and so decided that the ethically most contemptible character should not be nationality-wise "one of us": hence the choice of a non-English-speaking character to epitomize a betrayal of the professional code of conduct. The writer's selection of a German nationality for the skipper may have been also motivated by the deep-rooted hatred of Poles toward the partitioning powers,

Prussia being one of those. As Paul Wohlfarth argues: "Germany was to Conrad the power which had participated in three partitions of Poland; in *The Crime of Partition* he even foresaw the fourth ... Conrad was and remained a Pole, conscious and proud of his Polish descent ... His attitude to Germany, therefore, could only be full of enmity" (1963: 81). Although the critic continues by saying that this enmity "is not the whole story" and provides examples of "good Germans" in Conrad's fiction, arguing for a change in Conrad's attitude toward Germany resulting from the outbreak of war in 1914, the fact remains that the skipper, with his unspeakable act of cowardice, is a most despicable character. The ethically superior French lieutenant is likewise "not one of us" in terms of nationality but originates from a country representing prestige and high culture, and so by extension also professional and moral excellence.

The skipper's image and identity emerge through the narrators' comments and his own language in interactions with others. His speech is depicted through verbs customarily employed to refer to animal sounds: *growl* (" 'Shut up' growled the German") and *grunt* ("he emitted only a sulky grunt"). Accordingly, the skipper does not speak, but utters coarse dog- and pig-like sounds. His communication is compared to waste: "a torrent of foamy, abusive jargon that came like a gush from a sewer" (*LJ* 22). The lexemes describing his articulation dehumanize his utterances, although his speech is human. It seems that he is not worthy of being a human, though, which is reflected in the phrasings of those who describe him. But it is his own speech that vastly contributes to constructing his identity and negative perception of him as a person. His speech is marked by interference from his mother tongue, initially mispronunciations, as in the already quoted first exclamation, and then lexical intrusions: "From the thick throat of the commander of the *Patna* came a low rumble, on which the sound of the word *Schwein* [emphasis in original] fluttered high and low" (23). On board the ship, his communication is limited to commands in colloquial register—"Shut up" (23)—indistinct speech infused with emphatic expressions bordering on swearing—"He *mumbled* to himself; all I heard of it were a few words that sounded like '*confounded* steam!' and '*infernal* steam!'" (29)—and finally another animal-like sound—"Suddenly the skipper *howled*, '*Mein Gott!* [emphasis in original] The squall!'" (87). The selection of words to construct this character foregrounds his beastliness, both appearance- and sound-wise: "That greasy *beast* of a skipper poked his ... head ... and screwed his *fishy* eyes up at me. '*Donnerwetter!* [emphasis in original][4] You will die,' he *growled*" (99). Phonetic and grammatical interferences personalize his speech, but profane words vulgarize it, thus creating a brutalizing identity.

The stylization of the skipper's idiolect is best represented by a longer passage:

> *What are you to shout?* Eh? You tell me? *You no better* than other people, and
> that old rogue *he make Gottam* fuss with me … That's what you English always
> make—make a *tam'* fuss—for any little thing, because I *vass* not born in your *tam'*
> *coundry*. Take away my certificate. Take it. I don't want the certificate. A man like
> me don't want your *verfluchte* [emphasis in original] certificate. I *shpit* on it …
> I *vill* an *Amerigan* citizen *begome*. (37–8)

Ethically the lowest in the hierarchy of German-origin characters, the skipper
speaks a most vulgar variety of stylized English. Interference from his mother
tongue resurfaces as the skipper becomes more irritated, culminating in the
last sentence where both the phonological and syntactic levels are affected. The
infinitive is moved to the final position in the last sentence, according to German
grammar, since the modal verb is used, thus reflecting the skipper's origin.
He uses ungrammatical forms of negation, omits a third person singular verb
ending -s, and selects inappropriate question words. Such forms are, however,
also found in many local English dialects or are typical of people for whom
English is not their native language. Depending on the situation, they may be
a mark of lack of education in native English speakers. Yet their combination
with mispronunciations, which reflect a possible way of uttering English words
by a German, code-switching into German, especially when the intrusions are
swear words, foreground the skipper's linguistic Otherness, excluding him from
the circle of "one of us." The German profanities and the stylization involving a
phonetic aspect, which "contaminate" the sound of English in the skipper's case,
attribute a vulgar identity to the character, which corresponds with his behavior.

A contrasting position in the hierarchy of German-speaking characters in *Lord
Jim* is occupied by Stein. Unlike the skipper, Stein is personalized onomastically.
His surname may be treated as a telling name: Stein means a stone, a rock, or a
brick in English, and thus something solid that may be used as building material.
He, in a sense, builds up a new life for Jim in Patusan. Perhaps to counterbalance
the negative image of the German ethnicity as represented by the skipper, Conrad
decided to endow another German character with positive attributes, Germany
being, after all, a home to outstanding thinkers, philosophers, composers, and
writers. Stein is respected by Marlow since, as Ian Watt notices, he is "deeply
reflective, and even an avowed intellectual" (1981: 322). His linguistic identity is
distinct from that of the skipper, even though some stylizing solutions naturally
remain analogous, as, for instance, moving the verb in a sentence to the final
position or code-switching. However, Stein's idiolect is stylized with national

traces in the manner of a speech of an educated person. The interferences from German (syntactic, lexical, and phonological) are not vulgarizing in his case, for he is the expositor of the richest sociocultural capital of the three characters of German origin depicted in *Lord Jim*, and his speech clearly reflects this fact:

> So fine as he can never be. The memorable metaphysical eloquence which Conrad generates from his dislocation of English idiom reminds us of how deeply representative Stein is of German romantic idealism. There is the twin enthusiasm for geographical exploration and scientific discovery ... there is the fact that Stein ... is an exile from the 1848 revolution, and thus representative of German political liberalism; and there are his poetic quotations, which make him the spokesman of German Romantic literature. (Watt 1981: 323)

Conrad's "dislocation of English idiom" is the stylization applied to create a character with specific intellectual and personal attributes as well as nationality to ensure his views are credible. Thus Stein's linguistic identity is shaped by these features, but at the same time, his very language shapes our perception of him as a person, his language representing his intellect and experiences.

In many senses (national, professional, philosophical, economic), Stein is "not one of us" that Marlow or his listeners might identify with: neither English, nor a sailor, but a German "philosopher." Thus language might be viewed here as a tool for creating the linguistic and cultural Other whose function is to provide a fresh perspective on Jim. Stein is endowed with some prophetic features in firmly diagnosing Jim: "I understand very well. He is romantic" (*LJ* 161). In this and other pronouncements, Stein is actually equivocal. Without understanding his cultural background, it is hard to grasp what he means by being romantic, but even then, his statement remains ambiguous.[5] This ambiguity is signaled in his first utterance, including characteristic markers of Stein's idiolect: "'So you see me—so'. ... 'Only one specimen like this they have in your London and then— no more. To my small native town *this my* collection *I shall bequeath*'" (155). The salient syntactic feature here is moving the predicate to the final position, analogously with the skipper's speech. Yet here the choice of high-register sophisticated vocabulary marks the difference between the two characters, the syntax only stressing their nationality in each case. The marked syntax appears in metaphysical utterances, as in the one noted by Watt and at the beginning of the same digression concerning man's imperfection: "but *man he* will never on his heap of mud *keep still*" (161). The pleonastic combination of the singular proximal demonstrative pronoun *this* and possessive pronoun *my* in the first example and the noun *man* and pronoun *he* in the second indicate the speaker's foreignness. In English, these grammatical elements are not used side by side; yet this is also true for German. However, this structure reflects a combination possible in Polish, thus rendering Stein's idiolect somewhat confusing and not entirely credible to those who know German. It appears that Conrad's aim was not so much to faithfully render a specific linguistic interference in the speech of a bilingual German, as to generate a sense of linguistic Otherness, without compromising the notion of good education.

Hence Stein's German origin is mostly evident in code-switching. His first utterance features an interesting phenomenon: the discourse marker *so*, which may be perceived as both an English and a German word. It functions analogously in both languages in spoken form; in other words, Stein may begin his utterance with this word in either of the two languages, its meaning depending on how the word is pronounced. Since Marlow here refrains from making a comment on the word's pronunciation, and the word is not italicized (as is the case for many other German intrusions, though not all), we may argue that Stein's first word is English. Yet it is equally plausible that as a German, he begins with the German variant. As no definite answer can be provided, the opening utterance reflects Stein's ambiguity: in fact, he does not say anything definitive about Jim, and his ideas are enshrouded in metaphor. The double linguistic perspective makes Stein intriguing, simultaneously serving as an inclusive element (if one interprets *so* as an English word) and limiting or exclusive (if *so* is perceived as a German word). The resonant *so* additionally indicates the meditative nature of the character's utterances and foreshadows his other similarly ambiguous phrases.

When creating his German-speaking characters, Conrad did not introduce systemic stylization. The elements marked appear side by side with perfectly correct English sentences. In the skipper's case, error-free sentences are colloquial; Stein prefers a more sophisticated discourse. If the choice between standard and nonstandard varieties of language discloses power relationships, as claimed by sociolinguists, Stein's discourse empowers him and shows him to be far superior to the other German. Stein's sociocultural and linguistic identity is best evident in his most famous utterance:

> Yes! *Very funny this terrible thing is.* A man that is born falls into a dream like a man who falls into the sea. If he tries to climb out into the air as inexperienced people endeavour to do, he drowns—*nicht wahr?* … [emphasis and ellipsis in original] No! I tell you! The way is *to the destructive element submit yourself*, and with the exertions of your hands and feet in the water make the deep, deep sea keep you up … And yet it is true—it is true. *In the destructive element immerse*

... That was the way. To follow the dream, and again to follow the dream—and so—*ewig—usque ad finem* ... [emphasis and ellipsis in original]. (162–3)

His speech begins with a defamiliarizing effect through the reversed word order, which appears in two other sentences, endowing them with emphasis. These reflect Stein's metaphysical ideas. The atypical syntax becomes distinctive by its placement in the co-text of natural-sounding English. Linguistic Otherness is further marked by German intrusions of formal register, while Stein's intellectual capital, with formal vocabulary (*endeavor*, *exertions*) and a Latin maxim. Stein's oratory abilities correlative to his literary interests are expressed by repetitions and choosing a metaphor to give shape to his thoughts. Stein's various attributes (education, social, and economic position) are reflected in his language, and his language creates his identity. If he is seen as artificial, it is because his spoken language sounds artificial. The formal vocabulary preferred in written English often involves longer words or those whose origins are in Latin and Greek, whereas informal vocabulary usually employed in spoken utterances involves shorter words or words of Anglo-Saxon origin. Stein prefers the learned *endeavor* to *try*, *immerse* to *sink* or *plunge*, *submit* to *give in*, and *exertion* to *effort*. If he is perceived as stiff and lofty, it is because his language is such. If his ideas are difficult to penetrate, it is because he chooses linguistic forms that are ambiguous and metaphorical to express them. Thus the stylization selected by Conrad to create this character perfectly renders Stein's nature and identity and clearly distances him from the skipper.

A different identity is attributed to Schomberg, a character gradually developed in "Falk" and *Victory*. In *Lord Jim*, Schomberg utters a few sentences not marked by any interferences from German, either phonetic or syntactic, or amounting to code-switching:

> And, mind you, the nicest fellow you could meet ... Quite superior ... He is a very nice young man ... but the lieutenant is a first-rate fellow, too. He dines every night at my *table d'hôte* [emphasis in original], you know. And there's a billiard-cue broken. I can't allow that. First thing this morning I went over with my apologies to the lieutenant, and I think I've made it all right for myself. (*LJ* 150, 151)

Nothing indicates his foreignness here. He speaks fluent, colloquial English, neither vulgarized as in the skipper's case, nor overtly sophisticated as in Stein's speech, which is what differentiates the three characters from one another. Marlow's negative attitude toward Schomberg results from the latter's being "an irrepressible retailer of all the scandalous gossip of the place" (150), his chatty language reflecting, and at the same time shaping, his identity. Apart from pointing to Schomberg's gossipy nature, Marlow eschews negative comments about Schomberg, and his language remains ethnically neutral. In fact, if not for the descriptive "hirsute Alsatian" (150), nothing about Schomberg's speech would indicate his non-English origin. The adjective Alsatian makes Wohlfarth argue that he is "not a German proper" (1963: 81). Nevertheless, in the first preface to *Victory*, Conrad refers to Schomberg as an illustration of "the psychology of a Teuton" (*V* 6), and thus to his mind, he is of Germanic descent. In *Lord Jim*, Schomberg's informal English is almost impeccable and well suited to the communication with the multilingual crowd visiting his hotel. It is intriguing why Conrad should choose a German-origin person for this character here, given that Germany was much less active as a colonizing power in the Far East than England, France, or the Netherlands, and hence statistically, there were fewer Germans in that part of the world than representatives of the other colonizers. Perhaps he wanted some middleman between the utterly repulsive skipper and the haughtily superior Stein.

Conrad seems to have had some predilection for certain characters and made them reappear transtextually: Tom Lingard, in the "Lingard Trilogy," Marlow, in the works explicitly narrated by him,[6] and Babalachi being the most obvious examples. Often, such characters undergo transformations between the texts. As effectively argued by John G. Peters, the Marlow who narrates *Chance* "bears little resemblance to the Marlow of Conrad's earlier work" (2014: 131) and differs essentially in his employment of language, his method of storytelling, and world view. A similar claim about a transformation may be made for Schomberg. In his preface to *Victory*, Conrad wrote:

> Schomberg is an old member of my company. A very subordinate personage in *Lord Jim* as far back as the year 1899, he became notably active in a certain short story of mine published in 1902. Here he appears in a still larger part, true to life (I hope) but also true to himself. Only, in this instance, his deeper passions come into play and thus his grotesque psychology is completed at last. (5)

The short story mentioned is "Falk," and—as indicated by the writer—Schomberg changes from an episodic character to one of the key personages: his agency is more pronounced, his influence upon others more negative, and his metamorphosis reflected in his transformed linguistic identity. Schomberg's "completed" psychology constructs his new identity, and this identity is expressed through his language.

In "Falk," Schomberg is in a transitional phase. His language is still that of the gossiper of *Lord Jim*, with no German intrusions. However, his English undergoes some modifications: he talks more and is more active in disseminating gossip. His pronouncements about people become derogatory: "But Falk is, and always was, a miserable fellow. I would despise him" (F [D] 173); his attitude toward others is contemptuous: "I could tell him [Captain Hermann] something about Falk. He's a miserable fellow. That man is a perfect slave"; and he begins to swear: "any *damned* native" (174), "A white man should eat like a white man, *dash it all*." The more involved he is, the more excited he becomes, and this is reflected in his changed language that includes exclamations reflecting his attitudes, both in his direct speech: "I don't blame you, captain. *Hang me if I do*" (195), and in indirectly quoted passages: "wondering in a low mutter *who the devil* could be there at this time of the day" (180). Likewise, the narrator's unfavorable comments on the character are more numerous: "Schomberg, a brawny, hairy Alsatian, and an awful gossip" (155); "an untrustworthy humbug Schomberg"— the narrator's references to his language stressing its gossipy nature and hinting at an agency—"set Schomberg's tongue *clacking*" (164); "I sat half stunned by his *irrelevant babble*" (176); "it would have been plausible enough if there hadn't been always *the essential falseness of irresponsibility in Schomberg's chatter*" (177); "It was as if Schomberg's *baseless gossip had the power to bring about the thing itself*" (195); and "Schomberg's gastronomic *tittle-tattle was responsible* for these" (223). The accumulation of such explicit comments reveals the quality of Schomberg's language, but these remarks also present him as a driving force behind the events. Schomberg's transition from a somewhat innocent talebearer to someone who influences the perception of others through his talk is evident. His duplicity is reflected in the various masks he wears, as is clear both from his choice of discourse and his speech: "'Sit still,' he hissed at her, and then, in an hospitable, jovial tone, contrasting amazingly with the angry glance that had made his wife sink in her chair, he cried very loud: 'Tiffin still going on in here, gentlemen'" (179). Conrad eschews a radical linguistic metamorphosis, preferring to gradually develop Schomberg's speech by subtle touches: an occasional expletive, an emotional exclamation, a derogatory remark. Such shifts, accompanied by narratorial comments, are sufficient to create a negative image of the character. He is more powerful and scheming than Wohlfarth would have it by claiming that in "Falk" Schomberg "is not wicked, but ridiculous" (1963: 81) as there is nothing ridiculous in Schomberg's attitude toward his wife and Falk. Schomberg "wields language to recklessly damaging effect" (Greaney 2002: 28), and his use of language is tantamount to "discursive cannibalism" (Greaney 2002: 30).

In *Victory*, Schomberg's portrayal becomes explicitly negative, focusing on his wickedness, foulness, and unscrupulousness. In this novel, the narrator stresses his baseness—"The keen, manly Teutonic creature. He was a good hater. A fool often is" (36)—and dehumanizes him through animalistic imagery—"Big, manly in a portly style, and profusely bearded, he would approach, his glass of beer in his *thick paw*" (36). The repetition of the adjective "manly" is crucial: he is no longer a man; he is only man-like. Derogatory epithets appear; he is not just a fool but an "unfathomable" fool (36). He transforms into a vicious "bête humaine" (Jabłkowska 1961: 218). His beastliness, similarly to that of the *Patna* skipper, is underscored by words describing his speech—often animal-like: "Schomberg *snarled* unpleasantly" (132). Unlike Jim or even Falk, he directly contributes to Heyst's demise. In his transitional stage in "Falk," the narrator speculates on his influence on others: "I shouldn't wonder if Schomberg's tongue had succeeded at last in scaring Falk away for good" (240); in *Victory*, his talk kills not merely figuratively: Schomberg had "an ungovernable tongue which surely must have worked on a pivot" (31). But it is specifically his talk that induces Ricardo and Jones to seek Heyst.

The more negative the image of Schomberg and the more negative the attitude of the narrators toward him, the more his language changes. In *Victory*, his speech is occasionally marred by grammatical errors. When talking about Heyst, whom he detests, Schomberg confuses tenses: "I remember him for years" (62).[7] When speaking of his wife, whom he equally detests, he wrongly uses the modal verb in the third person singular: "*Hang her!* I've never cared for her. The *climate don't* suit her … And she will have to go, too! I will see to it. *Eins, zwei* [emphasis in original], march!" (94). Additionally, exclamatory swearing appears as in "Falk," but also—and this is a new stylizing element—German intrusions occur. Code-switching is more frequent, especially when Schomberg is emotionally aroused: "*Gott im Himmel!* [emphasis in original] … Will he stop here *immer* [emphasis in original]—I mean always" (136), "'*Gewiss,*' [emphasis in original] snapped Schomberg" (140). For the first time, Schomberg's German origin is visible in his language, and his bilingualism comes to the fore: he seems to switch into German as if unconsciously, and then, realizing that he is speaking a language that others do not understand, he provides the English equivalent.

Schomberg's development seems quite consistent: as in "Falk," in *Victory* he is also two-faced (and fork-tongued). He is coarse when addressing his wife—"'Get out of my sight,' he snarled" (100)—but exceptionally kind when scheming with Jones and Ricardo: "'Won't you have a drink with me before retiring?' went on Schomberg" (102). Hence Conrad's handling of Schomberg's transformation is plausible. In stylizing his speech, the writer increases the frequency of elements already introduced, such as exclamations, derogatory terms, and profanities. This vulgarization of language matches the vulgarization of Schomberg as a person. In stating, "I don't pretend to say that this is the entire Teutonic psychology but it is indubitably the psychology of a Teuton" (*V* 6), Conrad makes his character utter German words to make a link between his origin and barbarity. In contrast to Stein, whose intrusions involve sophisticated German, Schomberg's code-switching is analogous to that of the *Patna* skipper. The change in Schomberg's idiolect directly reflects his transition from an insignificant gossiper to a mastermind of tragic events, his "negative agency" represented by a baser language and code-switching.

Conrad had limited options when stylizing the speech of his German-speaking characters to invent their nationality (code-switching, syntactic shifts, and phonological interferences), yet employed them effectively. The three German-origin characters in *Lord Jim* speak three different idiolects, and in each case, their speech cannot be detracted from their identities. Foreign interferences and vulgarization of English in the skipper's idiolect is concordant with his unethical conduct, and his substandard language indicates his inferior social position. The lack of traces of the mother tongue in Schomberg's case and his fluent informal English is motivated by his identity as a gossiper. Stein's language not only underscores his cultural background, but also indicates his superior position in the world of the novel, be it intellectual, economic, or social. Schomberg's transtextual development is marked with gradual changes in his speech.

As is evidenced in his German-speaking characters, Conrad consciously employs language to construct the unique identities of the characters inhabiting his multicultural and multilingual worlds. This does not mean that his stylizations are faithful representations of the manner in which Germans speak English. He does not introduce a given type of interference systematically (for instance, devocalization of the same consonant) to generate a fully realistic effect, but resorts to occasional markers of foreignness to achieve desired effects. As a writer, he demonstrates an unusual grasp of the fact that language determines how people see themselves and how they are seen by others. Hence rather than striving for linguistic verisimilitude in the presentation of foreigners, he makes their foreignness evident to express a given character's identity and social position through language. When language becomes interactive and intersubjective in an encounter with the social world, identity becomes personalized, and Conrad appears to have constructed his characters with the awareness that language may reveal a lot about their identities and personalities.

Notes

1 Due to space constraints, I only discuss the major German-speaking characters in *Lord Jim*. As for the episodic characters, Jacob Schnitzler ("The End of the Tether") is only mentioned and does not speak; in the case of German-speaking characters such as Siegers in "Falk" and the Yucker Brothers from Switzerland in *Lord Jim*, stylization is mostly used for comic effect. The most interesting instance is the Hermanns family in "Falk," as in their case, language is used as a means of inclusion, exclusion, and manipulation.

2 This is based on my discussion of translation problems involved in characters' idiolects in *Lord Jim* (2011: 339–69).

3 All emphases and ellipses are added unless indicated otherwise.

4 *Donnerwetter* has a few equivalents in English, which differ in their expressive meanings (wow, gosh, my word, God damn), but judging by the skipper's features, it may be assumed that he uses this expression as a swear word.

5 For a thorough discussion of the notion of romanticism and the romantic as expressed by Stein, see Watt (1981: 322–31).

6 The unnamed narrator of "Falk" bears much resemblance to Marlow.

7 This may have stemmed from the fact that English was not Conrad's native language. Conrad had difficulties in using present perfect correctly since this tense does not exist in Polish. This aspect of his language is discussed by Ian Watt (2000: 46–7) as well as Mary Morzinski, who claims that "although inappropriate choices of verb forms are infrequent in Conrad's writing, this [the choice between simple past and the perfect tenses] is the area in which they most commonly exist" (1994: 56). Here the present tense is used inappropriately and reflects the Polish usage. Yet, occurring in Schomberg's speech, this mistake draws our attention as normally his language is error free.

References

Evans, David. 2016. *Language and Identity: Discourse in the World.* London: Bloomsbury.

Fairclough, Norman. 2001. *Language and Power.* 2nd ed. London: Longman.

Greaney, Michael. 2002. *Conrad, Language and Narrative.* Cambridge: Cambridge University Press.

Halliday, Michael A. K. 2003. *On Language and Linguistics.* London: Continuum.

Hasan, Ruqaiya. 2005. *Language, Society and Consciousness.* London: Equinox.

Jabłkowska, Róża. 1961. *Joseph Conrad (1857–1924).* Wrocław: Zakład Narodowy im. Ossolińskich, Wydawnictwo Polskiej Akademii Nauk.

Kujawska-Lis, Ewa. 2011. *Marlow pod polską banderą. Tetralogia Josepha Conrada w przekładach z lat 1904–2004*. Olsztyn: Wydawnictwo Uniwersytetu Warmińsko-Mazurskiego.

Morzinski, Mary. 1994. *Linguistic Influence of Polish on Joseph Conrad's Style*. Lublin, New York: Maria Curie-Skłodowska University, Columbia University Press.

Peters, John G. 2014. "'Let that Marlow talk': *Chance* and the Narrative Problem of Marlow." *The Conradian* 39, no. 1: 130–46.

Watt, Ian. 1981. *Conrad in the Nineteenth Century*. Berkeley: University of California Press.

Watt, Ian. 2000. *Essays on Conrad*. Cambridge: Cambridge University Press.

Wohlfarth, Paul. 1963. "Joseph Conrad and Germany." *German Life and Letters* 16, no. 2: 81–7.

Part 2

Transmedial and Transnational Negotiations

6

Time, Place, Scale, and Decorum:
Conrad and the Polish Romantic Drama

Laurence Davies
King's College London

To begin with, here is an English response to Conrad's work. It is atypical but not unique:

> One word comes before long to haunt the mind of any persistent reader of Conrad's stories—the word "melodrama." Why does he do it? What has he got against ordinary life? What is the purpose of all these feuds, assassinations, revolutionary plottings, these fearful disasters and betrayals—against which, it seems, only the stolid application to duty of the totally unimaginative can hope to hold "ground"? (Hopkinson 1957: 38)

These questions by the journalist and editor Tom Hopkinson appeared in a mostly admiring contribution to a centennial symposium on Conrad published by the *London Magazine* in November 1957. Hopkinson's attitude is surprising, given that from 1940 to 1950 he had edited the pro-Labour illustrated magazine *Picture Post*, which had reported on the horrors of Nazism and more recent atrocities in the Congo and Korea, and was about to take up the editorship of *Drum*, a South African magazine firmly opposed to apartheid. One explanation might be that Hopkinson had assimilated the postwar mood of down-to-earthness, of suspecting grand gestures, overheated language, and sensationalism.[1] Another would be that Conrad's life was never "ordinary." A third would be that Poland under partition was never ordinary either, and the critic's brief catalogue of literary excesses would just as well apply to the work of the great Polish Romantic authors, who lived in dire times.[2]

Anglophone students of Conrad have every reason to be thankful for the Polish and Polish American colleagues who have traced his affinities with Polish literature. To cite just a few of that cadre, we might point to Andrzej Busza, whose *Conrad's Polish Literary Background* has been an essential resource for over half a century; Gustav Morf, Adam Gillon, Zdzisław Najder, and Czesław Miłosz; and more recently, Jean M. Szczypien, whose *"Sailing towards Poland" with Joseph Conrad* (2017) teases out a dense network of allusions, motifs, echoes, intertexts, and covert characterizations. We can also point to the discussion of women in nineteenth-century Polish literature in Susan Jones's *Conrad and Women* (1999: 38–68) and Richard Niland's *Conrad and History* (2010), an investigation of nineteenth-century Polish historiography in the context of the political novels: both inspiring examples of what can be achieved by an anglophone scholar writing an influential monograph.

What follows in this chapter is pure speculation: an attempt to show (I hope in a spirit of humility) that there may still be aspects of Conrad's literary background to explore, not only in terms of verbal echoes or moral imperatives but as responses to narrative shape, texture, and experiment. This is not by any means to disparage cultural or political readings of, say, *Konrad Wallenrod*, or *Grażyna*, or *The Undivine Comedy*—quite the opposite—but to consider the nexus between artistry and circumstance. One of the glories of Polish literature is its long and rich history of double speech, outspoken and ironic, public and clandestine, coded and uncoded. With Conrad in mind, I propose to consider certain aspects of Polish dramatic prose and verse of the early nineteenth century with particular attention to their experimental vigor, wide tonal range, fierce irony, freedom from decorum, deployment of the absurd, abrupt shifts in time and space, daring sense of scale, and some at least of their metaphysical preoccupations. An enduring (and endearing) paradox of Poland's cultural heritage, in the visual as well as literary arts, has been that it so often melds tradition with drastic innovation. Zdzisław Najder has said, "It is a peculiar characteristic of nineteenth-century political thought that its dominant trends are at the same time traditionalist and progressive" (1997: 151). Such was also the case in Polish literature. Conrad himself traced the beginnings of Polish literature to Jan Kochanowski, *szlachcic* and, as a poet and dramatist, innovator (*CL2* 144).

Given his parents' pride in Polish history and culture, it is no wonder that "Konradek" had an early and rapturous exposure to the great Polish authors. As he recalled in 1914, in an interview with Marian Dąbrowski: "My father read *Pan Tadeusz* aloud to me and made me read it out loud on many occasions. But I preferred *Konrad Wallenrod* and *Grażyna*. Later I preferred Słowacki. Do you know why Słowacki? *Il est l'âme de toute la Pologne, lui*" (Busza 1966: 171). Jean Szczypien has recently discovered another interview, published in a Polish newspaper in 1915: "I surround myself with the Polish literature of long ago, Krasiński's, Mickiewicz's and Słowacki's. Their words are everything for me. I was raised and formed by them" (Szczypien 2017: 1, 8, n23). During the stay in Zakopane in 1914, the younger Aniela Zagórska's reading of Słowacki's "The Tomb of Agamemnon," a lament for the dismembered and confused state of Ancient Greece seen as an analogue of Poland, moved Conrad to "a violent, although silent emotional outburst" (Najder 2007: 455; also 1983: 217). In Lwów, at the age of ten, Konradek was already writing plays himself, staging his scripts at the home of the two Tokarska children, and he was fond of puppet plays and marionettes. Six decades later, Mrs. Jadwiga Tokarska-Kałusa remembered those "merry, carefree days," which took quite a toll on the family furniture.

> The themes of those plays were battles with the Muscovites. To rise to the occasion I had to dress in my brother's clothes ... "Insurgents" sat around a camp fire with their commander (in the red square-topped cap) and sang patriotic songs ... Then the Muscovites crept on us noiselessly. A fight would follow with the breaking of chairs and stools ... The little tyrant ruled over us and we obeyed our commander-in-chief. (Najder 1983: 139)

In a letter of February 27, 1919, about casting Basil Macdonald Hastings's adaptation of *Victory*, Conrad told Hastings about a long-ago meeting with the most famous of nineteenth-century Polish actors, Helena Modrzejewska: "I know nothing about the psychology of actresses and I don't think I have ever met three of them in my life, though I have a vague recollection of having been fed with chocolates by Mme. Modjeska somewhere back in the Middle Ages" (*CL6* 374–5).[3] This encounter with the fervent patriot and multilingual performer is a vignette in its own right, but it also happens that her memoirs include several tales of the censorship that harried actors, theater managers, and dramatists. At the Imperial Theater in Warsaw, the Chief Censor tried to block a benefit performance of *Hamlet* on the grounds that the play referred to the murder of a king: "Such things must not be put before the audience, because they may suggest disloyal ideas" (Modjeska 1910: 184). The Russian censors were not only authoritarian but stunningly ignorant. One of them refused a license to perform Słowacki's *Mazepa* because there was a Polish king in it. "He said to me: 'A Polish king. Who ever heard of such an absurd thing! Polish kings never existed. There are only Russian emperors of Poles and of all the Russias; you understand, Madame?'" (Modjeska 1910: 185). Thanks to a contact in Russian high society, a licence was eventually granted in exchange for finding a speaking role for the censor's *petite amie* from the *corps du ballet*. The censorship was capricious.

Despite its political agendas, Modjeska took the leading role in both Schiller's and Słowacki's versions of *Maria Stuart*, and one of her first parts at the Lwów Theatre was as an imp of lake and forest in *Balladyna*, Słowacki's tragicomedy about a peasant girl who turns into a homicidal queen (Modjeska 1910: 89). Apollo Korzeniowski's satirical comedy *Dla miłego grosza* was staged in several Borderland theaters, quite possibly gaining official approval because the satire was directed at arriviste merchant families and venal members of the *szlachta* rather than the Russian administration.[4]

Słowacki wrote *Balladyna* in 1839, eight years after going into exile. All three of the "National Authors" had left partitioned Poland: Krasiński and Słowacki in the aftermath of the 1830 uprising, Mickiewicz somewhat earlier.[5] They suffered anguish and frustration at seeing dreadful events from a distance and with minimal agency, longing for the homeland (surely nostalgia is too soft a word), and anger at the insolence and callousness of the occupying powers. Despite zealous surveillance, there was in Poland a clandestine readership for lyric poetry, visionary prose, and drama and a clandestine audience for forbidden music. Krasiński's unfinished play *1846* has a telling scene. The speaker is Kęta, a gifted pianist. At a recent name-day party in Warsaw, a young woman had begun to recite the "Vision of Friar Piotr" from Part III of *Forefathers' Eve*. When her memory faltered, a young clerk had stood up and finished the recital.

> The gendarmes came for him, at about two o'clock in the morning. They rifled through all his papers, and when they found a hand-copied *Forefathers' Eve*, Part III, among them, they dragged him off to the Citadel! It seems that the police already knew that he was the one who spoke the last words of the poem that the young girl had forgotten. So, among us that evening there was a traitor! A Judas! (Krasiński 2018: 401–2)

By and large, the exiles' plays may be called closet dramas, that is to say dramas that by design or force of circumstance were fated to be read rather than staged. Among examples from other European literatures are Milton's *Samson Agonistes* (published in 1671), Goethe's *Faust I* and *II* (1808, 1832),[6] Byron's *Manfred* (1817), Percy Shelley's *The Cenci* and *Prometheus Unbound* (1819, 1820), Wordsworth's *The Borderers* (1842), and, from more recent times, Ford Madox Ford's effervescent yet serious *Mister Bosphorus* (1923). When one considers the circumstances under which such works evolved, variety trumps uniformity: sometimes censorship or scandal, sometimes lack of funds or lack of technical knowledge.

The Polish closet dramas by Mickiewicz, Krasiński, and Słowacki have gone through several phases. First, they were published, mostly in Paris and mostly anonymously, and circulated among the Polish exiles;[7] in Poland itself, especially in the Russian territories, the plays became illicit goods, smuggled into the country or passed around from hand to hand in entirety or in copied extracts. In both situations, there was already an aspect of performativity. In other words, although the labels *closet drama* and *cabinet drama* promise literary solitude,[8] the Polish plays speak in a different idiom.[9] Rather than appealing to what Wayne Booth and Wolfgang Iser call the implied reader, they evoke what Benedict Anderson would recognize as an implied community. This community was sustained by a number of forces: cultural tradition and cultural innovation, clandestine experience, and grief and the exhilaration of flouting the status quo. As the passage cited above from Krasiński's *1846* suggests, the scripts had multiple lives. While readable (and powerful) in private, they provided a frame of reference among like-minded readers and even, at great risk, the possibility of fragmentary recitations in small, clandestine groups.

During the three years of his professorship at the Collège de France in Paris, Adam Mickiewicz lectured on Slavic literatures. In April 1843, he devoted a lecture to Slavic drama, citing Russian, Serbian, and Czech examples, but dwelling on current Polish theatrical writing as represented by Krasiński's *The Undivine Comedy* and offering a vision of the future that "*should unite all the elements of a truly national poetry*, just as the political institution of a nation should express all its political tendencies" (Mickiewicz 1986: 93; emphasis in original). In his advocacy for a national poetry, Mickiewicz shows no narrowing of the mind, no dog in the manger urge to exclude.[10] The scope of his argument includes ancient Greek comedy and tragedy, Spanish drama of the Golden Age, medieval mystery plays, old Celtic and Germanic poetry, and the works of Shakespeare. What is more, he embraces a whole range of registers and genres: oral narrative and operatic performance, lyric and epic, classical and popular, natural and supernatural, heavenly and hellish, and ancient and modern. He evokes the ancient ritual of communing with the spirits of the dead (which figures so memorably in Part II of *Forefathers' Eve*); his love of popular imagery and song recalls Herder; he says of *The Undivine Comedy* that "the marvelous, the supernatural world, is not simply poetic and popular here, it is also conceived according to ideas that have been developed in our century" (1986: 95). Anticipating the *Gesamtkunstwerk* (merging of all the arts) of later in the century, he imagines "the perfecting of the arts that serve the drama—such as architecture, painting, the play of lights, etc." (95). Yet all these marvels must wait for another time. Although Mickiewicz was all too well acquainted with that barrier, there is no reference to censorship here; the problem is the inadequacy of contemporary staging (for exceptions, see n9). It was not until the very end of the nineteenth century that this inadequacy was overcome and the closet left behind, with productions in Cracow of *Kordian* in 1899, *Forefathers' Eve* in 1901, and *The Undivine Comedy* in 1902.[11]

As a hybrid of the readable and the theatrical, these plays are notably fluid in milieu, time, and space, untrammeled by mimetic demands. Part I of *The Undivine Comedy* offers a case in point. The invocation to God begins: "Stars about thy head—beneath thy feet the waves of the sea—before thee on the waves a rainbow rushes, cleaving the mist—whatever thou beholdest is thine—coasts, cities and people are thy property—heaven is thine—'tis as if nothing can thy glory equal" (Krasiński 2018: 48). The play proper leads off with the Guardian Angel's blessing on the Husband (Count Henryk), followed by curses on the Husband by a Chorus of Evil Spirits. The stage directions place the Angel above a village church; a sentence later, the inside of the church appears, with a consecrated candle on the altar and a priest conducting the wedding ceremony. In short order follow a wedding party, the flight of the vampirical Maiden over a burial ground, a bedroom scene with the cold-shouldered Wife and the Husband, who craves to be with the Maiden, then a moonlit garden, and another domestic scene just prior to the christening of a child. Among the later settings of Part I are a cliff above a wild sea and a lunatic asylum. Of course, there is much more to come in the three other parts, most forcibly the apocalyptic struggle in and around the Castle of the Holy Trinity.

The shifts and staggering juxtapositions in the plays of the great triumvirate are not only happenings in time and space; they are also jolting contrasts in mode, register, and scale. In other words, within the vastness of their scripts, we encounter tragedy, comedy, satire, debate, bathos, madness, gothic horror, political sacrifice, and religious adoration. Regardless of decorum, these modes are expressed in the varied languages of spirituality, hermeticism, exorcism, suffering, eloquence, gallantry, redemption, learning, insanity, overweening pride and cruelty, and the rough and tumble of manual labor. We also find the macrocosmic and the microcosmic, the quotidian and the eternal. What is more, these interminglings and metamorphoses are intensely dramatic, whether in the great soliloquies, such as Kordian's speech on Mont Blanc, which takes him from suicidal thoughts to a vision of Godlike sublimity and on to his dedication to the Polish cause (Słowacki 2018: 165–9), or in the agonistic confrontation of Count Henryk and Pankracy (Krasiński 2018: 118–27).

Part III of *Forefathers' Eve* offers a plenitude of dramatic moments and swings of mood and mode between and during scenes. The Great Improvisation is a psychomachia on the highest level, a challenge to God Himself in the vastness of the cosmos, culminating in a wild fantasy of superhuman power:

KONRAD: On earth I'm brothered to an awesome nation.
I've armies and dominions, powers and thrones,
And if I choose to blaspheme,
I'll grip with Thee more bloodily than did Satan!

(Mickiewicz 2016: 3.2 213; emphasis in original)[12]

Yet the scene rounds off with a brace of squabbling evil spirits eager to feast on Konrad's corpse. In the following scene, Friar Piotr has to exorcize Beelzebub's multilingual nephew:

SPIRIT: Do you think that I'm Satan's right hand man?
Landrat, Gubernator, Kreishauptmann -
That's more the style: an unimportant clerk. (3.3 225)

With their macabre humor, the spirits in these scenes have a medieval quality, like demons in mystery plays, or frescos, or the *Malebranche* in Dante's *Inferno*, XXI–XXIII. They also have a part to play in the presentation of Senator Novosiltsov, a historical character responsible for the fabrication of evidence, arrest, torture, and exile of the Vilnius students and the representative of the Tzar at the Congress Kingdom of Poland's Council of State, the *Rada Stanu*. He appears first in a luxurious bedroom, where two junior devils, briefly joined by Beelzebub himself, plunge him into a nightmare of falling from the Tzar's grace, then send his soul packing for a night of torment on the frontier of Hell (Mickiewicz 2016: 3.6 245). Next we hear of him in a gathering at a Warsaw salon, where two grand ladies at a card table praise his social skills:

LADY 2: Ever since Novosiltsov left Warsaw
There hasn't been a single tasteful ball. ...
LADY 1: Our Warsaw needs just such a man, I say! (3.7 247)

By the door to the salon, a group of immeasurably more humane Poles hear of the atrocious treatment of Adolf Cichowski, broken by fifteen years of imprisonment and drastic interrogation. It is not until act 3, scene 8 that the senator appears in his full vileness, insulting a mother whose son has been flogged nearly to death, ordering the arrest and interrogation of a young boy so as to make his father confess, and sneering at "my black cherub" Friar Piotr (3.8 275), who refuses to grovel to the senator or betray the captives even when threatened with torture and execution. In terms of theater, scenes 6 to 8 are triumphs of choreography as well as an anatomy of rule by violence and insult.

The three plays engage to an intense degree with the cosmic and the spiritual. They also engage with work, family, personal testimony, and worldly rank. Citing Norwid, Donald Pirie has argued that Polish Romanticism had concentrated on "a fictitious and overwhelming concept of 'the suffering nation' to the detriment of day-to-day 'humanity'" (Pirie 1988, qtd. in Foster 1988: 335). The following examples suggest that the suffering nation and day-to-day humanity were in a dramatic sense symbiotic. Here are some examples: the recollections of the Polish Corporal in *Forefathers' Eve* 3.1 and 3.3 and the family retainer Grzegorz in *Kordian* 1.1; the painful scenes in Count Henryk's family and the blindness of Orcio in *The Undivine Comedy* I and II; the choruses of butchers, peasants, and artists in III; and the debate between Pankracy the revolutionary and the Count, defender of aristocratic privilege, also in III.[13] What these passages show is a savage deformation of day-to-day life in a suffering nation.

There is a further dimension to the plays, which embraces resistance by mockery and the unearthing of scandalous deeds. Among subjugated peoples, scandal and ridicule can become powerful agents of solidarity (in the twentieth century, similar tactics could be found in such countries as South Africa, Ireland, Nigeria, Argentina, and of course Poland itself). *Kordian* in particular is notable for such events. The scene on Mont Blanc already mentioned is a successful attempt to lift Kordian's spirits after an absurd and infuriating audience with the Pope and Luther, the Papal parrot. In Kordian's words on the mountain's summit, "My childlike faith has been slain by the Vicar of Christ" (Słowacki 2018: 167). The pope is not named, but the circumstances point to Gregory XVI, who had reprimanded priests for taking part in the rising of 1830–1 and instructed Poles under Russian rule to obey Tzar Nicholas I. The pope welcomes Kordian as the scion of a noble family but pays no attention to the gift of a "holy relic: A handful of my native soil" soaked in the blood of suffering men, women, and children (163). Instead, the less-than-modest Pope tells him to be:

> Sure to hear my next Urbe et Urbi
> Tomorrow—what a sight! The people lie
> Prostrate before me. Tell the Poles that I
> Bid them to pray and hold fast to the faith
> And honour their rightful Tsar unto the death.

(Słowacki 2018: 163–4)

This brief scene is rendered absurd as well as shameless by the parrot's counterpoint: squawking *Miserere* when his owner praises the Tzar, *Lachryma Christi!* (a white wine) when Kordian asks the pope to shed a tear for Poland, and *Clamavi* (as in *de profundis clamavi*) when Kordian is lost for words by the pope's ignoring his gift. All this is capped when the pope tells the story of a Prince of the Church who thought he was debating with a profound theologian rather than a parrot.

Several scandalous scenes in act 3 present the Tzar and his older brother the Grand Prince Constantine (who renounced his right to the Imperial throne when he joined in a morganatic marriage). Nicholas was a martinet who ruled the empire with military strictness; Constantine was de facto viceroy of Congress Poland, where he was much reviled and had gained notoriety for mistreating women. Their interactions in Słowacki's play make a display of crazed instability, cruelty, and mutual loathing. When the plot to kill the Tzar is uncovered and Kordian captured, Constantine threatens to dismember him with horses or crush him under an artillery caisson, while the Tzar thinks that his brother is behind the plot. All of a sudden, Constantine changes his mind and decides to show off the bravery of his Polish charges. So as to infuriate his brother,[14] he commands the trumpeters to play the anthem of the Polish legions, "Dąbrowski's Mazurka," whose first line is "Jeszcze Polska nie zginęła"—"Poland is not lost yet." Matters come to a head in scene 9, beginning with a soliloquy that suggests the Tzar is suffering from a bad case of megalomania:

Europe, I'll soon
Slice you like an apple, with a poisoned knife.
All you crowned heads! Your fealty or your life! (3.9 230)

As part of his Polish stratagem, the Grand Prince arrives, now wanting a reprieve for Kordian. The display of fickleness degenerates into a fierce spat between two blackmailers. The Grand Prince now claims that Nicholas was complicit in the murder of their father, Tzar Paul I, and should be branded and hauled off to Siberia in a penal convoy. The Tzar holds the Prince guilty of the rape and murder of a sixteen-year-old English girl. Eventually, Constantine wins the struggle with a threat to strangle the Tzar and leave his body to rot in a wardrobe, which had been the fate of the young woman. The Tzar signs the order of reprieve for Kordian with the formula, "A brother begs a brother's forgiveness," but his final line has him wringing his hands in dismay as he says, "My brother—is a Pole" (239–40). Słowacki never wrote a Part II, so Kordian's destiny is left unknown—an effect that leaves us without the melodrama of a last-minute rescue. In its stead, we have not only a series of narrative horrors, but a revelation of enough cruelties and more than enough wrongheadedness to recognize the utter missteps and inadequacies of Russian hegemony over Poland.

The Polish Romantic dramas show clear evidence of literary and dramatic antecedents. The staging of sacred ritual and humanity's place in the cosmos owes something to the plays of Pedro Calderón de la Barca: Słowacki learned Spanish in order to translate Calderón's *El principe constante* and may have known *El gran teatro del mundo*.[15] In a scene in act 2 of *Kordian*, Kordian appears sitting on a chalk cliff reading *King Lear*, one of many Shakespearean plays where time, space, and register are fluid. The handling of the supernatural in *Kordian* and *The Undivine Comedy* recalls the scenes in *Faust I* set in Auerbach's Cellar and on the Brocken. Mickiewicz brings in opera, aptly quoting Mozart's *Don Giovanni* in the ball scene of *Forefathers' Eve* 3.8. The orchestra begins with the stately minuet, but as thunderclouds gather outside, the musicians play the menacing chords of the Commendatore, whose statue will soon be dragging Giovanni down to Hell. Victor Hugo's long preface to the closet drama *Cromwell* places grotesque comedy at the heart of Romantic poetry. The work of Byron, who often refers to Poland's captivity, caught the attention of Poles who read his poetry (including *Manfred*) in English, French, or Polish (Trueblood 1981: passim; Banham 1992: 139–40).[16] Mickiewicz praised both his poetic and his political acuity (Żuławski 1981: 122; Cochran 2015: 313). Yet the Polish plays remain utterly distinctive. To quote one of the few anglophone critics with a long-term commitment to the field, "Polish Romantic drama differs from its counterpart in the West in the power and originality of its theatrical form and in the resonance of its social and political vision" (Gerould 1992: 779). For example, the moral and spiritual direction of Kordian, Konrad, and Count Henryk is from rage and isolation to commitment to a cause. Near the end of Part II of *The Undivine Comedy*, the Count, deranged by his son Orchio's blindness, stumbles through a dark night of the soul:

> I toiled many years to arrive [at] the very end of all knowledge, delight, and thought, and discovered nothing but the charnel vacuum of my heart. I know all feelings by name, but there is no desire, no faith, no love in me at all. (Krasiński 2018: 79)

At the very end of Part II, having listened to the Eagle and the Guardian Angel, the Count speaks tenderly to Orcio and is ready "to fight, to act," albeit "with the few against the many" (87). Byron's Manfred, on the other hand, defies the urgings of the Abbot and the Spirit, and chooses solitude even in the hour of his death:

> I knew, and know my hour is come, but not
> To render up my soul to such as thee:
> Away! I'll die as I have lived—alone.

(Byron 2005: 504)

At one end of the Romantic spectrum lies hard-won isolation, and at the other, hard-won solidarity.

Zdzisław Najder has said that a "structural" understanding of the Polish background has profound implications for reading Conrad's work:

> Because what may have seemed to be a private code, deciphered only by biographical investigations and pointing to esoteric meaning, turns out to be a cultural language, a public system of signs, which carry meaning independently from the reflections of the novelist's own personality. (1997: 15)

I heartily agree, but have chosen in this brief study to consider vehicle at least as much as tenor, since the dramaturgy of the plays has not often been explored in English. Each of these scripts has an encyclopedic quality, covering a huge range of human and cosmic experiences and the links among them. Conrad's work is not quite as expansive. There are no guardian angels in his books, and no infernal demons—though some of his nastier characters deserve to qualify. Nevertheless, there are strong spectral and metaphysical forces at work in his writings, his letters included. One frequent invocation is to the Shades, dwellers in the Classical underworld, and by extension to sailors and more recent ancestors, the souls of the faithful departed. Writing to Hugh Walpole in May 1917 and thinking of the devastating attacks on gentry houses in Ukraine, Conrad asks, "Are those gracious shades of my memory to turn into blood-stained spectres?" (*CL6* 92). More generally, there is a sense, as there is in the plays, of Nature's immense powers. He once told his son John, as they visited a church, that sailors by reason of the great dangers that they ran were at heart religious (John Conrad 1981: 152). Like the three "National Authors," Conrad is ever aware of scale, measuring the small against the massive, the sudden against the long drawn out, as seen for example in "Typhoon," "Heart of Darkness," and *The Shadow-Line* (Davies 2018). One might well agree with Stefan Żeromski's comment on Conrad's writing in English: "There must have remained in his ear that subconscious, vague note, the Polish manner of linking words together, the Polish enthusiasm of marveling at the sight of things unknown, mysterious, terrible, and lofty" (Gillon 1966: 428). The last part of the sentence is pertinent both to the Romantic plays and to Conrad's essays and fiction.

Another relevant comment comes from Conrad's friend Józef H. Retinger, who was at home with several European literatures. He claims that Conrad was unique among British authors in his handling of natural events, in contrast with Wordsworth, who presents "successive immobile landscape paintings. Conrad, on the other hand, puts movement into his words, and catches Nature in the act of changing from one mood into another." When Retinger said that this was "a typically Polish verbal procedure," Conrad responded by fetching his much-traveled copy of *Pan Tadeusz* to show the source of this agility (Retinger 1941: 95–6). That gift for rendering movement and transition is certainly there in Conrad's work as well as in Mickiewicz's enthralling poem and the plays covered in this present essay. The author of "The End of the Tether," and *Nostromo*, and *The Secret Agent* shows a masterly hand in his cunning deployment of narrative time and place, and also his remarkable juxtapositions of florid and terse, formal and colloquial language. Throughout Conrad's work, moreover, we find an oscillation between the ironic and the operatic (Davies 2004, 2009).[17] That irony is often tethered to the absurd, when the trivial undermines the serious, as with Captain Mitchell's obsession with his impounded timepiece in *Nostromo*, or when ignorance is blinding, as in the garrulous Verloc's total misprision of his wife's intentions with the carving knife.

Absurdity, grotesquerie, and cruelty also abound in the plays. Absurdity is brilliantly represented in the episode of Słowacki's Papal parrot. Krasiński's depiction of Pankracy is like a political lampoon: "His brow is high and expansive, without a single hair on his skull—all have fallen out, knocked out by thought … the skin has dried to his skull, his cheeks squeezing in between bone and muscle, and from his temples downward a black beard rings his face like a wreath" (2018: 89). This depiction might well be compared with that of the anarchists in *The Secret Agent* or the marauding interlopers in *Victory. Forefathers' Eve* 3.7 and 3.8 are shaped around cruel behavior, with the cynical and sadistic senator, the sufferings of blind Mrs. Rollinson, mother of the tortured boy, the ingratiating lies of the doctor, the story of the broken prisoner Cichowski, the bravery of Friar Piotr, and the indifferent chatter of revelers at the ball. It would be difficult to find such a harrowing pair of scenes in British fiction or drama of the late nineteenth and early twentieth centuries anywhere but in the work of the author of *Nostromo*.[18]

Suggesting that a novelist, and a great one, might owe part of his artistic formation to the drama might at first seem a little far-fetched, yet genres at their best are hospitable rather than strict. It is easier to find traces of sentiments and verbal echoes than to imagine a metamorphosis of larger structures, but it is worth the trying. A few meters from Apollo Korzeniowski's grave in the Rakowicki Cemetery in Cracow, there is an effigy of a grown man sitting at a school desk. He is Tadeusz Kantor (1915–1990), and he sat at just such a desk for performances of his spectral vision *Dead Class*. Actors playing the part of elderly grown-ups in formal clothes sat at other desks, behaving like schoolchildren and being ground down by a bitter war. Riding on their backs were dummy figures, eventually cast into a fire. The settings were the World Wars and the Shoah. The guiding themes were the evanescence of the past and the impossibility of return. It is fitting that the two playwrights should be so close together, participants in a great tradition of theater. When reading Conrad's stage adaptations, I have often thought that he might have been a great dramatist as well as novelist if it were not for the cramping protocols of the early twentieth-century London stage. In April 1909, he told Edward Garnett, whose plays often fell foul of the theatrical censorship, "Though I detest the stage I have a theatrical imagination—that's why perhaps I detest the stage—that is the actors who mostly poor souls, have no imagination" (*CL4* 218). Somewhere in his memory and heart was a dramatist longing to get out.

Notes

1 Exemplified in England by authors like Philip Larkin, Elizabeth Jennings, and Kingsley Amis, who belonged to the loose grouping known as the Movement. By contrast, the month after the symposium appeared, F. R. Leavis quoted this passage in a lecture to the Literary and Philosophical Society of Newcastle-upon-Tyne. He swatted Hopkinson's questions about melodrama aside "to be dealt with incidentally and by implication" (Leavis 1958: 186). Previously, in *The Great Tradition*, Leavis had observed, "The melodrama, of course, is completely controlled to the pattern of moral significance" (1948: 186).

2 Such wonderfully rich narrative poems as Słowacki's *Anhelli*, and Mickiewicz's *Pan Tadeusz* and *Konrad Wallenrod* have a powerful theatrical element and are relevant to my argument, but for lack of space, the focus is on three canonical dramas: *Forefathers' Eve*, *Kordian*, and *The Undivine Comedy*.

3 The most likely period of this encounter would be in the late winter or early spring of 1869, when Apollo Korzeniowski and his son moved to Cracow and Mme Modjeska was at the end of her contract at the Cracow theater (now known as Helena Modrzejewska National Stary Theater). Her husband, Karol Chłapowski, the editor of *Kraj*, helped Apollo with finding a place to live (Najder 1983: 127).

4 When the script was published in Saint Petersburg in 1859, however, it had been heavily censored (Miłosz 1983: 265–6). The first half of an earlier work, *Komedia*, 1854/5, had drawn upon a satirical play by the popular Russian dramatist A. S. Griboedov (Najder 2007: 8).

5 Between 1823 and 1829, Mickiewicz had been imprisoned and then exiled beyond the bounds of the old Commonwealth to Russia proper on account of his former membership in the Philomaths, an anti-imperial secret society at the University of Vilnius. As a conservative Polish nationalist and the son of an overbearing tzarist general, Krasiński's motives for leaving Poland were more conflicted.

6 "As a work for the theater, even Part One was generally regarded during its author's lifetime as unperformable, though it was widely read" (Luke 1987: xlvii).

7 The first edition of *Kordian* (Paris 1834), for example, does not give the author's name, but indicates that it was published at his expense (*Nakładem Autora*) and sold at the Polish bookshop on the *quai* Voltaire.

8 The phrase *dans le silence de mon cabinet* was a long-standing favorite of French authors describing just such an isolation. Conrad uses it in a letter to André Gide when about to read the latter's novella *La Symphonie pastorale* (*CL7* 211).

9 "Unlike many of his contemporaries such as Byron, however, Mickiewicz thinks as a theatrical practitioner" (Filipowicz 1999: 10). The discovery in a Kiev archive by Zbigniew Jędrychowski of a playbill from 1832 announcing a full production of *Forefather's Eve* Part IV under the name *Gustaw* is evidence of the earliest fragmentary performance during Mickiewicz's lifetime (Filipowicz 1999: 15, n.11). (See also Filipowicz 2001: 612.)

10 In notable contrast with the presentation of converted Jews as saboteurs in *The Undivine Comedy*.

11 All three were produced at the Municipal Theater, now the Juliusz Słowacki Theater. There is a consensus that the most daring and influential production was that of *Forefathers' Eve*, directed by Stanisław Wyspiański, who fulfilled Mickiewicz's hope for a theater of all the arts. It was not until 2016, however, that a full text was performed, staged at the Teatr Polski in Wrocław. With a script based on *Forefathers' Eve*, Tadeusz Konwicki's film *Lawa* appeared in 1989.

12 For the reader's convenience, act and scene numbers from Part III are cited here as well as page references to the Kraszewski translation.

13 For an extensive discussion of the intellectual background to this play, including substantial quotations from Krasiński's correspondence, see Lednicki (1959). Miłosz (1959) argues that the playwright "had a personal terror of the people" (77).

14 And to delight future generations of Polish readers and theatergoers with its ironic placing.

15 Much closer to our own times, Jerzy Grotowski's production of *El principe constant* (Wrocław 1968) swiftly became a legend in *avant garde* drama.

16 There are echoes of *Childe Harold* in Conrad's unfinished novel *The Sisters* (Najder 1997: 74).

17 For the manifold dissolution of boundaries in Conrad, see Lawtoo, in particular (2016: 228–39).

18 French literature is another matter, but a triangulation of French and British with Polish literature is for another time.

References

Banham, Martin, ed. 1992. *The Cambridge Guide to Theatre*. Cambridge: Cambridge University Press.

Busza, Andrzej. 1966. "Conrad's Polish Literary Background and Some Illustrations of the Influence of Polish Literature on His Work." *Antemurale* 10: 109–255.

Byron, Lord. 2005. *Selected Poems*, edited by Susan J. Wolfson and Peter J. Manning. London: Penguin Books.

Cochran, Peter. 2015. *Byron's European Impact*. Newcastle-upon-Tyne: Cambridge Scholars.

Conrad, John. 1981. *Joseph Conrad: Times Remembered*. Cambridge: Cambridge University Press.

Davies, Laurence. 2004. "'The Thing Which Was Not' and the Thing That Is Also: Conrad's Ironic Shadowing." In *Conrad in the Twenty-First Century*, edited by Carola Kaplan, Peter Mallios, and Andrea White, 223–37. London: Routledge.

Davies, Laurence. 2009. "Conrad in the Operatic Mode." In *Joseph Conrad and the Performing Arts*, edited by Katherine Baxter and Richard Hand, 127–45. New York, London: Routledge.

Davies, Laurence. 2018. "'With All That Multitude of Celestial Bodies': Conrad's Sense of Scale." *The Conradian* 43, no. 1 (Spring): 99–120.

Filipowicz, Halina. 1999. "Performing Bodies, Performing Mickiewicz: Drama as Problem in Performance Studies." *Slavic and East European Journal* 43, no. 1 (Spring): 1–18.

Filipowicz, Halina. 2001. "Mickiewicz: 'East' and 'West.'" *Slavic and East Euopean Journal* 45, no. 4 (Winter): 606–23.

Foster, Roy. 1988. *Romanticism in National Context*. Cambridge: Cambridge University Press.

Gerould, Daniel. 1992. "Poland." In *The Cambridge Guide to Theatre*, edited by Martin Banham, 778–82. Cambridge: Cambridge University Press.

Gillon, Adam. 1966. "Some Polish Literary Motifs in the Works of Joseph Conrad." *Slavic and East European Journal* 10, no. 4 (Winter): 424–39.

Hopkinson, Tom. 1957. "The Short Story." "Joseph Conrad: A Critical Symposium." *London Magazine* 4, no. 11 (November): 36–41.

Jones, Susan. 1999. *Conrad and Women*. Oxford: Oxford University Press.

Krasiński, Zygmunt. 2018. *Dramatic Works*. Translated and introduced by Charles S. Kraszewski. London: Glagoslav.

Lawtoo, Nidesh. 2016. *Conrad's Shadow: Catastrophe, Mimesis, Theory*. East Lansing: Michigan State University Press.

Leavis, F. R. 1948. *The Great Tradition*. London: Chatto & Windus.

Leavis, F. R. 1958. "Joseph Conrad." *Sewanee Review* 66, no. 2 (Spring): 179–200.

Lednicki, Wacław. 1959. "*The Undivine Comedy*." *Polish Review* 4, no. 3: 106–35.

Luke, David. 1987. Introduction to Goethe's *Faust* Part One. Oxford: Oxford University Press.

Mickiewicz, Adam. 1986. "Lecture 16. Slavic Literature, Collège de France, Paris, 1843." Translated and edited by Daniel Gerould. *Drama Review* 30, no. 3 (Autumn): 91–7.

Mickiewicz, Adam. 2016. *Forefathers' Eve*. Translated by Charles S. Kraszewski. London: Glagoslav.

Miłosz, Czesław. 1959. "Krasiński's Retreat." Translated by Wacław Lednicki. *Polish Review* 4, no. 4: 72–81.

Miłosz, Czesław. 1983. *The History of Polish Literature*. 2nd ed. Berkeley: University of California Press.

Modjeska (Modrzejewska), Helena. 1910. *Memories and Impressions*. London: Macmillan.

Najder, Zdzisław. 1983. *Conrad Under Familial Eyes*. Translated and edited by Halina Najder. Cambridge: Cambridge University Press.

Najder, Zdzisław. 1997. *Conrad in Perspective: Essays on Art and Fidelity*. Cambridge: Cambridge University Press.

Najder, Zdzisław. 2007. *Joseph Conrad: A Life*. Translated by Halina Najder. 2nd English ed. Rochester, NY: Camden House.

Niland, Richard. 2010. *Conrad and History*. Oxford: Oxford University Press.

Pirie, Donald. 1988. "The Agony in the Garden: Polish Romanticism." In *Romanticism in National Context*, edited by Roy Foster, 317–45. Cambridge: Cambridge University Press.

Retinger, Józef H. 1941. *Conrad and His Contemporaries: Souvenirs*. London: Minerva.

Słowacki, Juliusz. 2018. *Four Plays*. Translated and introduced by Charles S. Kraszewski. London: Glagoslav.

Szczypien, Jean M. 2017. "*Sailing towards Poland*" with Joseph Conrad. Frankfurt: Peter Lang.

Trueblood, Paul Graham, ed. 1981. *Byron's Political and Cultural Influence in Nineteenth Century Europe: A Symposium*. London: Macmillan.

Żuławski, Juliusz. 1981. "Byron and Poland: Byron and Polish Romantic Revolt." In *Byron's Political and Cultural Influence in Nineteenth Century Europe: A Symposium*, edited by Paul Graham Trueblood, 122–31. London: Macmillan.

7

The "Curve" of Time: Modes of Imaginative Inquiry in *Under Western Eyes*

Anne Luyat
Université d'Avignon

> Standing in the present on the highest point of a curve,
> you can look back and see the Past, or forward and see
> the Future, all in the same instant.
>
> —Maurice Maeterlinck, *The Fourth Dimension*

Although he insists from the first to the last page of *Under Western Eyes* that he is unable to comprehend the unknowable Russian mind, the Teacher of Languages scans the arc of the "curve" of time to find the multiple perspectives he needs in order to tell the conflicting stories of the Russian expatriates who are living, spying, and writing in turn of the century Geneva. Within the negative space that the Teacher of Languages creates around the Russian expatriates and himself, he is able to record with impassive detachment intimate aspects of their lives and their stories and yet reveal almost nothing about himself. He does mention in passing that at the age of nine he left the city of Saint Petersburg in the company of his parents (*UWE* [D] 184) but makes no mention of the reason for their departure. Why does the Teacher of Languages insist on remaining outside the narration? Do the stories that he narrates form for him, as they did for Maurice Maeterlinck, an expanse of serial time capable of illuminating the past and implicating the future?[1] Does history repeat itself, and can writing about the past create an understanding of the future? (Said 2008: 238).[2] Past suffering and serial time bind lives and future destinies in the tzarist spy Razumov's diary, which, according to the Teacher of Languages, "reads like the open book of fate" (*UWE* 103); but why has the retiring and discreet Teacher of Languages, who continues to insist that he is unable to understand the Russian mind, taken it upon himself to narrate the obscure story of a compromised tzarist spy?

Past suffering and serial time meet for the first time in the story told by the Teacher of Languages when Razumov, the natural son of a Russian nobleman, who has neither family ties, nor close friends, betrays a fellow student at Saint Petersburg University to the tzarist secret police. After the capture and execution for treason of the man he betrayed, time changes irrevocably for Razumov in the instant it takes for the chief of the secret police to quietly ask him: "Where to?" (96). Councilor Mikulin's shrewd assessment of Razumov's personal isolation enables him to force Razumov, a young man without political beliefs, to leave the university and become a spy for the tzarist regime in Geneva. Will the words of regret that Razumov confides to his diary in Geneva after he meets the sister and the mother of the man he betrayed enable him to break the chain of autocratic control and repression in which he has been caught up? Or will the words he writes in order to escape his fate become the confession that will betray him to tzarist agents operating in Geneva, where he risks becoming another in a series of victims of the autocratic tzarist regime?

In pointing out Conrad's choice of the city of Geneva as the setting in the novel for Razumov's exile, it is Zdzisław Najder, who asks the essential question about *Under Western Eyes*: "but then as Councillor M. asks Razumov … 'where to?' To Switzerland rather than Russia, but perchance why of all places, does Conrad send Razumov to Switzerland?" (1984: 198). At least part of the answer to Najder's question is to be found in the history of Poland, for both the city of Geneva and the country of Switzerland had long-standing political ties to the Polish nation. When the philosopher Jean-Jacques Rousseau was asked at the end of his life to define a form of government for the fledging Polish-Lithuanian nation, his response was his well-defined and thoroughly meditated *Considérations sur le gouvernement de Pologne et sur sa réformation projetée* (1782).[3] The volume was published in French, in Amsterdam, in 1782, four years after Rousseau's death. In his proposed constitution for the future government of Poland, Jean-Jacques Rousseau had defined in detail the duty of a government to protect its citizens and their welfare. Rousseau's statue in Geneva on L'Île Rousseau is a gravitating point in *Under Western Eyes* for the spy and compromised former student Razumov, who seeks solitude at the foot of the statue in order to renew the hope he had nourished as a student at Saint Petersburg University to become a writer of influence.

During the European wars of partition in the eighteenth century when Russia invaded Poland and the name of Poland disappeared from world maps, the neutral country of Switzerland gave Polish political refugees safe haven within its borders. After the defeat of the Polish uprising of 1831, the young Polish diplomat, lyric poet, and dramatist Juliusz Słowacki, who was admired by Conrad, more than any other Polish author (Zdrada 2008-9: 30-92), found refuge in Geneva, where he lived until 1836. Conrad read the works of the banished poet Słowacki at home as a boy in Cracow, for under Russian rule, Słowacki's poems and dramatic works were banned in Polish schools and Polish theaters. Conrad also found in Słowacki's poems his first glimpses of the country of Switzerland. Expressing his homesickness for Poland in the poem "Hymn" written during his Swiss exile, Juliusz Słowacki associated the landscape around him in Switzerland to his memories of Poland: "The flying storks above me I could see/In a stretched out skein soar,/That once I knew them on a Polish pasture, I am sad, Savior" (1953: 9). Another poem of Słowacki's "In Switzerland" has a couple admiring an alpine panorama during a morning walk at the meeting point of the Arve and the Rhône Rivers (which will figure prominently in *Under Western Eyes*): "In the Swiss mountains there is a cascade,/Where the Aar's blue waters from the heights glissade" (1953: 15). Like Conrad's character Razumov in *Under Western Eyes*, many Polish and Russian *emigrés* lived on the embankment of the Arve near the rue de Carouge in the quarter of Geneva, which, after Karl Marx lived there and organized the First International Congress in 1866, acquired the name of "La Petite Russie" as noted by Paul Kirschner in Gene Moore's *Conrad's Cities* (1992: 228).[4]

In a brief aside to the reader, the Teacher of Languages remembers that after leaving the apartment of Natalia Haldin and her mother on Le Boulevard des Philosophes, he was aware of the city's political dichotomy and the improbable existence of "La Petite Russie" in the city of Jean-Jacques Rousseau. Although the Teacher of Languages had not yet read the article in the *London Evening Standard* describing the arrest of Victor Haldin in Saint Petersburg, he remembers as he continues along Le Boulevard des Philosophes that he had felt a premonition of danger concerning Natalia Haldin and her mother: "The shadow of autocracy, all unperceived by me, had already fallen upon Le Boulevard des Philosophes, in the free, independent, and democratic city of Geneva, where there is a quarter called 'La Petite Russie'" (*UWE* [D] 104). The Teacher of Languages knew his city well. Le Boulevard des Philosophes had acquired its name from its proximity to L'Académie, an institution of higher learning whose most celebrated Professor of *Belles Lettres* (1739), and later Professor of Theology (1756), was the Presbyterian pastor Jacob Vernet.[5] As he continued walking along Le Boulevard des Philosophes, the doubting narrator of *Under Western Eyes* expressed his deep sense of mistrust in the Russian state as well as his belief that all Russians suffered from the actions of their government: "Whenever two Russians come together, the shadow of autocracy is with them, tinging [*sic*] their thoughts, their views, their most intimate feelings, their private life, their public utterances haunting the secret of their silences" (104–5).

Juliusz Słowacki's dark and powerful poetic drama *Anhelli*, portraying the suffering of Polish prisoners in Siberia, written in part in Geneva and published in Paris in 1838, gave voice to Polish prisoners who were forced to work in the Siberian coal mines where they were tortured and starved to the point of wishing for death. With force, dignity, and restraint, Juliusz Słowacki portrayed the Polish prisoners in chains who chose to eat the coal they were forced to mine in order to poison themselves and thus put an end to their suffering:

> Behold, these are the mines of Siberia!
> Walk here carefully, for this ground is covered with sleeping men.
> In other mines the criminals howl; but this mine is only the grave
> of the sons of the homeland and is filled with silence.
> The chain that clanks here has a sorrowful sound, and in the vault are
> various echoes, and one echo that says, "I pity you." (1999: 87)

For generations of Polish readers, the image Juliusz Słowacki had created in *Anhelli* of "the chain that clanks here and has a sorrowful sound" had been a recognized symbol of Polish suffering under Russian rule.

Although the loudly clanking chain worn in *Under Western Eyes* by Conrad's character Peter Ivanovitch, the best-selling author of a recently published Siberian escape memoir, is omnipresent to the point of comedy during the writer's escape across Russia from Siberia to the Pacific coast, its echoing sound seems, oddly enough, as the memoir progresses, to erase the pain of suffering rather than to intensify it. Neither dramatic power, nor restraint, nor solemnity will figure in Peter Ivanovitch's account of his flight from the Russian prison camps of Siberia to the Pacific coast. Unlike the lives of the Polish prisoners portrayed by Juliusz Słowacki in *Anhelli*, who suffer torture and deprivation to the point of wishing for death, Peter Ivanovitch's account of his escape has a happy outcome in which the sound, too often repeated, of his clanking chain becomes as banal and as irritating as a continuously ringing bell. Knowing that Juliusz Słowacki's portrayal of the Polish prisoners' suffering in Siberia was both remembered and admired and that the clanking chain in *Anhelli* was its recognized symbol in Poland, why did Joseph Conrad allow his character Peter Ivanovitch to overuse it in *Under Western Eyes?* Conrad knew the true story of suffering and exile under Russian detention from the example of his parents' condemnation by Russian authorities after the Warsaw uprising of 1863, and from their deportation, which, at the age of four, he had shared with them in Chernikov. Why would Conrad, who detested overwriting and was known to have criticized the French author Alphonse Daudet for his authorial "dotted i's" and "pointing finger," have chosen deliberately to allow his character Peter Ivanovitch, who seemed to have little or no experience of the writer's craft, to tell an important story with such an evident lack of finesse? (*NLL* [D] 28).

According to the Teacher of Languages, the memoir of Peter Ivanovitch had been translated into seven languages and was being marketed across the world as an accurate account of life in Russia, an account that Conrad knew to be untrue. Yet he allowed his character Peter Ivanovitch to describe Russian prisons as a place from which it was actually possible to escape. He also chose to have his character narrate his escape in an unintentionally comic register. Peter Ivanovitch takes himself quite seriously; yet he becomes the object of a burlesque reversal of tragedy when he gives an improbable account in his memoir of his intelligence, his strength, and his ability to avoid capture. The veneer of unintentional comedy Peter Ivanovitch creates when he attempts to promote his own heroism allows Conrad's readers to laugh at his pretense and also to question the veracity of the account he is giving them about Russia and its prisons.

Maurice Ebileeni in *Conrad, Faulkner, and the Problem of Nonsense* indicates his belief that readers of novels need stories—both stories that are lived and stories that are portrayed in fiction, even stories with events which may seem at first to have no discernible meaning—in order to discern the truth. Ebileeni's investigation of stories used by both Conrad and Faulkner, which may at first seem to have no meaning but are actually at the heart of the story, give us a better understanding of Conrad's efforts to portray a tragic sense of human consciousness by taking into account elements that might initially seem comic, irrational, or irrelevant. By giving nonsense its human significance and by explaining its necessary presence both in life and in works of fiction, Ebileeni gives a deeper understanding of the efforts that Conrad and Faulkner made to confront and understand even the most outrageous aspects of the real (2015: 131).

The Teacher of Languages criticizes Peter Ivanovitch's tone of self-importance, which reveals that from the beginning to the end of the memoir, Peter Ivanovitch has not only given the role of hero almost exclusively to himself, but has continuously exaggerated his own accomplishments. In the opinion of the Teacher of Languages, the memoir's conclusion is especially irritating because Peter Ivanovitch attempts to describe his escape from the clanking chain as a mystical, quasi-religious, quasi-political experience. The triptych Peter Ivanovitch creates describing himself at the time of his deliverance by a village blacksmith and the blacksmith's newly wedded wife is remarkable primarily for its series of curiously mixed metaphors:

> "My fetters," the book says, "were struck off on the banks of the stream, in the starlight of a calm night by an athletic young man of the people, kneeling at my feet while the woman, like a liberating genius, stood by with clasped hands. Obviously a symbolic couple." (*UWE* [D] 122–3)

The dewy bombastic style of Peter Ivanovitch's triptych scene seems to take its inspiration both from nineteenth-century religious painting by artists describing peasant life, such as Jean-François Millet,[6] and from political documents of the kind that were being written in Geneva in the nineteenth century by Karl Marx and Friedrich Engels.[7] Unimpressed by Peter Ivanovitch's attempts at elevated rhetoric and distressed by his style, the Teacher of Languages says that he will no longer continue his reading of the best-selling memoir, "the great literary success of the year," because "the rest of his escape does not lend itself to mystic and symbolic interpretation" (123).

The Teacher of Languages does add, with a visible wince of false modesty about the appropriateness of his role as a literary critic, his eye-witness confirmation that Peter Ivanovitch seeks constantly in Geneva to emphasize what he believes to be his personal heroic stature in order to increase the sales of his book:

> However, it is not becoming for an obscure teacher of languages to criticize a "heroic fugitive" of worldwide celebrity. I was aware from hearsay that he was an industrious busybody, hunting up his companions in hotels, in private lodgings and *I was told* conferring upon them the honor of his notice in public gardens when a suitable opening presented itself. (*UWE* 124; emphasis in original)

Peter Ivanovitch's unsuccessful efforts at self-promotion represent an unfortunate initiative and a personal miscalculation, which the Teacher of Languages, who has learned from well-placed friends in the city that the writer has become a creature of social ridicule, is delighted to confirm.

The British scholar Owen Knowles quotes the British novelist and critic Anthony Powell, who commented favorably in *Faces in My Time* (1980) on Joseph Conrad's ironic treatment of Peter Ivanovitch's pretentious posturing. Burgess believed, too, in the possibility of a Swiss source for Peter Ivanovitch's escape story and indicated that the Swiss philosopher Henri Frédéric Amiel in his

Journal of 1884 had revealed his personal knowledge about the escape of a Polish political prisoner from Siberia, a story which he personally had found extremely difficult to believe. Owen Knowles points out as well that the story told by Peter Ivanovitch in his memoir may have its origin in the autobiographical account of an escaped Polish prisoner, a certain Rufin Piotrowski, which had appeared in *La Revue des Deux Mondes* in 1862 (1985: 154–61). All the roads in the story told by Peter Ivanovitch would seem to lead to Poland: yet Peter Ivanovitch makes no mention of any other source than his own personal experience—a source that cannot be verified. To see the grotesque as a high form of comedy as defined by Charles Baudelaire in his *Curiosités Esthétiques* (1868; qtd. in Luyat 1986: 4–15), is to recognize fantastic creations and deformations as mirrored images of the real and to understand why Conrad has the Teacher of Languages describe in detail and comment unfavorably on Peter Ivanovitch's portrayal of his series of fortunate escapes from Russian prisons in Siberia. Because of the escape story that Peter Ivanovitch had published simply for world acclaim, he had become someone in Geneva to be avoided: "Miss Haldin, with her sure instinct, had refrained from introducing me to the burly celebrity" (*UWE* [D] 124).

Under Western Eyes is a novel about writing, whose stories and stories within stories reveal a system of internal political terror within Russia that extends to Russians abroad. Yet Peter Ivanovitch does not seem to be the object in Geneva of surveillance by Russian authorities, as might have been expected for the author of a memoir about an escape from Russian prisons. On the other hand, Razumov's diary, when he reveals its contents to the revolutionaries, becomes the source of vicious retribution and punishments that nearly end his life.

The Teacher of Languages has chosen to reveal parts of Razumov's diary to an unnamed listener or correspondent. Might the Teacher of Languages feel a personal obligation, for reasons of his own, to tell Razumov's difficult and painful story? The Polish critic Grażyna Branny does not treat *Under Western Eyes* in her examination of personal commitment, yet her work *A Conflict of Values, Alienation and Commitment in the Novels of Joseph Conrad and William Faulkner* (1997) is essential to our understanding of the Teacher of Languages. Telling Razumov's story appears to be a painful exercise for him, yet he continues the difficult narration until he reaches the last entry in Razumov's journal, at the point when Razumov's words disintegrate into an indelible black smear of solitude, terror, and pain.

To conclude, within the covers of Razumov's diary, the reader discovers what has become, according to the French critic Jacques Darras, "Razumov's country and unique place of refuge" (1978: 156).[8] The reduced perimeter of Razumov's life confined him to the pages of his diary, the only place where he could note the true nature of the violence inflicted upon him both in Saint Petersburg and in Geneva. His diary was the only place where he could attempt to live out a tragedy of silence and escape the constant observation of informers, the only place where his voice could express grief in order to access for a moment the life of writing for which he had trained and to which he would never again have access. With his awareness that the assembled revolutionaries in Geneva would decide to take his life when he revealed the truth about his betrayal of Victor Haldin, Razumov's confession to them is not unlike the suicide of the Polish prisoners in Juliusz Słowacki's drama *Anhelli*.

The readers of *Under Western Eyes* will never learn exactly why the Teacher of Languages has chosen to narrate Razumov's story on the razor-sharp edge of doubt, for the novel's surprising last words are not his. Conrad's character, the Russian spy Sophia Antonovna, states flatly that Peter Ivanovitch, the author of the one-dimensional best-selling Siberian prison escape memoir, is "an inspired man." At the novel's eleventh hour, she obliges the readers of *Under Western Eyes* to weigh Peter Ivanovitch's unverified and unverifiable personal account of Siberian prisons, from which it was actually possible to escape, against the sense of isolation and terror experienced under autocratic rule—from which there was no escape—which was recorded by Razumov in his journal, first in Saint Petersburg and then in Geneva. The Teacher of Languages seems to have realized—in spite of his unexplained personal reticence and his doubts about the viability of the Russian mind—that Razumov's story must be told and a future imagined for him on the "curve" of time, if only to prevent the promulgation of stories like the ones to be found in Peter Ivanovitch's best-selling memoir.

Notes

1 In *An Experiment with Time* (1934), John W. Dunne, a British soldier, aeronautical engineer, and philosopher, wrote about precognitive dreams and a theory of time he called "Serialism." The book was widely read but was never accepted by mainstream science. It continues, however, to influence imaginative literature. Dunne published four sequels: *The Serial Universe* (1938), *The New Immortality* (1938), *Nothing Dies* (1940), and *Intrusions* (1955).

2 Edward Said believed that Conrad wrote about the past in order to prevent it from disappearing.

3 Incidentally, the title of his work that he was most proud of was "Thoughts of Jean-Jacques Rousseau, Citizen of Geneva."

4 Conrad himself had traveled through Geneva and Switzerland after he left Poland at the age of seventeen on his way to Marseilles to join the French Merchant Marine, for as the son of condemned political prisoners, he faced forced conscription into the Russian army (Lesage 2003: 20), with a prospect of "harrassment and many years of military service," if he remained in Poland after he reached the age of eighteen (Najder 2007: 41).

5 Jacob Vernet (1698–1789) was a European scholar who corresponded with the philosophers Voltaire, D'Alembert, Montesquieu, and Jean-Jacques Rousseau. An advocate of liberal Protestantism, he believed that governments existed in order to respect the rights of their citizens. His writings, like the writings of his correspondents, could be studied freely in Geneva. Like his correspondents, Jacob Vernet proposed political solutions that were in direct opposition to the autocracy that governed Russia. His works: *Traité de la verité de la religion chrétienne* (1748), *Instruction chrétienne* (1756), and *Lettres critiques d'un voyageur anglois sur l'article Geneve du Dictionnaire éncyclopedique et sur la Lettre de Monsieur d'Alembert à Monsieur Rousseau touchant les spectacles* have been re-edited and are available in new editions on Amazon France. In collaboration with the Voltaire Foundation and Oxford University, Graham Gargett published *Jacob Vernet, Geneva and the 'Philosophes'* in 1994.

6 Jean-François Millet (1814–1875) was one of the founders of the Barbizon School of painting in rural France, which idealized religion and the poverty of peasant life.

7 Karl Marx's speech at the Geneva Congress in 1868 as well as his speech at the International Workingmen's Congress in Geneva in 1873 come to mind.

8 Cf. Said:

> The loss of home and language is always acute. Yet the moment one enters his [Conrad's] writing, the aura of dislocation, instability, and disorientation are unmistakable. No one could represent the fate of lost-ness and disorientation better than he did, and no one was more ironic about the effort of trying to replace that condition with new arrangements and accommodations, which invariably lured one into further traps such as those Lord Jim encounters. (Said 1998: 3)

References

Baudelaire, Charles. 1868. *Curiosités Esthétiques*. Paris: Michel Lévy Frères.

Branny, Grażyna. 1997. *A Conflict of Values: Alienation and Commitment in the Novels of Joseph Conrad and William Faulkner*. Kraków: Wydawnictwo "Sponsor."

Darras, Jacques. 1978. *Conrad and the West*. London: Macmillan.

Dunne, J. W. 1934. *An Experiment with Time*. London: Faber and Faber.

Ebileeni, Maurice. 2015. *Conrad, Faulkner, and the Problem of Nonsense.* London: Bloomsbury.

Kirschner, Paul. 1992. "Topodialogic Narrative in *Under Western Eyes* and the Rasoumoffs of 'La Petite Russie.'" In *Conrad's Cities: Essays for Hans van Marle*, edited by Gene Moore, 223–54. Costerus New Series Library 82. Atlanta, GA: Rodopi.

Knowles, Owen. 1985. "*Under Western Eyes*: A Note on Two Sources." *The Conradian* 10, no. 2: 154–61.

Lesage, Claudine. 2003. *Joseph Conrad et le Continent: Biographie Critique.* Paris: Michel Houdiard, La Librarie.

Luyat, Anne. 1986. "Conrad's Feminine Grotesques." *The Conradian* 11, no. 1: 4–15.

Moore, Gene, ed. 1992. *Conrad's Cities: Essays for Hans van Marle.* Costerus New Series Library 82. Atlanta, GA: Rodopi.

Najder, Zdzisław. 1984. *Under Familial Eyes.* Translated by Halina Carroll-Najder. Cambridge: Cambridge University Press.

Najder, Zdzisław. 2007. *Joseph Conrad: A Life.* Translated by Halina Najder. New York: Camden House.

Powell, Anthony. 1980. *Faces in My Time.* London: William Heinemann.

Rousseau, Jean-Jacques. 1782. *Considérations sur le gouvernement de Pologne et sur sa réformation projetée.* Amsterdam: Marc-Michel Rey.

Said, Edward. 1998. "Between Worlds." *London Review of Books* 20, no. 9 (May 7): 3.

Said, Edward. 2008. *Joseph Conrad and the Fiction of Autobiography.* New York: Columbia University Press.

Słowacki, Juliusz. 1953. *In Switzerland.* Translated by Kenneth Mackenzie. London: Eyre and Spottiswoode for the Association of Polish Writers.

Słowacki, Juliusz. 1999. *Anhelli: Ta siła fatalna,* or *This Fateful Power.* Translated by Michael J. Mikos. Lublin: Norbertinium.

Zdrada, Jerzy. 2008-9. "Apollo Korzeniowski, Poland and Muscovy." *Yearbook of Conrad Studies (Poland)* 4: 30–92.

8

Conrad's Afterlife: Adaptations of Conrad's Biography in Contemporary Polish Culture

Agnieszka Adamowicz-Pośpiech
University of Silesia

As a writer, Joseph Conrad has been present in Polish culture since 1897. What is unique about this presence, however, is the fact that not only have his novels and short stories been revisited but also his biography. Furthermore, this process of the incorporation of Conrad's life into Polish culture has intensified since the 1980s. As far as Conrad's biography is concerned, Polish writers and artists have chosen its crucial points and fictionalized them—for example, Wacław Biliński in his novel *The Marseilles Affair* (1982)[1] concentrates on Conrad's residence in Marseilles; Leszek Prorok's novel *The Radiance Line* (1982) focuses on Conrad's time in Mauritius; Andrzej Braun's short story "The North Sea" (2003) revolves around Conrad's journey on a Q-boat; Ingmar Villqist's drama *Conrad* (unpublished manuscript) describes the writer's sojourn in Zakopane; Tomasz Man's *Wyspiański/Conrad* (unpublished manuscript) dramatically presents the meeting of the two artists aboard a ship sailing to New York. The purpose of this chapter is to examine the transtextual transformations of Conrad's biography and its absorption into contemporary Polish culture across various media forms. I distinguish three types of reworkings of the writer's life for different purposes: firstly, literary works of lasting artistic merit (e.g., Andrzej Braun's short story "The North Sea"); secondly, theatrical adaptations of Conrad's life (e.g., Ingmar Villqist's *Conrad*); and thirdly, popular culture productions (the comic book *The Thrilling Tales of Joseph Conrad* by Łukasz Godlewski and Maciej Jasiński; the graphic installation *Conrad: The Nostromo Passenger*—graphics Krzysztof Ostrowski, script Robert Zieliński) and the advertising film *Joseph Conrad: A Pole, Catholic, and Gentleman* by Rafał Geremek. Due to space constraints, the chapter examines two types of these transformations in detail: literary and popular culture ones, with the theatrical versions only mentioned briefly.

Biography as a Text of Culture

What we can observe in contemporary Polish culture is a process of Conrad's biography being transformed into a text of culture—reworked and revisited by various artists using different media for the purpose. The first to observe that Conrad's biography pertains to a study of culture was Zdzisław Najder. He argued that the writer's life was deeply steeped in Polish history, culture, and political affairs (1997: 14) and called for an expansion of the study of Conrad's biography into a broad study of culture (15). A number of Conrad's apparent "individual idiosyncrasies," which seemed to be a "private code," turned out to be "a cultural language,"[2] and his biography may have proven to be so attractive to Polish artists and may have so appealed to them as a complex cultural text that they approached it transmodally. Najder argues that the investigation of the writer's life deeply rooted in Polish community should not be limited to biographical research alone but ought to be expanded to social and intellectual history, ethics, and politics of contemporaneous partitioned Poland (17). How does it bear on the works of Polish artists? It seems that Conrad's tangled biography was identified as a stereotypical yet non-obvious cultural text that was symptomatic of the predicament of a number of Poles at the time of partitions. In other words, it appealed to Polish artists since, interpreted from various angles, it could illuminate different aspects of Polish cultural capital and become emblematic for many artistically talented Poles who emigrated from Poland to be able to pursue their own line of development (e.g., Juliusz Słowacki, Adam Mickiewicz, Fryderyk Chopin, Ignacy Paderewski).

Another aspect of textualizing Conrad's biography was raised by John Stape, who classified Conrad biography as a "fine art" and asked for "thickening the texture" of the narrative of his life (e.g., by "drawing on resources" about the Great Dock Strike of 1889, or the London Conrad had lived in, among others [2007: 67–8]). The scholar persuasively argued that "an appreciation of the circumstances in the outer world, and affecting his [Conrad's] daily life, offers insights and perspectives" and has "explanatory power" (67). In his overarching essay on Conrad's biographers, Stape identified the lacunae in Conrad's biographies, which mostly comprised "a sense of period and place":

> Without indulging in picture-painting, this is, perhaps, where Conrad biography most becomes a fine art, the essence of which is *shading, lighting, colour*, modulation, whereby archival sources are used to create a sense of layered reality and even, perhaps, the sights and sounds of daily life. (67; emphasis added)

Obviously, Stape meant extensive archive studies, but the method he highlighted is significant for *my* exploration of the artists' reworkings of Conrad's life and consists in "shading," "lighting," and adding "colour" to raw biographical data. This is exactly what the adapters do: take "an imaginative leap" (69) and see Conrad as a young man at a Marseilles opera house (the Grand Théâtre), or at a casino roulette table in Monte Carlo, or, as an elderly writer, surveying navigation charts of the North Sea. It was Stape's wish to see Conrad "the lodger in his late twenties, still no doubt mastering … his third language in the atmosphere of a North London boarding house alive, even fairly bursting with children" (69); and it has been the adapters' aim to depict it. Some questions about Conrad's biography will probably remain unanswered—for instance, the details of his sojourn in Marseilles (the gambling and smuggling episodes, his love affairs) or his courting in Mauritius. And these are precisely the moments that the fictional biographers pick and start spinning their own stories from.

Adaptation

Julie Sanders defines adaptation as "an updating or the cultural relocation of a text to bring it into greater proximity to the cultural and temporal context of readers/audiences" (2006: 163). It has to be stressed that Conrad's biography not only became a text of culture in Poland, but also abroad. As Nathalie Martinière demonstrates, Joseph Conrad is used as a trope, a figure by a number of contemporary novelists who fictionalize him as a character (2018: 24, 28–33): "They introduce him in their fictions, thus literalizing the fantasy of the author for their own purposes. It seems that for them, Conrad the author becomes 'a variable and complex function of discourse' (Foucault 1998: 221)" (Martinière 2018: 24). Adaptation studies recognize the demands of a globalizing world and problematize the notions of objectivity and fidelity as well as emphasize the significance of perspective (Raw 2012: 3).[3] This is a fundamental premise when we study the fictionalized accounts of Conrad's vicissitudes: the point is not to verify the extent to which they are congruent with the writer's life but rather which elements of his biography have been chosen and/or modified to bring the writer closer to the cultural and temporal context of contemporary audiences. Do those elements recur in the works of various authors? Do they overlap across cultures (Polish versus Western artists)?[4]

Literary Transformations

Conrad's biography has been widely discussed by Polish scholars and has instigated intense public debate.[5] Perhaps unsurprisingly, therefore, it has also become popular with Polish artists. Andrzej Braun (1923–2008) is emblematic of a whole generation of writers who chose Conrad as their mentor in life and literary career (others include, e.g., Jan Józef Szczepański, Gustaw Herling-Grudziński, Jan Parandowski, and Leszek Prorok).[6] All of them reworked Conrad's biography in one way or another and, on that, built their own fictionalized accounts of his adventures. A paragon of that kind of writing is Andrzej Braun's short story "The North Sea," which will serve as an illustration of literary adaptations here. Braun, a writer, journalist, scholar, and reporter, traveled to the Far East and visited Vietnam, China, Japan, Indonesia, Australia, and South America. It is in the East that his lifelong fascination with Conrad's prose began. He published more than twenty volumes of fiction, poetry, and essays, including three books on Conrad: *Conrad—dotknięcie Wschodu* (Conrad: Touching the East), 1970, *Śladami Conrada* (In the Footsteps of Conrad), 1972, and *Kreacja Cotaguany* (The Creation of Costaguana), 1989.

In his short story "The North Sea" (2003), Braun focuses on Conrad's cruise on the HMS *Ready* in October and November 1916. It is based on the recollections of Captain John Sutherland (1922) and Jessie Conrad (Conrad 1935: 202–5) and on Conrad's letters (*CL5*). It fictionalizes the writer's service on a Q-boat, a seventy-year-old brigantine that was rebaptized the *Freya* and later the *Lightning* and sailed—contrary to international law—under a Norwegian flag. In the story, the voyage starts sometime in September 1916 at St. Andrews Bay and ends in November at Bridlington. Conrad set sail across the North Sea to work on the trade routes between Scotland, Norway, and Denmark, where German U-boats at that time were most active. The commander was J. Sutherland, and the first mate, H. Osborne, with Conrad sharing the post with the second mate (responsible for navigation, coding messages, and communication). The writer spends a lot of time with the crew, the skipper Moody, and the chief engineer Rampling. They tell stories of their war experiences: Conrad of being trapped in Vienna with his wife and children; Sutherland of the monotony of minesweeping;

and Moody of his schooner that was sunk by the enemy. The wireless operator Musgrave teaches Conrad to operate the radio. Conrad participates in round table conferences with the captain and the first lieutenant, advising them what precautions to take in case they see a U-boat. The expedition was eventful: they sighted U-boats four times but were unable to destroy any due to their distance or rapid submersion.

When Conrad is alone in his cabin, he reflects on his past. It is interesting to note which elements of the author's biography Braun chose to incorporate into the story. It is, first of all, the writer's colorful past with a spice of adventure to it, such as smuggling arms for the supporters of Don Carlos or rebels in Columbia (Braun calls Conrad an "ex-smuggler"; 116). Next, come Conrad's momentous decisions: first, his resolution to leave Poland, which met with the derision of his family, and, on the side of Conrad, parrying the accusations of quixotic behavior (to prove his opponents wrong, Conrad is reading ships' certificates with the assessment of his service as "sober," thus demonstrating his success in life [Braun 2003: 157–8]); second, his decision to write—the morning in Bessborough Gardens and the reminiscence of Almayer, who "came to me stripped of all prestige by men's queer smiles and the disrespectful chatter of every vagrant trader in the Islands" (Braun 2003: 140; *PR* 83); third, Conrad's perseverance in the arduous process of writing: in Rouen, aboard the *Adowa* (Braun 2003: 149), his recollection being of the general's daughter entering his study and annihilating the whole world of Costaguana:

> He remembered the moment when he was engrossed in the last chapters of *Nostromo*, wrestled with the Lord for his creation, for the headlands of the coast, for the darkness of the Placid Gulf, the light on the snows, the clouds on the sky, and for the breath of life that had to be blown into the shapes of men and women ... There was not a single brick, stone, or grain of sand he had not placed in position with his own hands; all the history, geography, politics, finance—and out of the blue comes a daughter of some general and asks innocently: "And you sit like this here writing your—your ... "—And all that he was thinking about came down crashing on his head. (Braun 2003: 150; *PR* 100)

I have quoted this passage *in extenso* to illustrate the method of composition that Braun frequently employs: he incorporates (sometimes with slight modification) fragments of Conrad's works to depict the writer's past experiences. There are longer or shorter excerpts from *A Personal Record*, "Typhoon," *The Shadow-Line*, and *Lord Jim* interwoven seamlessly with Braun's story, and, since he does not use quotation marks, only an advanced reader of Conrad's fiction can detect these concealed intertextual references (Genette [1982] 1997: 1).[7]

These colorful vignettes are intertwined with Conrad's reveries on the ship. Braun follows in Conrad's footsteps and mythologizes those activities by which the writer wanted to be lionized (in *A Personal Record*, among others). This confirms his reverential attitude toward the writer and the great esteem Conrad was held in by Braun and his generation (Zabierowski 1988). The facts Conrad mentions in his reminiscences (and other works such as *An Arrow of Gold*) are taken at face value, without a single one being questioned. Interestingly enough, several biographical episodes chosen by Braun overlap with those selected by other Polish writers fictionalizing Conrad's biography,[8] but they do not coincide with those of Western novelists (Winfried G. Sebald, Juan G. Vásquez, Mario V. Llosa, and Graham Swift). For reasons of space, let me briefly enumerate only some of them: Conrad's decision to leave Poland and its consequences are depicted in Biliński's and Prorok's novels as well as the dramatic representations of Conrad's life by Villqist and Man; the Marseilles episode is discussed in Biliński; Conrad's perseverance in writing—in Biliński's and Prorok's fictions and in the dramas. By contrast, Western authors focus on the African episode (Sebald), Conrad's Caribbean voyages (Vásquez), the writer's English citizenship (Llosa), or the beginning of his English naval service (Swift). On the basis of the analyses I have carried out elsewhere, it can be concluded that Polish authors, even while discussing later episodes in Conrad's mature life (his sojourns in Mauritius or Corsica, or the voyage on a Q-boat), inscribe them with the events and people from his Polish years (Adamowicz-Pośpiech 2022).

Graphic Adaptations

By graphic adaptations, I mean the representations of Conrad's life by means of visual images. I have traced three instances of this type of adaptation in Poland,[9] all of which locate themselves in the realm of popular culture productions: the comic book *The Thrilling Tales of Joseph Conrad* by Łukasz Godlewski (graphics) and Maciej Jasiński (script) (2015); the graphic installation *Conrad: The Nostromo Passenger* (Ostrowski and Zieliński 2017); and the advertising film *Joseph Conrad: A Pole, Catholic, and Gentleman* (Geremek 2017).

The album *The Thrilling Tales of Joseph Conrad* transforms Conrad's biography and some of his works into an appealing visual story for young audiences in an unconventional way. Although at first glance those young audiences may seem to be the sole target readers, after a closer study, one can note more than fifty intertextual references to Conrad's life and works in the album (most of them covert, without explicit reference markers).[10] Ultimately, therefore, the comic appears to be also addressed to advanced readers of Conrad who can decipher those allusions. I shall analyze some of them to demonstrate the intricacy of the scheme on which the narrative is constructed.

The story begins in a similar manner to "Heart of Darkness": four men sit at a table and talk aboard a ship on the Thames. Over a game of bridge one of them comments on the press news he has just read and alludes to his own life. On the basis of the stories he tells, we see a globetrotter (with sojourns in Africa and Australia) and an incredibly lucky writer (he almost lost the manuscript of his first novel), but also an ill-timed traveler who arrives in the wrong place and at the wrong time (Conrad's arrival in Kraków on August 28, 1914, the day the war broke out between Austro-Hungary and Serbia). The whole action of the story takes place on one day (July 8, 1915), during a cruise on the Thames.

Godlewski's images are basically in black and white, which harmonizes well with sepia shades reflecting the antiquated character of the stories. One of the narrative techniques used by the authors is to intermingle the original frame story of the comic with some of Conrad's tales.[11] For instance, at the beginning of the comic, the cruiser passes a barque, and through a porthole in close-up, we can see a woman watering flowers, which constitutes one of the allusions to Conrad's works. To clarify what she is looking at, the perspective changes in the next panel, and we get the view from behind her back: she sees a man standing on a barge. These frames are not accompanied by any speech bubbles or explanatory narrative, so the reader has no hints as to how to interpret the drawings. Only if one knows Conrad's short story "Falk" can they recognize Hermann's niece:

> The tiny white curtains and the greenery of the flower-pots behind the glass …
> On one or two occasions when passing under her stern I had detected from my
> boat a round arm in the act of tilting a watering-pot, and the bowed sleek head
> of a maiden whom I shall always call Hermann's niece. (F 108)

There is, however, one tiny intertextual marker that may shed light on the presented sequence of frames—that is, the name of the barque painted across her stern: *Diana.*

The subsequent series of panels refers to the ending of *The Secret Agent.* One of the gentlemen sitting at the table with Conrad reads up a press note titled "Suicide of Lady Passenger from a cross-Chanel Boat," which relates the mysterious disappearance of a woman from the deck of a boat. Jasiński used a fragment of the novel with a slight modification: "This act of madness or despair will remain forever an impenetrable mystery" (Godlewski and Jasiński 2015: 5)—the line in the novel running as follows: "An impenetrable mystery seems destined to hang forever over this act of madness or despair" (307).[12] Additionally, he changed the ending of the press note to "the steamer was stopped immediately and the anchor was cast" (Godlewski and Jasiński 2015: 5) in order to introduce another intertextual allusion to *The Mirror of the Sea*, in which Conrad complains about the nautical language used by journalists. Jasiński deliberately uses the wrong term "to cast anchor," which triggers an immediate reaction in Conrad (the passenger), who voices his criticism of the inaccuracy of the terminology:

> It's one of the commonest mistakes. Have you ever seen sailors taking the anchor in their hands and throwing it overboard? ... The captain's order is "Let go!", and not "Heave over!" ... For years I have been dividing newspapers into these whose journalists "let go" the anchor or "cast" it. The latter I don't read so as not to lose my temper. (Godlewski and Jasiński 2015: 5)

This is a reference to *The Mirror of the Sea*, where Conrad claims that part of the initiation into the naval craft is in learning its jargon that has been "wrought into perfection by ages of experience":

> Before an anchor can ever be raised, it must be let go; and this perfectly obvious truism brings me at once to the subject of the degradation of the sea language in the daily press of this country [Great Britain]. Your journalist, whether he takes charge of a ship or a fleet, almost invariably 'casts' his anchor. Now an anchor is never cast, and to take a liberty with technical language is a crime against the clearness, precision, and beauty of perfected speech. (*MS* 13)

The motif of the anchor seamlessly links to the next panel in which Jasiński focuses on the biographical episode when, while serving as a first mate aboard the *Torrens* in 1892, Conrad lost the boat's anchor (Godlewski and Jasiński 2015: 6). A diver had to be employed to recover it, which is all shown on the frames. Aboard that ship Conrad had the opportunity to meet the educated (non-sailing) Englishmen John Galsworthy and Edward L. Sanderson, among others, with whom he could discuss art, literature, and politics and with whom he developed lasting friendships (Najder 2011: 178–82). The narrative situation, with Conrad sitting with the other gentlemen at the table discussing literature and politics, echoes the talks he had with Galsworthy and Sanderson on the poop deck.

Another set of panels refers to the vicissitudes of the manuscript of Conrad's first novel *Almayer's Folly*. Godlewski draws a dynamic picture of Conrad rushing for a train leaving for Ukraine, with a railway porter knocking on the carriage window at the last minute and handing him in his Gladstone bag with the eight chapters of his first book, which he had left in the waiting room. The manuscript is a springboard to the next episode in the Belgian Congo, in which we see Korzeniowski's boat capsized and the baggage sunk (Godlewski and Jasiński 2015: 10–11). It was only by chance that one of the paddlers fished out the captain's bag with the novel's handwritten pages (Galsworthy 1927: 101–3).

This motif is developed further into the story of Korzeniowski's sojourn in Africa and initiated by a one-page panel picturing a black river winding like a ribbon. In this way, Godlewski depicts a significant passage from "Heart of Darkness," which refers to a river on a map as a snake, thus building up the symbolism of Inferno and ubiquitous evil. It is only around the small steamboat going up the river that one can see a bright spot, apparently an image of the professed civilizing mission of the white colonizers. Korzeniowski's journey to Africa is well presented (and well known) in mass culture (thanks to the film by Francis F. Coppola, *Apocalypse Now*, or the graphic novel by Catherine Anyango and David Zane Mairowitz (2010), to mention just a few of the popular culture intermodal transformations of the novella),[13] hence only two pages of the album are devoted to it and the story is condensed into two motifs: the director of the central station plotting against Korzeniowski (grounding his boat) and the gossip about Kurtz (the colonizers do not really know whether he is a real man or a legend [Godlewski and Jasiński 2015: 13]). Korzeniowski talks to a sailor who met a man (near madness) who claimed that he knew Kurtz. When the sailor asks what they talked about, the madman answers: "You don't talk to that man, you just listen" (Godlewski and Jasiński 2015: 13). The account of Kurtz is doubly mediated (the sailor—the madman—Kurtz), and Korzeniowski himself never meets him in person. Hence the tale becomes yet another yarn spun by some mariner, where one will never know what is true and what is not: "These are just tall stories," the authors of the comic seem to be saying.

Interestingly enough, two narrative planes of the comic overlap structurally: the voyage up the river Congo and the cruise on the Thames, which is another example of the narrative technique of intermingling mentioned earlier. In "Heart of Darkness," just before the climactic point of reaching Kurtz's station, dense fog descends, and Marlow's steamer has to stop. A similar event takes place in the comic: while Conrad is telling the story of his adventures in Africa, the captain of the tourist boat informs the passengers of an unplanned layover due to London mist (Godlewski and Jasiński 2015: 14). The African tale is disrupted and never finished. This might, to a certain extent, be a visual mode of inserting epistemological uncertainty into the narrative texture of the comic, since the listeners (and readers) will not know how the adventure in Africa ended. Likewise, in "Heart of Darkness," when a dense fog shrouds the river, Marlow and the crew have to stop the boat and do not know what will happen when the fog clears.

The next sequence of panels, which I will only discuss briefly due to space constraints, hinges on "The Inn of Two Witches." The story takes twelve pages, which, in comparison with the space devoted to "Heart of Darkness," is a lot more. The reason for such a quantitative distribution of panels might be related to the fact that "Heart of Darkness" has been illustrated (Conrad 2012) many a time (Matt Kish, Jean-Philippe Stassen, and Sylvain Venayre; Tom Tirabosco and Christian Perrissin; Stephane Miquel and Loic Godart; Catherine Anyango and David Mairowitz, among others). Jasiński seems to have decided to select the less-known works by Conrad and also those abounding in sensational or thrilling elements. "The Inn of Two Witches" may be classified as a gothic, or horror, story with haunted places, traps, unresolved mysteries, and sudden deaths. Godlewski and Jasiński present Conrad as the frame narrator who found an old manuscript with missing pages (which deepens the mystery of the story). A number of details are left out, so that the reader is at a loss as to the meaning of certain events. The scenery that is essential for a gothic tale is expertly depicted and involves a sense of terror, fear, surprise, and confinement. In one of the frames, we see a ghostly house against a dark backdrop, the rain pouring down and flashes of lightning forking the black sky. The whole page, together with the other panels, builds up an atmosphere of fear and terror: in one frame, we have a close-up of a contorted face of a wanderer looking through the window into the strange house; in another, two humped and hooded black figures without faces, stirring some slime in a cauldron over fire (Figure 2). In the previous panel, the figures are seen from a distance, through the frame of a window, so the authors skillfully, step by step (or rather frame by frame), build up suspense. Although the comic's narrative sets up suspense for horrific events, they all, in the end, have natural explanations.

The same method of intermingling of Conrad's biography with his works is used in the presentation of the story of a typhoon. It is Conrad who has to face the impending hurricane, and it is he who comes up with a clever idea of how to divide the mixed dollars among the Chinese coolies. The story of the typhoon unfolds across eight pages, mostly focusing on the catastrophic aspect of Conrad's

Figure 2 The wanderer approaches a lonely house; upon entering he meets the two faceless figures. From Godlewski and Jasiński (2015: 21). Courtesy ©Wojewódzka i Miejska Biblioteka Publiczna w Gdańsku.

tale. Structurally, it is composed on the juxtaposition of contrastive panels. To give just one example of this contrast, on one page we see pedantically folded ceremonial robes, incense sticks, chopsticks, cups, and dollars—everything sorted out in separate boxes. The only detail that might disturb an alert reader is the positioning of these objects in between the frames; they are never contained within one panel but reach over 'the gutter' to the neighboring one. What is the reason for such graphic representation? It might be that the authors want to graphically signal the future events in this way. This contrasts with the pages featuring the hurricane (Godlewski and Jasiński 2015: 33–5), which are very dynamic and disruptive. Contrary to the neatly ordered belongings, in the "hurricane panels," one cannot distinguish one thing from another: the bodies reduced to a mass of convoluting parts, the floor strewn with mixed-up goods (Figure 3). Interestingly enough, the authors add their own twist to that story: the Chinese waiter who tends to the gentlemen on the cruiser overhears the story. He confesses that he was aboard that ship during the typhoon that Conrad was reminiscing about, and so we have access to his side of the story—a different perspective from the lower deck. This seems to be the artists' way of representing the fragmented mode of narration in "Typhoon," where the readers are exposed to various epistemological perspectives and learn about the hurricane from three kinds of letters (Adamowicz-Pośpiech 2008).

The other biographical elements that are, among others, portrayed in the comic include the Captain McDonald episode, the sinking of the "Karain" manuscript on the *Titanic*, and Conrad's sojourn in Kraków. To conclude, Godlewski and Jasiński rework Conrad's biography through the prism of his quasi-autobiographical stories or portray the adventures in some of his short stories as if the writer himself took part in them. In a similar manner to Braun, they apply implicit intertextual references to Conrad's works.

Dramatic Adaptations

In the final section of this chapter, I wish to briefly mention adaptations of Conrad's biography for the stage. In his essay on biography as a fine art, Stape points out that in his later career Conrad was interested in dramatic adaptations (Hand 2005) and argues that the writer should be considered a dramatic adaptor in that phase. Unsurprisingly then, theater directors and script writers have turned Conrad's works to dramas (Stape 2007: 72). Yet, at present, a new trend can be observed in contemporary Polish culture when Conrad's life comes on

Figure 3 The coolies fighting below deck tossed by the typhoon. Korzeniowski asking Hopkins to call in the other members of the crew. From Godlewski and Jasiński (2015: 36). Courtesy ©Wojewódzka i Miejska Biblioteka Publiczna w Gdańsku.

stage: the novelist's biography has given rise to plays: Ingmar Villqist's *Conrad* (Teatr Śląski [Silesian Theatre], Katowice, 2017) and Tomasz Man's *Wyspiański/Conrad* (Teatr Dramatyczny [Drama Theatre], Warszawa, 2020, performative readings).

In the first play, the playwright combines elements of Conrad's life with the storyline of "Tomorrow." The action of the play takes place in Zakopane in 1914, and Conrad is presented as a tired elderly man who has to meet a number of eminent Poles. In this dramatic transformation of Conrad's life, we can observe, similarly to the previously discussed two categories, the porosity between biographical reality and fiction: Villqist freely modifies facts from Conrad's biography with fictitious details (e.g., the talk with Józef Piłsudski at the villa of Konstantynówka in Zakopane, or the ship broker's proposal to steer a tourist boat on the Thames). In between the encounters in Zakopane, Conrad dozes off in his armchair, and the audience sees scenes from the writer's early life in his sleep (his visit to Tadeusz Bobrowski in Kazimierówka, in Ukraine [Figure 4], his encounters with friends in Kraków, his first visit to a ship broker in London). The intertwining and binding theme of the play is related to the scenes with two Austro-Hungarian secret agents spying on Conrad during the Great War

Figure 4 Tadeusz Bobrowski handing Conrad the *Memorial*. Ingmar Villqist, *Conrad*, 2017. Courtesy ©Photo: P. Jendroska, Teatr Śląski im. St. Wyspiańskiego in Katowice.

(Figure 5). They write reports on the writer's meetings, discuss speeches he made in Zakopane, and denounce intellectuals who paid him a visit.[14] The last part of the drama makes use of Conrad's short story "Tomorrow." It employs the convention of a play within a play: the "Złoty Róg" (Golden Conch) theater group from the Jagiellonian University performs fragments of the storyline while Conrad sits in the audience. This is an echo of an actual university performance in the 1980s by a student theatrical group from the English Philology Department. As with Braun, Villqist intersperses the main biographical incident (Conrad's sojourn in Zakopane) with episodes from the writer's early Polish years.

As Stape perceptively observed, Conrad was a man of protean capacities (2007: 71), and each generation of biographers has accentuated different aspects of his personality and life. Arguably, the contemporary generation of artists-cum-fictional biographers paints a diverse picture of the writer in accordance with changing cultural values and concerns. In other words, each generation of adapters shows the Conrad relevant for their time and thus achieves its goal of bringing the writer and his biography closer to contemporary audiences. In conclusion, however, it must be stressed that there is one distinctly Polish feature of the adaptations of Conrad's biography: even if they discuss episodes from Conrad's mature life, Polish authors inscribe them with the events and people from his Polish years.

Figure 5 The two secret agents spying on Conrad in Zakopane. Ingmar Villqist, *Conrad*, 2017. Courtesy ©Photo: P. Jendroska, Teatr Śląski im. St. Wyspiańskiego in Katowice.

Acknowledgments

Several publishers, writers, and right holders very generously gave permission to reproduce the illustrations, photographs, and unpublished fragments of their scripts in this chapter. I wish to thank Jarosław Zalesiński, director of The Voivodship and Municipal Joseph Conrad Library in Gdańsk; Ingmar Villqist, theater director, and Miłosz Markiewicz, literary director, of the Teatr Śląski in Katowice.

A version of this essay was presented at the 46th Annual International Conference of The Joseph Conrad Society (UK), St. Mary's University, Twickenham, July 2019.

Notes

1 See the Reference list for original titles.

2 By "cultural language," I mean "a public system of signs which carry meaning independently of the reflections of the novelist's own personality" (Najder 1997: 15).

3 Adaptation studies in recent years has emerged as a full-fledged discipline, with its own corpus of theoretical texts and journals (Raw 2012: 1). It no longer focuses solely on textual transfer and adaptation of text to film but undertakes interdisciplinary questions of transmodal transfer (from one medium to another).

4 For an in-depth analysis of Conrad's life fictionalized by Polish artists, see Adamowicz-Pośpiech (2022); for the Western writers' perspective, see Martinière (2018).

5 For the discussion of those debates, see Adamowicz-Pośpiech (2003).

6 Cf. Zabierowski (1988).

7 Genette introduces an elaborate classification of transtextuality, but the most general division is into an "obvious" and "concealed" relationship between texts (Genette [1982] 1997: 1).

8 Cf. my detailed discussion and numerous examples in Adamowicz-Pośpiech (2022).

9 For the discussion of French and English graphic novels visualizing Conrad's life and works, see Adamowicz-Pośpiech (forthcoming).

10 The referential *marker* signals the intertextual relation (Ben-Porat 1976: 109).

11 Being a "juxtaposed pictorial and sequential visual art" (McCloud 1993: 9), comics not only represent reality graphically, but also use sophisticated narrative techniques (Badman 2010: 91–111; Groensteen 2007: 5–23).

12 The line borrowed from the Polish translation of *The Secret Agent* runs even closer to the comics version.

13 Those include Tom Tirabosco and Christian Perrissin's *Kongo*, Stephane Miquel and Loic Godart's *Au Coeur des ténèbres*, and Peter Kuper's *Joseph Conrad's "Heart of Darkness"*; see Adamowicz-Pośpiech (forthcoming).

14 The play abounds in numerous allusions to the contemporary sociopolitical affairs in Poland.

References

Adamowicz-Pośpiech, Agnieszka. 2003. *Joseph Conrad: Spory o biografię* [Joseph Conrad: Debates on His Biography]. Katowice: Deni-Press.

Adamowicz-Pośpiech, Agnieszka. 2008. "Letters and Books in Conrad's *Typhoon*—or on Writing and (Mis-)reading." *Yearbook of Conrad Studies (Poland)* 4: 119–32.

Adamowicz-Pośpiech, Agnieszka. 2022. *Adaptacje życia i twórczości Josepha Conrada w kulturze współczesnej* [Adaptations of Conrad's Life and Works in Contemporary Culture]. Katowice: Wydawnictwo Uniwersytetu Śląskiego.

Adamowicz-Pośpiech, Agnieszka. Forthcoming. "Adaptations of Conrad's *Heart of Darkness* in French and English Graphic Novels."

Anyango, Catherine, and David Z. Mairowitz. 2010. *Heart of Darkness: A Graphic Novel*. London: SelfMadeHero.

Badman, Derik. 2010. "Talking, Thinking, and Seeing in Pictures: Narration, Focalization, and Ocularization in Comics Narratives." *International Journal of Comic Art* 12, no. 2: 91–111.

Ben-Porat, Ziva. 1976. "The Poetics of Literary Allusion." *PTL: Journal for Descriptive Poetics* 1: 105–28.

Biliński, Wacław. 1982. *Sprawa w Marsylii* [The Marseilles Affair]. Łódź: Wydawnictwo Łódzkie.

Braun, Andrzej. 2003. "Morze Północne" [The North Sea]. *Apogeum*. Gdańsk: Wydawnictwo Oskar. 107–67.

Conrad, Jessie. 1935. *Joseph Conrad and His Circle*. New York: E. P. Dutton.

Conrad, Joseph. 2012. "Heart of Darkness." Illustrated by Matt Kish. Portland, Oregon: Tin House Books.

Foucault, Michel. 1998. "What Is an Author?" In *Aesthetics, Method, and Epistemology*, edited by James D. Faubion, translated by Robert Hurley, vol. 2, 205–22. New York: The New Press.

Galsworthy, John. 1927. *Castles in Spain*. New York: Ch. Scribner's Sons.

Genette, Gérard. [1982] 1997. *Palimpsests*. Translated by Ch. Newman. La Vergne, TN: University of Nebraska Press.

Godlewski, Łukasz, and Maciej Jasiński. 2015. *Niesamowite opowieści Josepha Conrada* [The Thrilling Tales of Joseph Conrad]. Gdańsk: Wojewódzka i Miejska Biblioteka Publiczna im. Josepha Conrada-Korzeniowskiego.

Groensteen, Thierry. 2007. *The System of Comics*. Translated by B. Beaty and N. Nguyen. Jackson: University Press of Mississippi.

Hand, Richard. 2005. *The Theatre of Joseph Conrad*. London: Palgrave Macmillan.

Man, Tomasz. "Wyspiański/Conrad." Unpublished manuscript.

Martinière, Nathalie. 2018. "Multiple Contemporary Images of Joseph Conrad." In *Joseph Conrad's Authorial Self Polish and Other*, edited by Wiesław Krajka, 21–35. Lublin: M. Curie-Skłodowska University Press.

McCloud, Scott. 1993. *Understanding Comics*. New York: HarperCollins.

Najder, Zdzisław. 1997. *Conrad in Perspective*. Translated by Halina Najder. Cambridge: Cambridge University Press.

Najder, Zdzisław. 2011. *Joseph Conrad: A Life*. Translated by Halina Najder. New York: Camden House.

Prorok, Leszek. 1982. *Smuga blasku* [The Radiance Line]. Warszawa: Czytelnik.

Raw, Laurence, ed. 2012. *Translation, Adaptation and Transformation*. London: Bloomsbury.

Sanders, Julie. 2006. *Adaptation and Appropriation*. New York: Routledge.

Stape, John. 2007. "On Conrad Biography as a Fine Art." *The Conradian* 32, no. 2: 57–75.

Sutherland, John. 1922. *At Sea with Joseph Conrad*. New York: Houghton Mifflin.

Villqist, Ingmar. "Conrad." Unpublished manuscript.

Zabierowski, Stefan. 1988. *Autor-rodak: pisarze polscy wobec Conrada* [Author-Countryman: Polish Writers Responding to Conrad's Works]. Katowice: Wydawnictwo Śląsk.

9

Communication with Marconi's Electric Waves: Conrad and Wireless Telegraphy

Kazumichi Enokida
Hiroshima University

The period of Conrad the seaman coincides with the expansion of the worldwide network created by telegraph cables. The first telegraph cable between England and France was laid in 1851. Fifteen years later, the first transatlantic telegraph cable designed for commercial use was completed. After the nationalization of the telegraph industry in Britain in 1868, a network of undersea cables was extended to India, Australia, Southeast Asia, East Asia, and Africa. By the time Conrad started his career as a seaman in the mid-1870s, the global telegraph network had been serving an essential role as a means of high-speed exchange of information. In other words, Conrad—similar to today's contemporary society living in the age of the internet—lived in the age of the telegraph, dubbed the "Victorian Internet" by Tom Standage (2009), in an era when information traveled faster than humans and commodities.

The impact of the information network created by new media technologies was also found in literature in the nineteenth and twentieth centuries. Richard Menke saw Victorian fiction as "a critical part of the shifting media ecology in which it arose, circulated, and had meaning and value" (2008: 12). David Trotter (2013) discussed how contemporary media technologies, such as the telephone, radio, airplanes, and automobiles, affected British literature during the interwar period in the early twentieth century.

It seems that Conrad was no exception regarding the influence of wired telegraphy. As can be expected from the sailor-turned-novelist, who, according to Matthew Rubery, "was unusually informed about scientific issues for a man of letters" (2009: 239), Conrad frequently relied upon his familiarity with contemporary wired telegraphy in his literary and nonliterary works. Direct or indirect references to wired telegraphy can be found in "An Outpost of Progress," "Heart of Darkness," *Lord Jim, Nostromo, The Shadow-Line,* and *The Mirror of the Sea.*

The period of Conrad the novelist coincided with the birth and prevalence of wireless telegraphy. The shift from wired to wireless telegraphy began at the turn of the century. Guglielmo Marconi relocated to Britain in 1896, where he successfully performed the first transatlantic radio transmission in 1901, after which the Marconi Company played an important role in the proliferation of marine radio communication technology. Of interest are the following: (1) how writers at the turn of the century responded to Marconi's technology, (2) how Conrad's attitudes toward wireless telegraphy can be compared with that of his contemporaries, (3) how his attitudes toward wireless telegraphy can be compared with his attitudes toward the wired systems he was more familiar with as a former marine professional, and (4) whether or not his references to wireless telegraphy had any significance in his literary career.

This essay explores how Conrad responded to contemporary wireless telegraphy compared to his response toward wired telegraphy. First, I examine "An Outpost of Progress" as an example of how information played a key role in Conrad's fiction in the age of global communication networks promoted by wired telegraph messaging systems. I then compare how Conrad's writing contemporaries responded to wireless telegraphy, with specific references to *The First Men in the Moon* (1901) by H. G. Wells and "Wireless" (1902) by Rudyard Kipling. Finally, I explore Conrad's response to wireless telegraphy.

Compression and Discrepancy: Information in "An Outpost of Progress"

"An Outpost of Progress" is based on Conrad's shocking personal experiences during his travels to the Congo Free State as a steamboat captain in 1890. The proliferation of electric telegraphs—along with steamboats and railways—was essential for the colonial expansion of European powers. The Congo Free State, notoriously known as a private property of Belgian King Leopold II, was no exception. Henley Morton Stanley reported on the communication network in Central Africa that a "telegraphic cable lies across the mouth of the great river, and Europe is within twenty-four hours' communication of the state" (1886: 59). Twelve years later, in 1898, the telegraph cable network extended to Leopoldville.

However, Stanley Falls, where Conrad traveled in 1890, was still beyond the limits of the information network in the nineteenth century.

According to Roland Robertson, the electric telegraph accelerated the globalization that brought about "compression of the world and the intensification of consciousness of the world as a whole" (1992: 8). However, it had also produced discrepancies between places where information did and did not arrive. The remote outpost of the story's protagonists, Kayerts and Carlier, is 300 miles from the nearest telegraph station. It is one of the "uninformed" places where occasional steamships served as the only lifeline to the rest of the world. Although telegraphy does not appear in this story, the narrator's description of Kayerts as one who worked at "the Administration of the Telegraphs" (*TU* 78) effectively underlines the ironic contrast between telegraphs as a means of communication on the one hand and Kayert's isolation at his outpost on the other: "There is a nice irony in the mention of his previous occupation: as a means of communication. 'Telegraphs' are a striking contrast to the isolation of Kayert's outpost, whose real administrator is Makola" (Lothe 1989: 54). Situated 300 miles from the nearest trading post, the outpost remains far beyond the contemporary telegraph network, and the steamships of the Great Trading Company hold life-or-death authority over Kayerts and Carlier.

Also, the alienation lies *within* the outpost, as can be found in the description of the drums beating in the night when Makola is working on his plot to sell ten station men to the traders from Loanda to make up for poor ivory yields:

> All night they were disturbed by a lot of drumming in the villages. A deep rapid roll near by would be followed by another far off—then all ceased. Soon, short appeals would rattle out here and there, then all mingle together, increase, become vigorous and sustained; would spread out over the forest, roll through the night, unbroken and ceaseless, near and far, as if the whole land had been one immense drum booming out steadily an appeal to heaven. (*TU* 86)

In Africa, drums have often been used as a means of communication known as "talking drums." The "rapid roll near by" followed by "another far off" and the "short appeals" rattling out "here and there"—all this "mingling together" may represent an African version of telegraphy. Again, our two white men are not only uninformed of Makola's plot but also alienated from the interaction of drum beats that parallels communication via language.

Consequently, "An Outpost of Progress" can be read as a story depicting the frailty of Europeans in the late nineteenth century while living at the dawn of an information-oriented society. Although the absence of information plays a key role in the destruction of the two men, it does not imply, however, that other surroundings connected by telegraphy would have allowed them a better chance to survive. In "An Outpost of Progress," the amount of information that one can obtain is linked to the usefulness and diligence of that person. Kayerts and Carlier are left in a worthless outpost because they are useless and lazy themselves. In this respect, their destruction was predestined from the onset of the story, thus enabling readers to remain detached from the two men while experiencing their suspense and anxiety.

Beyond Space and Time: Wireless Telegraphy for Conrad's Contemporaries

While wired telegraphy seemed worthy of Conrad's attention, the next-generation wireless technology had started to appear in fiction written by his contemporaries, including H. G. Wells and Rudyard Kipling. In Wells's *The First Men in the Moon*, the narrator Bedford explores the moon together with Cavor, an inventor he met in a small town on the southern coast of England. Cavor discovers a gravity-defying substance he names *cavorite* with which he invents a sphere-like spacecraft. After a successful landing on the moon, they are captured by lunar inhabitants named Selenites. Only Bedford manages to escape, and he returns to earth alone. Cavor had previously disappeared after suffering an injury while trying to escape to their spacecraft and was left on the moon. Back on earth, Bedford is informed that fragmented messages have been sent wirelessly from Cavor on the moon:

> It is well the reader should understand the conditions under which it would seem these messages were sent. Somewhere within the moon Cavor certainly had access for a time to a considerable amount of electrical apparatus, and it would seem he rigged up—perhaps furtively—a transmitting arrangement of the Marconi type. (Wells 2017: 143)

Imaginative technologies like gravity-defying cavorite and interplanetary wireless transmission using a "Marconi-type" apparatus served as tools for the colonial expansion beyond the earth. Aaron Worth noted that communication technologies in this context were central to the construction of an imperial chronotope linking colonial expansion with cultural fragility (2014: 70). It was as if wireless telegraphy in this text was parallel to wired telegraph in the actual world, through which Conrad also linked colonial expansion with cultural fragility in "An Outpost of Progress."

Cavor's messages from the moon are first discovered by a Dutch electrician named Julius Wendigee, who has experimented with a "certain apparatus akin to the apparatus used by Mr. Tesla in America with hopes of discovering a method of communicating with Mars" (Wells 2017: 141). Nikola Tesla was a Serbian American engineer and inventor who was a rival of Marconi in the late nineteenth-century radio race. In the 1890s, he succeeded in generating electric waves using his "Tesla coil" that was based on electrical conduction and induction. The reference to Tesla in *The First Men in the Moon* seems to reflect the inventor's actual dream of communicating with the planet Mars (Tesla 1901: 8). At the time, his dream was not irrelevant to the contemporary public narrative related to the existence of Martians, spurred by society's misguided belief of "Martian canals." One might be inclined to associate the enthusiasm of Tesla, born one year before Conrad, with Marlow's reference to Martians in "Heart of Darkness." When he is stuck at the Central Station, Marlow feels that the existence of Kurtz is so unreal that he "believed it in the same way one of you might believe there are inhabitants in the planet Mars" (HD 69). Tesla's aspiration to communicate with the planet Mars via wireless telegraphy parallels Marlow's desire to meet Kurtz and hear his voice with the help of a steamship, another essential technology that became indispensable during the formation of a global network of information and commerce.

In Kipling's "Wireless," the narrator visits a chemist friend who is experimenting with his Marconi installation. The chemist is trying to communicate with a friend who lives in Poole, Dorset, between thirty and forty miles away. His assistant, Shaynor, falls into a trance after taking medicine for his tuberculosis. During his master's wireless experiment, Shaynor suddenly rises to his feet and starts writing fragments of a poem that are very similar to John Keats's "The Eve of St. Agnes." When he wakes up, he tells the narrator that he does not know Keats.

> "I suppose I must have been dreaming," said Mr. Shaynor.
>
> "I suppose you must," I said. "Talking of dreams—I—I noticed you writing—before—"
>
> He flushed consciously.
>
> "I meant to ask you if you've ever read anything written by a man called Keats."
>
> "Oh! I haven't much time to read poetry, and I can't say that I remember the name exactly. Is he a popular writer?"

"Middling. I thought you might know him because he's the only poet who was ever a druggist. And he's rather what's called the lover's poet." (Kipling 2011: 375)

Here, wireless telegraphy beyond space is depicted as parallel to the mystical literary inspiration beyond time. The story thus ends with their successful communication with Poole. The juxtaposition of wireless telegraphy and the mystic phenomenon in this story is in line with the coincidence, identified by Robbie McLaughlan, between the invention of the former and the booming popularity of mesmeric fiction in the 1890s (2012: 186). Wireless telegraphy as "non-scientific science" was an easy subject of skepticism (188).

Both Wells and Kipling were very quick in responding to Marconi's wireless telegraphy during its experimental stages. Wireless telegraphy in their works involves communications beyond time and space; for example, the observations of the Selenites and the supernatural inspiration in the form of Keats's poem. Both have a strong affinity with contemporary science fiction and mysticism.

It is difficult to find Conrad's responses to wireless telegraphy in his literary works. Therefore, in this section, some of the nonliterary texts by Conrad and his contemporaries are examined. Most were written in the 1910s and 1920s when wireless technology was becoming a household name, after a couple of well-known historical events—namely, the Dr. Crippen case and the sinking of the RMS *Titanic*.

Conrad and Crippen: Conrad's Indignation

The homoeopath Hawley Harvey Crippen was the first suspect to be arrested with the aid of wireless telegraphy. He was captured in 1910 while crossing the Atlantic Ocean with his lover on their way to Canada after the police found that his wife was murdered and her body parts were buried in the basement of his house. This is how Archibald Marshall, an editor of *The Daily Mail*'s Literary Supplement, described Conrad's reactions when the paper asked him for comments on Crippen's sea library: "What happened was that poor dear Conrad exploded in epistolary fury at being asked to do such a thing and severed his connection with our journal" ([1933] 1990: 65). Borys Conrad recalls his father's indignation with *The Daily Mail* differently:

> The fact that wireless telegraphy had made [the arrest of Dr. Crippen] possible was, of course, a "front page" story and the Editor of the *Daily Mail* had asked

my Father to write an article on some aspect of the event. The effect of an incident of this sort upon him when he was suffering from a spell of gout was sometimes quite contrary to our expectations. In this case we naturally expected it to aggravate the attack but his indignation was so great at, as I overheard him telling Mother, the Editor's "Confounded impertinence in arbitrarily summoning me all the way to Ashford, while suffering from gout, in order to listen to such a bizarre proposal" that it seemed to have the opposite effect and the attack quickly passed off. (1970: 68–9)

As Borys Conrad suggests, the power of wireless telegraphy was the center of attention for the press when reporting about the Crippen case. If so, would Conrad have had something to say regarding wireless telegraphy if his gout had not been so painful and had it not been for the bizarre nature of *The Daily Mail* proposal? All we can note here is his jocular tone when talking with his wife Jessie about the editor's "confounded impertinence." Conrad made no other comments or remarks about the case in his essays or letters. It is unlikely that, for him, wireless telegraphy as the latest technology was the center of attention in the Crippen case.

"The Welter of Marconi Lies": The Sinking of the RMS *Titanic*

In contrast to the Crippen case, the sinking of the RMS *Titanic* on April 14, 1912, cast a negative shadow on wireless telegraphy. The *Titanic* used installations of the Marconi Company, with failures in radio communication leading to the death of 1,513 passengers and crew members. In an essay released the same year titled, "Some Reflections on the Loss of the *Titanic*," Conrad only briefly mentioned the Marconi installations:

> I venture to suggest that to take advantage of so many pitiful corpses, is not pretty. And the exploiting of the mere sensation on the other side is not pretty in its wealth of heartless inventions. Neither is the welter of Marconi lies which has not been sent vibrating without some reason, for which it would be nauseous to inquire too closely. (*NLL* 177)

Conrad criticized the press for pursuing "the mere sensation" and inquiring about "the welter of Marconi lies," calling such activities "not pretty." According to the notes of the Cambridge edition of *Notes on Life and Letters*, the phrase

"Marconi lies" in this context refers to various irregularities committed by Marconi Company wireless operators in reporting the *Titanic* disaster as well as the insider trading scandal involving the Marconi Company and the government, including David Lloyd George (*NLL* 442). To mourn the victims in peace and silence, detachment from the excessive attacks on "Marconi lies" seemed more desirable for Conrad. His attention in this case was not directed toward the treatment of wireless telegraphy after this accident. Similar to his reaction after the Crippen case, Conrad left no specific remarks about the new technology related to the *Titanic* disaster.

Pudding over Marconi: The Sinking of the RMS *Empress of Ireland*

In his 1914 essay titled "Protection of Ocean Liners," Conrad commented on the sinking of the *Empress of Ireland* that occurred that year, only two years after the *Titanic* disaster.

> They are discussing bulkheads, boats, davits, manning, navigation, but I am willing to bet that not one of them has thought of the humble "pudding" … Perhaps they may think the thing too rough and unsightly for this scientific and æsthetic age. It certainly won't look very pretty but I make bold to say it will save more lives at sea than any amount of the Marconi installations which are being forced on the shipowners on that very ground—the safety of lives at sea. (*NLL* 199)

In this case, the Marconi installations as a symbol of the "scientific age" contrast sharply with the "pudding" used as a shock absorber when ships accidentally contact other ships or objects. After the *Titanic*, wireless marine communication was considered essential for safe navigation, and the government was very keen to promote its use. As a result, as Conrad stated, the Marconi installations were "being forced on the shipowners." (The aforementioned insider trading scandal was the byproduct of the government's policy.) Conrad said, however, that the puddings must be more useful than the installations, even though they are "too rough and unsightly for this scientific and aesthetic age." It is not clear how seriously Conrad thought of the puddings as something practical, but one can certainly identify his detachment from the enforced prevalence of shiny new installations.

Conrad Meets Wireless

I have thus far shown how Conrad kept silent on wireless telegraphy throughout the 1900s and the early 1910s. The silence was broken in 1916 when Conrad, upon a request from the Royal Navy, experienced marine wireless communication on a ten-day voyage in the HMS *Ready*, a Q-ship designed to lure and destroy German submarines. In his memoir about Conrad, John G. Sutherland, captain of the *Ready*, stated that Conrad "did not ask to send any wireless messages, nor did he receive any," although he "certainly had all a father's anxiety for his eldest son Borys" who was on campaign in France (1922: 74–5). According to Sutherland, Musgrove, the wireless engineer of the *Ready*, taught Conrad about the technology while at sea:

> Musgrove was a wonderful little fellow … I don't believe he ever slept, as when he had absolutely nothing else to do he was teaching Conrad wireless, both in the working of the instruments and the Morse code … I asked him what progress Mr Conrad was making under his tuition. Musgrove's reply was: "He knows it now from A to Z, sir." (1922: 124)

Conrad was taught about the functionality of wireless instruments and Morse code at the age of fifty-eight, only six years before his death. While Sutherland did not explain the reasons for Conrad's reluctance to communicate by wireless (in fact, he did send one telegraph on-board to his agent J. B. Pinker), it seems reasonable to assume that Conrad's experience with wireless telegraphy had not been as rich as it was for wired telegraphy for most of his life.

Conrad's profound experience with wired telegraphy and cables is reflected by their relatively frequent appearances in his fiction, such as in "An Outpost of Progress" and *Lord Jim*. These works involved the discrepancy between networked space and unwired, uninformed space. Conrad often chose the latter as settings for his fiction, including ships or secluded places like Patusan. Airborne wireless telegraphy had allowed information to reach anywhere in the world for the first time, perhaps explaining why Conrad may have felt it could undermine his fictional worlds. The nostalgic tones that are often found in his novels and stories seem to have served as a strategy to bring their settings into existence in an age of cutting-edge contemporary technologies.

"The Unlighted Coast": Wireless as the "Grouped-letters War Talk"

A month after the voyage, Conrad wrote an essay titled "The Unlighted Coast." It was posthumously published in *Last Essays* and intended as a propaganda essay in response to a request by the Royal Navy. It is the only essay in which Conrad wrote about his own experience with wireless communication. In "The Unlighted Coast" in *Last Essays*, Conrad ponders the differences of war talk transmitted wirelessly compared to "on the lips of men" (*LE* 38) that obscures "the one and only question: To be or not to be—the great alternative of an appeal to arms" (38).

> The other, the grouped-letters war-talk, almost without sound, and altogether without fury, is full of sense, of meaning, and single-minded purpose; inquiries, information, orders, reports. Words, too. But words in direct relation to things and facts, with the feeling at the back of it all of the correct foresight that planned and of the determination which carries on the protective work. (38–9)

Interestingly, Conrad's insight into new media was based on his views on the aesthetics of language rather than as a propagandist. As Mark Wollaeger states, his "characterization of coded wireless messages as 'grouped-letters war talk,' in other words, evoking not only the transparent language of fact but also the alphabetic opacities of Mallarmé, resonates with literary accounts that locate modernism at the confluence of naturalism and symbolism" (2006: 36). Here, as a novelist, Conrad's wireless experiences on the *Ready* seem to have inspired him to explore the potential of the "words, too" that is foregrounded in the new media.

"Grouping" and "Lightning"

In a letter to Richard Curle written on July 14, 1923, Conrad tried to explain his narrative methodology in his original terms "grouping" and "lightning."

> It is in those matters gradually, but never completely, mastered that the history of my books really consists. Of course the plastic matter of this grouping and of those lights has its importance, since without it the actuality of that grouping and that lighting could not be made evident any more than Marconi's electric waves could be made evident without the sending-out and receiving instruments. In

other words, without mankind my art, an infinitesimal thing, could not exist. (*CL8* 131)

Conrad believed that to visualize the "actuality of that grouping and that lighting" in his art, it was important to make his reader aware of "the plastic matter." Ivo Vidan saw Conrad's adumbration as a highly modern, relativistic, structured but open approach to art, similar to Umberto Eco's (1976: 190). J. Hillis Miller stated that Conrad aimed to provide a necessary material base for transforming something invisible into something visible through an artful arrangement of that material (2001: 112).

It is interesting to see how Conrad used the metaphor of wireless telegraphy to explain, as described by Jeremy Hawthorn, his "narratological analysis of an extremely high degree of sophistication" (2008: 167). The "grouping" and "lightning" were as invisible by themselves as "Marconi's electric waves" and were never visualized without the author as transmitter and the readers as receivers. Using wireless telegraphy to visualize the invisible was directly exploited by Wells and Kipling as a tool for describing communication beyond space and time. Conrad, in contrast, was not interested in incorporating the technology into his fiction. Not only was it unfamiliar to him, but the new technology might also have been seen as a threat to his fictional world. However, in the final stages of his life, Conrad finally embraced wireless telegraphy, which by then had become commonplace technology, as the best method to explain the nature of his art.[1]

In this essay, I have tried to determine whether and how Conrad communicated with contemporary wireless telegraphy, even though it did not overtly appear in his literary works. The mainstream use of wireless communication came slightly too late for Conrad, although the sailor-turned-novelist was familiar with the technologies of the era in general. It is quite understandable that novelists create fictional worlds that are based on, and limited to, their knowledge, references, and experiences. Still, it does not seem without reason that Conrad kept his fictional worlds distant from wireless telegraphy and that he tried to find its aesthetic nature during the final stage of his life.

Acknowledgments

The reprint of this article, first published in *The Conradian* 45, no. 1 (Spring 2020): 116–27, under the same title, has been made possible courtesy of *The*

Conradian. A version of this essay was presented at the 46th Annual International Conference of The Joseph Conrad Society (UK), St. Mary's University, Twickenham, July 2019.

Note

1 Wireless telegraphy was more than commonplace technology for the Conrad family in the 1920s. In 1922, Borys was involved with the Surrey Scientific Company, an ill-fated wireless appliance venture (cf. *CL8* 7n; Borys Conrad 1970: 156).

References

Conrad, Borys. 1970. *My Father: Joseph Conrad*. New York: Coward-McCann.

Hawthorn, Jeremy. 2008. "Review of *The Collected Letters of Joseph Conrad: Volume 8, 1923–1924*." *The Conradian* 33, no. 2: 158–69.

Kipling, Rudyard. 2011. *The Man Who Would Be King: Selected Stories from Rudyard Kipling*, edited by Jan Montefiore. London: Penguin Books.

Lothe, Jacob. 1989. *Conrad's Narrative Method*. Oxford: Oxford University Press.

Marshall, Archibald. [1933] 1990. "Conrad and Crippen." In *Joseph Conrad: Interviews and Recollections*, edited by Martin Ray, 64–5. London: Macmillan Press.

McLaughlan, Robbie. 2012. *Re-imagining the 'Dark Continent' in fin de siècle Literature*. Edinburgh: Edinburgh University Press.

Menke, Richard. 2008. *Telegraphic Realism: Victorian Fiction and Other Information Systems*. Stanford, CA: Stanford University Press.

Miller, J. Hillis. 2001. *Others*. Princeton, NJ: Princeton University Press.

Robertson, Roland. 1992. *Globalization: Social Theory and Global Culture*. London: Sage.

Rubery, Matthew. 2009. "Science and Technology." In *Joseph Conrad in Context*, edited by Allan H. Simmons, 237–44. Cambridge: Cambridge University Press.

Standage, Tom. 2009. *The Victorian Internet: The Remarkable Story of the Telegraph and the Nineteenth Century's On-line Pioneers*. New York: Walker Books.

Stanley, Henley Morton. 1886. *Incidents of the Journey through the Dark Continent*. London: Wm Clowes & Sons.

Sutherland, John G. 1922. *At Sea with Joseph Conrad*. New York: Houghton Mifflin.

Tesla, Nikola. 1901. "Nikola Tesla Promises Communication with Mars." *Richmond Times* (January 13): 8.

Trotter, David. 2013. *Literature in the First Media Age*. Cambridge, MA: Harvard University Press.

Vidan, Ivo. 1976. "Ford's Interpretation of Conrad's Technique." In *Joseph Conrad: A Commemoration*, edited by Norman Sherry, 183–93. London: The Macmillan Press.

Wells, H. G. [1901] 2017. *The First Men in the Moon*, edited by Simon J. James. Oxford World's Classics. Oxford: Oxford University Press.

Wollaeger, Mark. 2006. *Modernism, Media, and Propaganda: British Narrative from 1900 to 1945*. Princeton: Princeton University Press.

Worth, Aaron. 2014. *Imperial Media: Colonial Networks and Information Technologies in the British Literary Imagination, 1857–1918*. Columbus: Ohio State University Press.

10

Representing Conrad in Modern China

Gloria Kwok Kan Lee
School of Oriental and African Studies, University of London

Introduction

In the foreword to Gérard Genette's *Palimpsests: Literature in the Second Degree*, Gerald Prince states that all texts are imitations of an earlier text, "any writing is rewriting; and literature is always in the second degree" ([1982] 1997: ix). He does not mean that the object of study should be changed to "any text that plays off an older, pre-existent text" (Phelan and Rabinowitz 2008: 549), as a "second-degree text" is generally defined. Rather than the form and content of a text, as his argument goes, the focus should be on the text's "links with other texts"—transtextuality. In this way, attention is drawn to the relationality of all texts, and literary discourse is considered in terms of an aesthetic practice, which involves pragmatic choices and decisions made by human agents in the production process (Prince [1982] 1997: x). Such a paradigm shift is significant to the study of translated literature, where the image of the authors and their works in the target culture is a result of a series of decisions made by agents at a specific time and place.

The introduction of Joseph Conrad to China in the early twentieth century is a case in point. In the nineteenth century, Chinese intellectuals had looked for ways to save the nation in the face of challenges coming from the West. Translation was regarded as a means of importing modern and scientific knowledge meant to reform the government and the political systems. Some intellectuals began to see the need to change the people's mindsets by reforming Chinese language and culture. Thus, at the dawn of the twentieth century, China witnessed a proliferation of translations of foreign literature. Writers like Shakespeare, Ibsen, Dickens, and Wilde were introduced to promote new concepts (e.g., democracy, feminism) and new literary genres (e.g., fiction, drama) that would popularize the vernacular and enrich rhetorical devices for modern Chinese literature. Translations were either done by famous literary figures or commissioned by literary groups with specific aesthetic or political agendas. In these cases, the originals could be adapted and "rewritten" to a large extent to fit into the literary discourse prescribed by translators or literary groups of writers. These translations met with mixed reviews; they were welcomed by fellow members and criticized by the opposition. The discussions often ended up in abusive remarks between both sides while the original works and the authors became irrelevant.

This was not the case for Joseph Conrad. His name was first seen in an obituary published on the front page of a literary journal on August 11, 1924. He was then simply called "a noted writer of sea literature" who was eager to break away from despotic rule and seek freedom (Song 1924). More details were given in another article of a different journal in October 1924, in which he was described as a realist and praised for his powerful narratives filled with uniquely human emotions (Fan 1924). Although Conrad was mentioned in a smattering of articles after that, he was not given as much attention as other English novelists, such as Charles Dickens, John Galsworthy, and Thomas Hardy. In fact, in a 1929 article on his works, he was criticized for being obscure and unreadable (Zhao 1929). The first translation, "The Lagoon," appeared five years later. It was contributed by a reader to the journal *Xinyue* [The Crescent Moon] without any commentary on the author or the story. Considering the lukewarm reception Conrad received in that period, it is surprising that as many as seven translations of his stories and novels were published in book form, or serialized in newspaper supplements, over seven years. Four of those translations were commissioned by the Committee on Editing and Translation of the China Foundation for the Promotion of Education and Culture, within a project to translate European classics and history, launched and supervised by Hu Shi.

While there is no record indicating how Joseph Conrad was selected by the committee, alongside Shakespeare and Hardy, it is quite clear that the English novelist of Polish decent was recommended by Liang Yuchun (1906–1932), who was the first one to translate "Youth" and annotate its text in 1931. Liang's translation of *Lord Jim* was published posthumously, after his premature death in 1932 at the age of twenty-six. More than just making Conrad's works available in Chinese, Liang created a discourse on the author and his writing style, using both the epitexts in the form of prose collected in literary journals and the peritexts that come with the translations.

Introducing Conrad

When the Chinese translation of "Youth" was brought out in 1931, Liang Yuchun had already translated over twenty foreign works, including Vsevolod Garshin's "The Scarlet Flower," Elizabeth Gaskell's "The Squire's Story," Mary Russell Mitford's *Our Village*, and W. N. P. Barbellion's *A Last Diary*, as well as those by John Galsworthy, William Hale White, George Gissing, and Maxim Gorki, all published by Beixin Bookstore between 1930 and 1931. He had also established himself as an upcoming essayist in literary circles. Joseph Conrad's name was frequently quoted in his own writings, such as "'Huan wo toulai' jiqita" ["Return My Head" and Others] and "Wenxue yu rensheng" [Literature and Life] (Liang 1930: 58, 119–20), where he praised the novelist's style and his views on literature and life. In his article on vagabonds and adventurers, "Tan 'liulanghan,'" [On Vagabonds] alongside Pierre Loti, James Fenimore Cooper, and Frederick Marryat, Liang cited Conrad as a distinguished writer who composed sea stories that won the reader's sympathy (1930: 209).

In Liang's translations of "Youth" and *Lord Jim*, such features are highlighted conscientiously but recreated in a different style. Most of the nominalized clauses and passive structures in the original are rewritten with verbs of action and the agents properly restored to present captivating scenes of adventures in the ocean. The tension of the chain of events is further enhanced by an addition of adverbs marking the turning points. The diegetic levels in *Lord Jim* are differentiated in English by tenses and the respective narrators' knowledge of the events. Marlow as a heterodiegetic narrator, for example, has a restricted access to past events, and his narrative is marked by words indicating a subjective perception and speculation. In Liang's translation, however, the narrators on different levels all speak with confidence, revealing the characters' thoughts and emotions as if from an omniscient perspective.

Conrad's writing style is outlined in Liang's three-page postscript to "Youth" as well as a preface to *Lord Jim* written by Yuan Jiahua (1903–1980), who continued with the project after Liang had passed away. In these peritexts, the biography of Conrad is given in detail, projecting him as a sailor-turned-writer, whose representative works include such novels and stories as *Lord Jim*, *The Nigger of the "Narcissus," Nostromo*, "Youth," "Typhoon," and "Heart of Darkness" and such essays as *A Personal Record*, *The Mirror of the Sea*, and *Notes on Life and Letters*, all associated with sea voyages and the author's *personal* experiences and reflections on the human condition, all tinged with a mysterious mood and a note of deep sadness. In the preface to *Lord Jim*, the ocean is said to be the backdrop of different stories about ocean-going ships, sailors, merchants, and the indigenous people of the East (Liang 1934; Yuan 1934: 5). The themes of Conrad's novels include loneliness of the soul and a sense of fatalism that prevails in a losing battle of humankind against Nature (6). This melancholic mood colors *Lord Jim*, the novel itself, and its protagonist. Through the book's translations and commentary, the Chinese reader is led to focusing on the universal character of Conrad's fiction.

The linguistic and cultural gaps, if any, are filled in by the explanatory notes. The Chinese translation of "Youth" is printed in the form of a parallel text, with the English original on the left page and the Chinese translation on the right, to facilitate language learning. The nautical jargon and technical expressions are paraphrased in the translation, and some are explained in the footnotes. "To square the foreyard" is translated as "to adjust the yard" (Liang 1931: 73; author's own translation) and explained as "to bring the foreyard to a right angle with the mast 使帆桁與桅成為直角" in both English and Chinese at the bottom of the page. In fact, the English source text is richly annotated with 147 footnotes, 107 of which are on the English expressions or general usage. The remaining entries are mostly Liang's interpretations of selected fragments. The note on the phrase "the blaze of vivid color," for example, says that it refers to "Asians' preference for clothes in bright colors, so dazzling and eye-catching as the blaze" (126; author's own translation). At times, the translator also wears the hat of a reviewer and urges the reader to appreciate the excerpts from specific perspectives. In the note to the last paragraph that concludes the story, Liang shares his view: "These few sentences can summarize the whole life. Who wouldn't feel the sadness? Wouldn't the reader at this point pause and contemplate?" (132; author's own translation). Such remarks echo the portrayal of Conrad and his style commented on in the postscript, strengthening a melancholy impression of the story set against the backdrop of the ocean.

Translating Conrad

Although Yuan Jiahua translated the remaining thirty chapters of *Lord Jim* and wrote the preface, he was not listed as a co-translator to Liang Yuchun when the translation was published in 1934. It was not until the publication of the Chinese translations of *The Nigger of the "Narcissus"* in 1936 and *Typhoon and Other Stories* in 1937 that he was officially named as the translator on the front cover. Compared with the two earlier Conrad translations, that is, of "Youth" and *Lord Jim*, Yuan's translations configure a different relationship between the "author/translator" and the reader. While the previous translations prescribe the image of Conrad and his sea stories mainly through the translators' direct commentary in the explanatory notes, prefaces, and postscripts, Yuan Jiahua makes an effort to lay out linguistic traits in the translated text, inviting readers to use their imagination to reconstruct the world of the seamen. A network of nautical terms and expressions is carefully developed, and special words are used to match specific parts of the ship. The parts that are generalized as 桅杆 (yards) in "Youth" and *Lord Jim* are now given separate names: 帆桁 for "yard," 桅桁 for "spar," 桅檣 for "mast," and 船頭斜桅 for "bowsprit." More complicated terms such as "in ballast," "anchor-watchman," and "paddle-tug" are sometimes expanded in explanatory phrases like 載着壓艙的重物 (lit. carrying loads to weigh down the hold), 夜泊值班水手 (lit. nightshift sailors), and 雙翼的拖輪 (lit. tug with double wings). The mere appearance of technical terms alerts the readers to the fact that the ship and the ocean are more than just the setting of these stories; this is the language that the readers need to acquire so as to understand the characters and their world.

The effect of lexicalization is more intense in *The Nigger of the "Narcissus,"* initially subtitled *A Tale of the Forecastle* (Knowles and Moore 2000: 248). A story about the unity and bondage among the ordinary seamen living in the forecastle of the *Narcissus*, as the novella is, it is loaded with terms referring to various parts of the ship, together with eye dialects representing the accents of sailors coming from different parts of the country. Chinese characters indicating body parts are incorporated into the translations, and the ship is described as if she were a living creature: "midship" is rendered into 船腰 (lit. ship waist), "haul and hulk" into 船殼 (lit. ship shell), and "wheel box" into 舵輪殼 (lit. wheel shell). The key terms such as 船頭 (ship head/bow), 船尾 (ship tail), 甲板 (deck), 艙 (cabin), 桅 (mast), 桁 (pole), 帆 (sail), and 蓋板 (hatch) are repeatedly used throughout the Chinese narrative, together with basic nautical concepts like 上風 (up wind), 下風 (down wind), and 受風 (toward/facing the wind), as in the instruction "把船頭調到下風去" (lit. lead/adjust the bow down wind), which is a translation of "wear ship" in the English source text. Along with the technical phrases come numerous notes attached at the end of the translation. There are a total of 189 endnotes, eighty-three of which describe ship parts, instruments, and ship types, with eighteen explaining the expressions used by sailors in steering or maneuvering a ship.

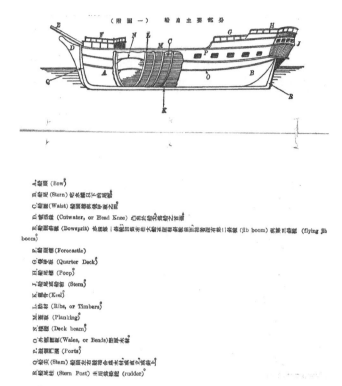

Figure 6 An illustration of ship parts (*Heishuishou* [*The Nigger of the "Narcissus"*], Yuan, 1936b, pp. 178–9). Public domain.

Yuan Jiahua's translation also contains two illustrations of ship parts (Figure 6) and of different kinds of masts and rigs (Figure 7). The readers learn from the sailors about the craft of seafaring, gaining a new perspective on the adventures in Conrad's texts.

The titles of the officers and seamen are also translated with respect to the interactions among the characters. The captain is mostly called 船長 (head of the ship), but it is changed to 船主 (master/owner of the ship) toward the end of the story, a term that underlines his role as the leading figure and the respect accorded him after the voyage has ended. The cook is called 廚師傅 (chef master) or 大師傅 (big/great master) for "doctor" in the source text after he makes his way back to the galley to prepare coffee for the exhausted shipmates. "The sail maker" is translated as 帆工 (sail worker), but as 帆子 (sail boy) when Belfast uses the term, indicating intimacy when they are preparing the corpse of the West Indian sailor for his funeral. The crew is mostly called 水手 (lit. water-hands, the Chinese term for "sailors"), but at times 夥計們 (fellows) and 船友

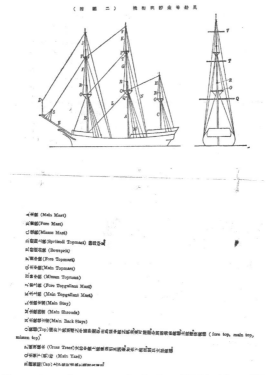

(mates, shipmates) are used to show a degree of affinity. The various names given to the characters in different contexts and situations help to shape the sense of hierarchy in the community on board the ship. With the nautical jargon and phrases, Yuan hints at the symbolic bondage of the English sailors, "who hath known the bitterness of the Ocean" (F [D] 145).

The translator not only provides technical knowledge that allows the readers to enter the fictional world, but also attempts to reduce the distance between them and the author. In the Chinese translation of *The Nigger of the "Narcissus"* (1936), Joseph Conrad's photograph, with his autograph beneath it, appears right after the title page, bringing in an authentic touch. In the thirteen-page preface that follows, Conrad is depicted as an "international writer" who traveled widely as a sailor, but also a "cultural invader, who was at the same time assimilated by other races" (Yuan 1936a: 1; translation mine). His views on and achievements in fiction writing can be compared to those stated by writers of Anglophone novels, such as Hardy, James, Stevenson, Galsworthy, and Bennett, who were widely known in China at that time. Yuan cites particularly Conrad's view on the mission of the novelist, which is to discover the truth of the universe and human life and to convey it in the most efficient and skillful way. The novelist traces the emotions back to their roots, and such sentiments, Yuan says, can be comprehended only by a reader as sympathetic as the translator, who acts as the author's representative. He then goes on to explain the effect of the "oblique method of narration" (cited in English in the preface) used by Conrad in figurative language:

> Hitting and knocking at the sides, as if coming close, then drifting away, [the reader] is trapped in a mesmerized alien land … At the end, suddenly a flash of light, the profile and demeanor of the characters are projected clearly. [This] accidental glimpse leaves you with an impression which can never be erased. (Yuan 1936a: 8; translation mine)

The emotions of the sailors are those experienced by the author or the narrator, and they will become the experience of the readers as they savor the actions and ambience through Conrad's description of the setting and the natural environment. The readers can "immerse themselves in, be permeated and inebriated with a spiritual aura" (11; translation mine). The translator appeals to the readers' sensibilities and encourages them to read the text as if they were present in the fictional world themselves. As in the previous prefaces, Yuan does not explain or defend his translation strategy as if this was the only way to read the novel. This forms a stark contrast to the translation style found in his Chinese version of *Typhoon and Other Stories* published the following year.

Interpreting Conrad

The notion of "the implied author" was first coined by Wayne Booth in 1961 to serve as the definitive image of the author. It is the second self of the author as projected in a novel, as opposed to the flesh-and-blood writer. In theory, it is the sum of the decisions made by the author in terms of his or her writing style and ethical judgments, and it dictates the only correct interpretation of the text (Booth 1983: 74–5). Seymour Chatman defines the concept in similar terms, referring to it as "the invention and intent" of the novel (1990: 85). Based on this image inferred from the novel, the readers are guided to a specific reading of the text as if it were intended by the "author." This image of the author is "implied" in the sense that the readers have to follow the traits laid out in the text and (re) construct it by themselves.

The implied author is a controversial concept in narratology. Gérard Genette argues that the image is identical to the real author as long as the image presented is a faithful one. The faithfulness of such an image hinges on two factors: its production by the author and its reception by the reader. However, according to Genette, the author here is only an agent who produces the text. He or she cannot be separated from the text, nor can he or she dictate its interpretations to the reader (Genette 1988: 143). In other words, the interpretative task is vested entirely with the reader. Mieke Bal shares this view, pointing out that the implied author is "the *result* of the investigation of the meaning of a text, not the *source* of that meaning" (2009: 17; emphasis in original). The reader's input is likely to be marginalized if too much emphasis is put on a "correct" understanding of the text. This argument would hold as long as the narrative text is the original work of the author, and the reader's interpretation is based on a text that has not been mediated by a second party.

The case is different for a translated narrative. It is assumed that the translator would rewrite the original narrative, using another language for readers who do not have access to the source text, and claim his or her translation to be a "correct" or "faithful" representation of the original. In Bal's words, it is a translator's job— like that of a teacher or a critic—to claim the "authority of knowing 'what the author meant to say'" (2009: 17). The Chinese readers who do not understand English or own copies of the English original can only evaluate the reliability of the translated narrative by judging whether the narrator is speaking for or acting "in accordance with the norms of the work" (Booth 1983: 158–9; see also Chatman 1978: 233; Rimmon-Kenan 2002: 101). In this respect, the paratexts, which facilitate "a better reception for the text and a more pertinent reading of it," according to Genette (1997b: 2), play a significant role in ensuring the reliability of the translated narrative for the target reader by defining the implied author.

In the Chinese translations of "Youth," *Lord Jim*, and *The Nigger of the "Narcissus,"* the translator, the author, and the narrator speak in one voice, directing the reader to construct an image of Conrad as an accomplished novelist of sea fiction. The translated texts are written only in Chinese characters, with English words or phrases limited to the translators' notes and prefaces. While this may simply be a rule stipulated by the editors, a translation without foreign words would appear more coherent.

Yuan's style changes in the translation of *"Typhoon" and Other Stories* (1937b). In "Falk, a Reminiscence," for example, German words are inserted in the main text as direct quotations from Captain Hermann, with the Chinese translation provided in brackets:

我聽見他自言自語地咕咕道，『Himmel! Zweidreissig Pfund! [*sic*]』（老天爺！三十二鎊呢！）我損失數目給了他深刻的印象。(Yuan 1937b: 144–5)

我好幾次聽得說『Mench』[*sic*]（人）；還聽得說『fressen』，末了這個字，後來我查了查字典，纔明白意思就是『吞吃』。(201)

The German words in the original are used to reinforce the perspective of the English captain, the homodiegetic narrator, who does not understand German and has difficulty figuring out the meaning of the speeches delivered by Hermann and Falk. This is an important element of the narrative since it is also this English captain who relays Falk's confession of "having eaten men" in indirect discourse, allowing the reader to doubt the narrator's report. This leitmotif can also be seen in the English captain's comments on Hermann's English as "fairly comprehensible" and on Falk, who "spoke English, of course on my account." When these phrases are translated directly into Chinese as 雖然他說的英國話還讓人聽得懂 (Yuan 1937b: 137; lit. although the English he speaks is still comprehensible) and 他從頭到尾都是說的英語, 當然是為我方便 (198; lit. from the beginning to the end he speaks in English, naturally for my convenience), the contradiction between the semantic content (i.e., the reference to "English" being spoken by the characters) and the translated text (being actually written in Chinese) would no doubt remind the Chinese readers that they are reading a text mediated by the translator (Hermans 1996). Later on in the translation, English words are also found in brackets next to the Chinese translation (最好的 [the best] and 最強韌的 [the toughest]) as if the Chinese-speaking narrator (or the translator, who provides the original English text in brackets) also had doubts about his interpretation and asked the readers to decide for themselves.

The voice of the Chinese-speaking narrator/translator is more discernible in the translation of "Typhoon" when the Chinese coolies enter the story as "a cargo" shipped back to their home village. The Chinese are characterized by their dark clothes, yellow faces, and pigtails. They are called 天朝人民 (lit. people of the heavenly dynasty), a translation of the English term "celestial," which is marked by Yuan as "a sarcastic expression" in the endnote (Yuan 1937b: 261). The Chinese clerk who acts as the interpreter on board is being mocked by Jukes, the chief mate, who communicates with him in Pidgin English. Just like the German words in "Falk, a Reminscence," Jukes's speech in Pidgin English is retained in the main text, followed by the Chinese translation in parentheses:

他粗率地說，『Come along, John Make [sic] look see!』。（來，老贛兒。去瞧瞧罷。）這話引得那個<u>中國</u>人跟在他後面走動了。

『Wanchee look see, all same look see can do.』，（你要想瞧瞧的話，這就可以瞧啦，）<u>朱可士</u>說；他沒有說外國話的本領，便任意胡謅了一套洋涇浜英國話。他指點着敞開的艙口。『Catchee number one piecie place to sleep in, Eh!』（你瞧，這地方睡覺是再好沒有的了。呃！）

『No Catchee rain down there-savee?』（那下面漏不着雨——你明白麼？）<u>朱可士</u>指點說。『Suppose allée same fine weather, one piecie Coolie-man come topside.　』，（假使天氣照現在這樣好，那麼你們這般苦力不妨輪流着到上面甲板來。）他繼續講，興會似乎濃起來了。『Make so-phooooo!』（就這樣罷——吷——呼！）他擴大了他底胸部，吹鼓了他底面頰。『Savee, John? Breath—fresh air, Good, Eh? Washee him piecie pants Chow-chow topside-see,　John?』（你明白麼，老贛兒？呼吸——新鮮空氣。好呃？洗條褲子，待在上面吃吃飯——懂麼，老贛兒？）　(Yuan 1937b: 10–11).

While the translator does not provide any explanation for the decision or notes on the use of Pidgin English in this context, it is quite clear that the Chinese-speaking narrator/translator is distancing himself from Jukes by giving a verbatim report of what he cannot fully comprehend. The translator relinquishes his authority to interpret the original text and suggests a possible translation for the reference of more competent bilingual readers. The changing strategy may render the translated narrative unreliable, as the narrator, the translator, and the author are no longer speaking in the same voice.

The tendency of the translator to dissociate himself from the original text, or even the author, can also be observed in the preface. Yuan still provides scholarly reviews of and his personal opinion on the book, but his authoritative tone is much weakened. As he appraises Conrad's literary achievement and criticizes his monotonous style and lack of organization, he points out the redundancy and verbiage exhibited in "One Day More," a play adapted from the story "Tomorrow," both collected in the translation. In addition, Yuan acknowledges the help of his wife and admits that there are possible blemishes in this translation as a result of his incompetence. He then goes on to state that there are gaps between languages that cannot be bridged, a remark that echoes the German words and Pidgin English left intact in the translation. The translator cannot speak for the author, and the readers should decide for themselves what the original really means. In the end, Yuan surrenders his authority to represent the author, admitting that he is but a meek translator:

These explanatory notes do not necessarily help the reader. Sometimes, they may cause hindrance. Therefore, I hope that the readers will ignore them if they can help it … I have to admit that a translator's interpretation is not necessarily superior to the readers' understanding. (Yuan 1937a: 5; translation mine)

Instead of making himself into a spokesperson of Conrad as he does in the previous prefaces, Yuan now aligns himself with the Chinese readers and encourages them to look for their own interpretations of Conrad's works.

Conclusion

Genette uses the notion of "transtextuality" to address the "textual transcendence of the text" and examine the relationships that exist between texts (1997a: 1). However, he considers translation merely a form of hypertext, a translator undertaking a failing task of choosing between "a wrongful emphasis" and "a forced neutralization" (216). However, the translators who brought Joseph Conrad to the Chinese literary scene had more tools at their disposal. In addition to translating his works, they also introduced Conrad's literary views and writing style, foregrounding his achievements by comparing him with his contemporaries in the West. They negotiated with editors and publishers who commissioned translation projects and selected Conrad's maritime fiction to configure him as a skillful sea-story writer whose works would instill universal human truths in Chinese readers. The translators made use of Chinese rhetoric devices and rendered the English originals into action-packed adventures catering to Chinese readership. With their explanatory notes and diagrams, they provided knowledge about the English language, culture, and nautical terminology, extending the reader's imagination beyond the texts. When the cultural conflicts between the English sailors and Chinese coolies became more sensitive as political tension built up in society in the late 1930s, the translators did not choose to delete or rewrite the passages. Instead, they took the position of humble translators, encouraging their compatriots to come up with their own interpretations and thus enriching the transformative meanings of Conrad's narratives.

Conrad's major works continued to be translated and retranslated after the political upheaval in the 1940s. His influence on Chinese literary circles can also be seen in a different form. Apart from Liang Yuchun, Shu Qingchun (1899–1966), a novelist and dramatist who was better known by his pen name

"Lao She," had also praised and learned from Conrad's style during his stay in London as a teacher at the School of Oriental and African Studies from 1924 to 1929. It is widely known that his 1929 novel *Er Ma* (*Mr Ma and Son*, translated by W. Dolby, 2013) and his 1931 *Xiaopo de Shengri* (lit. Xiaopo's Birthday) are partly inspired by Conrad. However, he also states clearly that he is against the Eurocentrism in Conrad's novels and wants to subvert what he called "chauvinism" in Western literature by writing stories about Chinese and South Asian people, thus allowing them to speak in their own voices. In this respect, the two translators take a similar approach as they construct Conrad in the image of a novelist whose powerful narratives of seafaring, peopled with distinct personalities, would inspire Chinese readers' imaginations to reflect on their own experiences, foregrounding the universal values of humankind. It is in this image that Joseph Conrad has taken root on foreign soil and will continue to inspire readers and writers for generations to come.

References

Bal, Mieke. 2009. *Narratology: Introduction to the Theory of Narrative*, 3rd ed. Translated by Christine van Boheemen. Toronto: University of Toronto Press.

Booth, Wayne. [1961] 1983. *The Rhetoric of Fiction*, 2nd ed. Chicago: University of Chicago Press.

Chatman, Seymour. 1978. *Story and Discourse: Narrative Structure in Fiction and Film*. Ithaca: Cornell University Press.

Chatman, Seymour. 1990. *Coming to Terms: The Rhetoric of Narrative in Fiction and Film*. Ithaca: Cornell University Press.

Fan, Z. Y. 1924. "Kangladepingzhuan—jinianzhegexinsi de yingguodazuojiaerzuo" [A Critical Biography of Conrad: In Memory of the Great English Writer Who Died Lately]. *Xiaoshuo Yuebao* 15, no. 10: 2–10.

Genette, Gérard. [1983] 1988. *Narrative Discourse Revisited*. Translated by J. E. Lewin. Ithaca: Cornell University Press.

Genette, Gérard. [1982] 1997a. *Palimpsests: Literature in the Second Degree*. Translated by C. Newman and C. Doubinsky. Lincoln: University of Nebraska Press.

Genette, Gérard. [1987] 1997b. *Paratexts: Thresholds of Interpretation*. Translated by J. E. Lewin. Cambridge: Cambridge University Press.

Hermans, Theo. 1996. "The Translator's Voice in Translated Narrative." *Target* 8, no. 1: 23–48.

Knowles, Owen, and Gene. M. Moore, eds. 2000. *Oxford Reader's Companion to Conrad*. Oxford: Oxford University Press.

Liang, Y. C. 1930. *Chunlao Ji* [*Spring Wine Collection*]. Shanghai: Beixin Bookstore.

Liang, Y. C. trans. 1931. "Qingchun" ["Youth"]. Shanghai: Beixin Bookstore.

Liang, Y. C. trans. 1934. *Jimu ye* [*Lord Jim*]. Shanghai: Commercial Press.

Phelan, James, and Peter. J. Rabinowitz, eds. 2008. *A Companion to Narrative Theory.* Malden, MA: Blackwell Publishing.

Prince, Gerald. [1982] 1997. Foreword. In *Palimpsests: Literature in the Second Degree*, ix–xi. Translated by C. Newman and C. Doubinsky. Lincoln: University of Nebraska Press.

Rimmon-Kenan, Shlomith. 2002. *Narrative Fiction*. 2nd ed. London: Routledge.

Song Yu. 1924. "Xinjinqushi de Haiyang wenxuejia—Kanglade" [The Late Writer of Sea Literature—Conrad]. *Wenxue* 134: 1–2.

Yuan, J. H. 1934. "Yizhexuyan" [Translator's Preface]. In *Jimu ye* [*Lord Jim*], 3–6. Translated by Y. C. Liang. Shanghai: Commercial Press.

Yuan, J. H. 1936a. "Yizhexu" [Translator's Preface]. In *Heishuishou* [*The Nigger of the "Narcissus"*], 1–13. Translated by J. H. Yuan. Shanghai: Commercial Press.

Yuan, J. H., trans. 1936b. *Heishuishou* [*The Nigger of the "Narcissus"*]. Shanghai: Commercial Press.

Yuan, J. H. 1937a. "Yizhefuji" [Additional Note from the Translator]. In *Taifengjiqita* [*"Typhoon" and Other Stories*], 1–5. Translated by J. H. Yuan. Shanghai: Commercial Press.

Yuan, J. H., trans. 1937b. *Taifengjiqita* [*"Typhoon" and Other Stories*]. Shanghai: Commercial Press.

Zhao, J. S. 1929. "Xiandaiyingmeixiaoshuo de qushi" [Trends in Modern Anglo-American Novels]. *Wenxue Xunkan* (July): 98–109.

11

The Man Who Foresaw It All:
Joseph Conrad and India

Narugopal Mukherjee
Bankura Christian College (Bankura University)

"I am the world itself, come to pay you a visit," says Mr. Jones to Heyst in Joseph Conrad's *Victory* (371). Nothing could better express Conrad's global perspective, his universal sensibilities, and his all-encompassing vision of the future. Mr. Jones's words quoted above echo Conrad's conviction that a writer has to move across spatial and temporal boundaries and predict some universal and global aspects of the human world. An extensive reading of his fiction reveals that Joseph Conrad was not simply a European writer writing on European perceptions and experiences; rather he was a philosopher who advocated transculturalism and a prophet who foresaw the issues that would haunt or affect peoples across the globe in times to come. Maya Jasanoff in her seminal book *The Dawn Watch* (2017) rightly says, "From the deck of a ship, Conrad watched the emergence of the globally connected world" (6). Conrad might not have written anything directly on the Indian way of life, but the issues and the perspectives that he tackles in his fiction touch upon almost all major aspects of life in India these days: colonial and postcolonial nuances, gross marginalization or "othering," terrorism and violence, corruption in politics, crude forms of nationalism, and so on.

"Everything about my life in the wide world can be found in my books," Joseph Conrad wrote to Marguerite Poradowska in his letter dated August 18, 1894 (*CL1* 171), and critics like Richard Curle and Gérard Jean-Aubry (1927), or later ones like Edward Said and Ian Watt, found Conrad's life and philosophy to be contained in the very writings of the novelist. To Conrad, fiction is but a record of the actual experiences of life. "Fiction is history, human history, or it is nothing," he said in "Henry James: An Appreciation" (*NLL* 17). His fiction traces his journey through the continents, and metaphorically, this journey is an inward journey as well, as is the case of Marlow in "Heart of Darkness" or in *Lord Jim*. The journey unraveled the world to him, both physically and psychologically, and he could, as said earlier, envisage the future while sitting on the deck of his ship. Jasanoff observes,

> Conrad wouldn't have known the word "globalization," but with his journey from the provinces of imperial Russia across the high seas to the British home countries, he embodied it. He channelled his global perspectives into fiction based overwhelmingly on personal experience and real incidents … Conrad cast his net across Europe, Africa, South America, and the Indian ocean. (2017: 7)

He served as a professional mariner on at least a dozen ships and was later promoted to the position of Captain. Conrad took the vast sea as the mighty world. Sailing was for him like exploring the world and the land ahead, as he would explore future time and the future world. He served for sixteen years in the British merchant navy and, later, obtained British citizenship and chose London as his home.

It was not just his vast experiences at sea, but also his national and linguistic identities that made Conrad a citizen of the world. The long attachment to Britain made him choose English as the language for literary venture, although it was only his third language, after Polish and French. His wide experience of different lands and close familiarity with different languages helped Conrad overcome all provincial and linguistic inhibitions and turned him into a global citizen.

Conrad's popularity is always on the rise, particularly in this century, because of the issues that he dealt with in his fiction. Before the term "globalization" became ubiquitous, he had been able to anticipate certain issues that would haunt human civilization in the late twentieth and the early twenty-first centuries. He foresaw economic imperialism, racism, marginalization, the pangs of the imagined communities of the diaspora, rampant violence, and most importantly, terrorism that would traumatize human life in the future. These experiences, as said earlier, relate to the issues of human civilization in general, and are thus prevalent here in Asia as well. Hence, Conrad has always been relevant, and he has been gaining popularity in India, a land beset by corruption, terrorism, marginalization, and exploitation.

Conrad's four major works—"Heart of Darkness," *Lord Jim*, *The Secret Agent*, and *Nostromo*—deal with issues that are largely at the core of life in India. "Heart of Darkness" takes up the issues of colonialism and imperialism that India experienced in the past and is experiencing now, albeit in a different way. India's colonial legacy and economic imperialism are extant even today. *The Secret Agent* takes up the issues of nationalism, diasporic experiences, and terrorism that have always been relevant to India. *Lord Jim* speaks of marginalization and othering, both of which are very common in India. It also speaks of industrialization, which has had both positive and negative effects on all Indians. *Nostromo* deals with revolution, politics, and financial irregularities, all of which determine Indian perspectives as well.

Conrad has thus been very popular as a writer, a philosopher, and a prophet in India and has been widely read and researched across the nation for his global and transcultural perspectives. There have been hundreds of doctoral and postdoctoral theses written on Conrad in different universities in India. There could be quite a treasure house of PhD dissertations on Conrad successfully completed in the last decade of this century alone. Subhadeep Ray (Kalyani University) in his PhD dissertation brought into discussion "Heart of Darkness," *Lord Jim, The Secret Agent, Nostromo,* and *Under Western Eyes.* A. M. Hulubandi (Karnatak University) focused on identity crises in six different works of Conrad—"Heart of Darkness," *Lord Jim, The Secret Agent, Under Western Eyes, The Nigger of the "Narcissus,"* and "Typhoon." Indrani Bora Bhuyan (North-Eastern Hill University) in her PhD dissertation made an attempt to look into the soul of the narrator, Marlow. Anjana Srivastava's (Jawaharlal Nehru University) PhD dissertation made a semiotic study of the journey motif in Conrad's tales. If we go back to the previous century, there too we find a long list of dissertations on Conrad. Suchismita Biswas (The University of Burdwan) in her PhD dissertation (1997) discussed the issue of colonialism in three different Conrad texts: "Heart of Darkness," *Lord Jim,* and *Nostromo.* Md Shirajul Islam (Panjab University, 1981) explored the self and its perfect communion in Conrad's novels. Mohd. Asaduddin (Aligarh Muslim University) in his thesis (1988) dealt with the political and cultural nuances of Conrad's works in "Heart of Darkness," *Almayer's Folly, The Secret Agent, Nostromo,* and *Under Western Eyes.* The list would be a pretty lengthy one if we were to name all. Almost all the universities in India, from premier institutions, like Jawaharlal Nehru University, Delhi University, Hyderabad University, and Jadavpur University, to the newly established universities, like Bankura University and SKB University, have included Conrad's texts on their respective curricula, either at the undergraduate or postgraduate level of studies. Thus Joseph Conrad has been very much relevant to Indian academia.

Conrad has been so popular throughout the world not because of the romanticism or exoticism that has been found in a number of his writings, or the varied experiences of his extensive sea travels that he records in his fiction, but because of the uncompromising moral standpoint that he assumes. In a letter to Sidney Colvin, Conrad said in a complaining tone: "I may say that I have not been very well understood. I have been called a writer of the sea, of the tropics, a descriptive writer, a romantic writer—and also a realist. But as a matter of fact all my concern has been with the 'ideal value' of things, events and people" (*CL6* 40). Indeed, Conrad has been widely accepted in India because of his insistence on the "ideal value" of things. His voice against imperialism and colonialism, his strong opposition to marginalization and exploitation of all kinds, his repulsion for all kinds of corrupt practices, his staunch criticism of terrorism, and above all, his transcultural ideas have endeared him to millions of Indian readers. Conrad's narrators literally undertake a journey, and metaphorically, that journey aims at exploring the soul, the hidden truth. This soul-searching is what appeals to Indians and in that sense Conrad comes close to the Indian heart.

One of the works that has won Conrad millions of Indian readers is definitely "Heart of Darkness" (1899). Frances B. Singh considers the novella to be "one of the most powerful indictments of colonialism ever written" (1988: 268). He observes that "as a child Conrad was a victim of Russia's colonialistic policies toward Poland" (268). Conrad projected this novella as a critique of colonialism and imperialism. Hugh Clifford interpreted it as a "study of the Congo" (qtd. in Raskin 1967: 113), and Edward Garnett referred to it as "an impression taken from life, of the conquest by the European whites of a certain portion of Africa, an impression in particular of the civilizing methods of a certain great European Trading" (qtd. in Raskin 1967: 113). It was Conrad's firm belief expressed in "Henry James: An Appreciation" that a "novelist is a historian, the preserver, the keeper, the expounder, of human experience" (*NLL* 17). In "Heart of Darkness," Conrad records his real-life experiences: the brutality of the European colonizers that he noticed in Africa. Jasanoff points to the traumatic experience of Conrad in the Congo:

> He saw in Congo a European regime of appalling greed, violence, and hypocrisy, and left Africa in a state of psychological and moral despair. Nine years later, when he'd settled down in England and Anglicized his name to Joseph Conrad from Józef Teodor Konrad Korzeniowski, he channelled his experience into a novel called *Heart of Darkness*. (2017: 3)

Marlow, the narrator in the novella, discovered that Kurtz, the prophet of civilization had become a savage lord who could scrawl a crazed injunction, "Exterminate all the brutes!" (HD 125). In connection with this Jonah Raskin remarks, "Conrad transformed a personal experience into a fiction of general historical and cultural significance. With little sense of strain, he moved from self to society" (2011: 115–16).

However, Conrad's anonymous narrator on the *Nellie* described Marlow as someone for whom "the meaning of an episode was not inside like a kernel but outside, enveloping the tale which brought it out only as a glow brings out a haze" (HD 50). J. Hillis Miller observes that the narratives of Marlow are not meant for conveying an obvious message that can be extracted out of the tale like a kernel; rather, the meaning is made obscure in darkness. Similarly to parables, remarks Miller, Marlow's tales are "in preordained correspondence or in resonance with the meaning. The tale magically brings the 'unseen' meaning out and makes it visible" (2017: 233).

Nevertheless, Chinua Achebe makes a searing attack on Conrad by labeling him "a thoroughgoing racist" and is not ready to accept "Heart of Darkness" as a great work of art (1977: 257). He objects to its gross underestimation of the Africans:

> *Heart of Darkness* projects the image of Africa as "the other world," the antithesis of Europe and therefore of civilization, a place where man's vaunted intelligence and refinement are finally mocked by triumphant bestiality … The real question is the dehumanization of Africa and Africans which this age-long attitude has fostered and continues to foster in the world. (Achebe 1977: 252–7)

I pointed out earlier in my article "Joseph Conrad and E. M. Forster in Search of a Transcultural Space" (Mukherjee 2017) that "Conrad does not narrow down his novella simply to the discussion of the evils of imperialism or colonialism. He has something more significant to contribute. The journeys that Marlow undertakes to the 'heart' of 'darkness' take us on to the discovery of our real character, the 'darkness' within, the evil within us" (Mukherjee 2017: 163). Caryl Phillips aptly remarks:

> Conrad uses colonisation, and the trading intercourse that flourished in its wake, to explore [the] universal questions about man's capacity for evil… Conrad was interested in the making of a modern world in which colonisation was simply one facet. (2003)

Jasanoff is more than right when she remarks, "Conrad's book has become a touchstone for thinking about Africa and Europe, civilization and savagery, imperialism, genocide, insanity—about human nature itself" (2017: 4). "Heart of Darkness" has had a perpetual appeal not just in Europe and Africa, but also in India.

India witnessed the evils of the human heart during the colonial period. The British colonizers committed all kinds of atrocities and brutalities to carry on with their colonial aggression and the plundering of natural resources. The country has since attained freedom, but the colonial legacy of exploitation still exists, and its effects are to be found in every walk of life. Linguistic hegemony creating a divide between those who know English and others, the hegemony of bureaucracy, the harassment of the common people by the diplomats in different government offices, corporeal and psychological abuse going on because of different levels of discrimination, and a continuation of the colonial system of education and administration—are all reminiscent of British colonialism and the colonial hangover that we have not yet overcome, although the country celebrated its seventy-fourth Independence Day very recently.

Conrad expressed his displeasure with Belgian imperialism in the Congo in "Heart of Darkness" and anticipated imperialism of different kinds in the days to come. Colonial rule has come to an end, but the aggressive economic imperialisms of the United States and China are threatening the very stability of third-world countries like India. Conrad realized that it was not just one particular colonial rule or one imperialist force that presented a threat to the African community, as evil is always very much inside the heart of humans; it is a person's "heart of darkness." The evil in India is lurking in casteism, which is no less than a variant of racism that we come across in "Heart of Darkness." The oppression and subjugation of Dalits and the inhuman brutality directed against the marginalized even in this century remind us of Conrad's appalling experiences in the Congo. It is thus that Conrad comes close to the hearts of Indians.

Almost half of the writings of Conrad have South-East Asia as their background. With Malaya, Conrad introduced British readers to a remote place about which few would consider writing. He took every care to introduce the Malaya as accurately as possible. *Lord Jim* (1900), the greatest of Conrad's novels set against the backdrop of Asia, deals with the life of a European sailor taking a ship to Asia, which is where the action starts. Conrad mentions Indian and Asian cities while referring to Jim: "He was known successively in Bombay, in Calcutta, in Rangoon, in Penang, in Batavia" (*LJ* 10). Jim took a berth as chief mate on the *Patna*, a steamship on the Indian Ocean. The ship "was owned by a Chinaman, chartered by an Arab, and commanded by a sort of renegade New South Wales German" (17). This very description speaks of the global feature of Conrad's novels. The story is based on a true tale Conrad might have heard in Singapore. In the month of July, 1880, a steamship named the *Jeddah* had departed from the Asian city of Singapore, with 953 pilgrims on board, bound for Mecca. But on the way, because of extremely foul weather, the captain and the engineers abandoned the ship, anticipating that it would sink. Surprisingly, the *Jeddah* was just lost, not sunk. It reached Aden with the passengers and the crew on board. This incident brought Conrad close to Asia, and he turned into a citizen of this continent as well when he started working on the novel, *Lord Jim.*

Lord Jim is a study in racism as well as colonialism. The binaries of white versus dark, right versus wrong, West versus East, and so on are there all along. By 1900, the year in which this novel was published, European nations and America had colonized almost the whole of Africa and Asia. The novel is thus steeped in the language of colonialism. Expressions like "apparelled in immaculate white" (9), "the white man" (212), "white lord" (253), "white from head to foot" (153), and "*them* meaning all of mankind with skins brown, yellow, or black in colour" (255) perfectly fit in with a colonial discourse. With Marlow's help, again, Jim took up a job in a remote district of a native-ruled state, known as Patusan, where he was trusted by the natives and obtained the title "Tuan Jim," or "Lord Jim." This very title opens up a discourse on racism, where a white is upheld as "Lord," superior to the natives. Jim fell in love with Jewel, an Eastern bride, part Asian and part European. When Jim chose to die, she cried in despair: "He has left me ... you [the white people] always leave us—for your own ends ... Ah! you are hard, treacherous, without truth, without compassion" (261–2). She voices the deprivation and the exploitation of the natives by the white colonizers.

The novel also deals with marginalizations of different kinds. Jim is first marginalized by the officials on board the *Patna*, and then, after the *Patna* incident, he goes into self-exile and chooses for himself a remote corner of the world to live in where there would be no discussion of the scandal. Marginalization is also there with respect to skin color. The novel speaks of industrialization as well: a steamship taking the place of a sailing ship and bringing about radical changes in the lives of the people. Jasanoff observes: "*Lord Jim* ruminated over values in crisis: the demise of the seafarer's craft in an age of steam" (2017: 145); as a result of industrialization, "hypocrisy, selfishness, and greed triumphed over honesty and hard work. Communities fractured. People broke promises" (Jasanoff 2017: 149). All the evils accompanying industrialization affected the common man. William Lee Hughes in his essay "(Post)colonial, Queer: *Lord Jim*" labels Jim a colonized figure instead of an agent of colonialism. Hughes also observes that Marlow's narration of Jim and Jim's story construct "a homosocial triangle" in which Jim becomes the apex that unites Marlow with his audience (2012: 71–83). Because of the themes of marginalization, industrialization, and colonialism, *Lord Jim* has been widely acclaimed. Marginalization on the basis of caste, class, and community is very common in India. Caste-based discrimination has been present in India since ancient times, and the Hindu caste system has been referred to even in the great Indian epics, *The Ramayana* and *The Mahabharata*. Al Biruni, a medieval writer, in his book *India* ([1988] 2018) also spoke of discrimination in Indian society on the basis of caste. Industrialization has been a major issue of debate since the nineteenth century. Even in the present century, there has been much debate surrounding the benefits of perpetuation of an agrarian economy versus an industry-based economy. India experienced colonialism for almost 200 years. Even after India gaining independence, colonial policies and system of administration still persisted. Because of all these issues *Lord Jim* has been very popular in India.

Nostromo (1904), recognized as "a work of genius" (Jasanoff 2017: 277), presents a prescient picture of the future world. Here, Conrad prophesied the dominance of the United States in the world economy and its economic imperialism. The novel predicts what we are actually experiencing now. With his visionary powers, Conrad anticipated the emergence of the United States as a superpower. Wilson Follett significantly remarks that Conrad in this novel created "the world in miniature" (1915: 58). The novelist takes us to the fictional world of Costaguana, but this is not a novel about a place where Conrad had been himself; rather, the novel describes every place Conrad had been to and in that way comprises Conrad's philosophy of the world and his vision of the future. Costaguana was a world created by the writer for his fiction. Until then Conrad had always given expression to his own experiences in different lands. This was the first time he created a completely fictional world. Jasanoff observes, "The invention of Costaguana was Conrad's declaration of independence as a writer" (2017: 245). *Nostromo* deals with what the reputed geographer Sir Halford Mackinder predicted and announced as the dawning of a new age in geopolitics. Jasanoff, while referring to Halford Mackinder, remarks, "For centuries, European powers had played out their ambitions in other parts of the world. Now, suddenly, the world was full up" (Jasanoff 2017: 279). There was "scarcely a region left for the pegging out of a claim of ownership" (Mackinder, qtd. in Jasanoff 2017: 279). Mackinder had earlier observed, "Other empires have had their day, and so may that of Britain… The European phase of history is passing away … and a new balance of power is being evolved" (Mackinder, qtd. in Jasanoff 2017: 281). *Nostromo* heralded the arrival of a new overseas empire, the United States, and marked the commencement of US imperialism.

The novel is about Italian immigrants in South America. Conrad relied on his close friend, Cunninghame Graham, for all the information on the settlements in Latin America. In the novel, Charles Gould has been based on his friend, Graham. The novel revolves around the story of Sam Tome silver mine, the inheritance of the mine by Charles Gould, and his efforts to modernize the mine so that it once again becomes profitable. Conrad introduces Nostromo, an Italian sailor who works as the head longshoreman for the shipping company. His original name is Gian' Battista Fidanza. The word *fidanza* means "trust." Gould places upon him the trust of safeguarding his silver mine. All consider him to be incorruptible. But the word "Nostromo" is also pronounced by the unsophisticated British people as "nostro uomo," meaning "our man" (*N* 36). Ironically, Nostromo turns into one of us as he takes the decision to keep the buried silver, not for Gould but for himself. The decision brings about his downfall. Nostromo emerges as a common man, with all the greed of a common man, and indeed he turns into "nostro uomo," an everyman guided by self-interest. Conrad made this novel a sequel to every other novel that he had written earlier: "By pouring his experiences from Europe, Asia, and Africa into Latin America, Conrad turned the past into prologue" (Jasanoff 2017: 257).

The novel exhibits two competing empires in respect of economic imperialism—Britain and America. The American mining magnate, Mr. Holroyd, into the making of whom all Europe had been blended—English, Danish, German, French, and Scottish—offers a "theory of the world's future." According to him, the Americans would sit and wait till all others get exhausted:

> There's no hurry. Time itself has got to wait on the greatest country in the whole of God's universe... some day we shall sleep in. We are bound to... We shall be giving the word for everything, industry, trade, law, journalism, art, politics, and religion... We shall run the world's business whether the world likes it or not. (*N* 62–3)

This very assertion of Conrad foresaw American imperialism of the twentieth and present centuries.

India has been a victim of this economic imperialism of the United States. Indian economy is largely dependent on American economy. There is always a threat of financial sanctions to be imposed on countries like India. The United States exercises its hegemony over all developing countries, including India. In spite of being a sovereign country, India looks to the United States for all major decisions related to its neighboring countries or other nations. Millions of Indians are working in US companies:

As of 2019, about 2.7 million Indian immigrants resided in the United States. Today, Indian immigrants account for approximately 6 percent of the U.S. foreign-born population, making them the second-largest immigrant group in the country, after Mexicans and ahead of immigrants from China and the Philippines. (Hanna and Batalova 2020)

These statistics show how Indians are dependent on the American economy. This dependence is what Conrad was able to foresee in his novel. Nostromo's turning into a common man also speaks of the average mentality of the people across all nations and times.

The novel that also speaks for the general concerns of the Indians and the diasporic people is *The Secret Agent* (1907), with its focus on terrorism, anarchism, violence, corruption, and anguish of a diasporic community as well as familial commitments. However, the issue that poses the most serious threat to the global community these days is definitely terrorism. After 9/11, there has been a growing concern with combating terrorism, both cross-border and internal, and protecting the lives of innocent people. Not just India, but almost all the countries of the world have been severely affected by terrorism. Conrad's novel theorizes terrorism and discusses at length various issues related to it—anarchism, politics, corruption, involvement of foreign embassies, concern about livelihood, and so on.

The novel is based in London, Conrad's haven. The traumatic experiences that he and his parents had to go through in Russia would never have occurred here in London. Apollo and Ewa, Conrad's parents, who were Polish patriots, were exiled to Vologda, in Siberia, together with their 5-year-old son, which left Conrad an orphan at the age of eleven, under the care of his grandmother. Jasanoff observes:

> London was the best place to disappear... There were no restrictions on who could come into the country: no passports or visas required, no need to prove that you had means of support. Nobody could be forced into military service. Nobody could be jailed merely for saying or writing something against the establishment. Nobody got extradited on political grounds. Freedom turned London into Europe's beachcomber, collecting refugees washed up by political change: Poles from the insurrection of 1830–31, Germans and Hungarians from 1848, Italians who'd fought alongside Garibaldi in the 1850s and '60s, French radicals from the Paris Commune of 1871, even France's ex-emperor Napoleon III. (Jasanoff 2017: 60)

Conrad found London to be a safe heaven and a haven for continental Europeans. He saw London through Charles Dickens's novels as he arrived in the city, his very idea of London shaped, especially, by *Bleak House* and *Nicholas Nickleby*. London as described by Conrad has dim light, mud, soot, and fog, as in Dickens's novels. Inspector Bucket in Dickens's *Bleak House* becomes Inspector Heat in Conrad's *The Secret Agent*. Conrad comments in *The Secret Agent*: "The vision of an enormous town presented itself, of a monstrous town more populous than some continents ... There was room enough there to place any story, depth enough for any passion, variety enough there for any setting, darkness enough to bury five millions of lives" (*SA* 10). The product was this novel, *The Secret Agent*. The novel is based on a historical fact, a failed attempt in February 1894, by Martial Bourdin, a Frenchman, an anarchist, and a member of the Autonomie Club, to blow up the Greenwich Observatory, an icon of science in Britain. By 1906, when Conrad started writing the novel, "anarchism had already become an anachronism" (Jasanoff 2017: 80). Although Conrad had "no idea to consider Anarchism politically," as he wrote to John Galsworthy on September 12, 1906 (*CL3* 354), and wanted his novel to be considered simply "the story of Winnie Verloc," or "a domestic drama, it acquired a political angle." *The Secret Agent* deals with the political interference of foreign embassies in engineering the explosion and the consequent death of Winnie's brother, Stevie, who was carrying the bomb that exploded near the Greenwich Observatory. The action was undertaken by anarchists to force the British Government to take firm and exemplary action against political activists—that is, socialists—operating in England, rather than allowing them to take refuge in England. Mr. Vladimir in the novel makes his mission very clear: "What we want is to administer a tonic to the Conference in Milan... Its deliberations upon international action for the suppression of political crime don't seem to get anywhere. England lags. This country is absurd with its sentimental regard for individual liberty" (*SA* 33). While talking to the under-secretary, the assistant commissioner says, "the existence of secret agents should not be tolerated" (117) and, again, "the existence of these people in the pay of foreign governments destroys in a measure the efficiency of our supervision" (118).

Through Mr. Verloc, an immigrant to England, Conrad brings into discussion the issue of free immigration and the experiences of diasporic people. The little shop that is mainly run by Verloc's wife, Winnie, is a testament to the hardship that the diasporic people have to go through in a foreign land. Toward the end, Verloc plans to leave the country and settle down either in France or California. His life, like that of any immigrant, is a tale of despair and hardship, familial duties, and loss of the charm of life. *The Secret Agent* speaks of the tragic irony in the life of the novelist himself. Born of Polish parents in the Ukraine when Poland did not formally exist on the map of Europe, "He'd adopted a country to which he could never fully belong, because he remained in certain ways an alien, and to some extent by choice… There's no place that's home" (Jasanoff 2017: 84). Verloc seems to echo this very diasporic experience of the author.

The issue of terrorism is definitely very pertinent to India. Since the 1960s, India has been seriously troubled with cross-border terrorism, with loss of innumerable lives and property. As many as 12,002 incidents of terrorism have occurred in India since 1970 ("Global Terrorism Database" 2018). A number of political assassinations, like that of Prime Minister Indira Gandhi or Rajiv Gandhi, can be related to what Mr. Vladimir says to Verloc in Conrad's novel: "An attempt upon a crowned head or on a president is sensational enough in a way, but not so much as it used to be… It's almost conventional—especially since so many presidents have been assassinated" (*SA* 35). He instructs Verloc to target the Greenwich Observatory as "science is at the source of their material prosperity… The demonstration must be against learning—science… The whole civilized world has heard of Greenwich" (36–7). This suggestion of Vladimir reminds us of 9/11 in America, when the Taliban terrorists targeted the Twin Towers of the World Trade Center in New York City. *The Secret Agent* thus remains a relevant text for both Indians and the global community.

Conrad has thus become an author relevant to readers across the globe. Academia in India has always found immense interest in studying his oeuvres, such as "Heart of Darkness," *Lord Jim*, *Nostromo*, and *The Secret Agent*, for their particular prescience: "He brought to the page a more international and multiethnic assortment of voices than any other writer of this day … Joseph Conrad was one of us; a citizen of a global world" (Jasanoff 2017: 12). Conrad was indeed a visionary whom every scholar of English literature in India, adores and admires.

References

Achebe, Chinua. 1977. "An Image of Africa: Racism in Conrad's *Heart of Darkness*." *Massachussetts Review* 18: 252–7.

Asaduddin, Mohd. 1988. "Cultural and Political Dimensions in Conrad's Major Novels." PhD Diss. Aligarh Muslim University. http://hdl.handle.net/10603/52700. Accessed October 15, 2020.

Bhuyan, Indrani Bora. 2018. "The Role of the Narrator in Selected Novels of Conrad, Melville and Bronte." PhD Diss. North-Eastern Hill University. http://hdl.handle.net/10603/194768. Accessed October 11, 2020.

Biruni-Al. [1988] 2018. *India*, edited by QeyamuddinAhmad. 2nd ed. New Delhi: National Book Trust. Accessed August 23, 2020.

Biswas, Suchismita. 1997. "A Study of Conrad's Novels as a Critique of Colonialism." PhD Diss. The University of Burdwan. http://hdl.handle.net/10603/65894. Accessed November 16, 2020.

Follett, Wilson. 1915. *Joseph Conrad: A Short Study*. Garden City, NY: Doubleday, Page & Co.

"Global Terrorism Database." 2018. National Consortium for the Study of Terrorism and Responses to Terrorism. University of Maryland. https://www.start.umd.edu/gtd. Accessed October 27, 2020.

Hanna, Mary, and Jeanne Batalova. 2020. "Indian Immigrants in the United States." https://www.migrationpolicy.org/article/indian-immigrants-united-states-2019. Accessed September 17, 2020.

Hughes, William Lee. 2012. "(Post)colonial, Queer: *Lord Jim*." *Conradiana* 44, no. 1 (March): 71–83.

Hulubandi, A. M. 2012. "Identity Crisis in the Select Novels of Joseph Conrad." PhD Diss. Karnatak University. http://hdl.handle.net/10603/8395. Accessed November 10, 2020.

Islam, Md Shirajul. 1981. "Self and Community in the Fiction of Joseph Conrad." PhD Diss. Panjab University. http://hdl.handle.net/10603/90475. Accessed October 12, 2020.

Jasanoff, Maya. 2017. *The Dawn Watch*. London: William Collins.

Jean-Aubry, G. 1927. *Joseph Conrad: Life and Letters*, vol. 2. London: William Heinemann Ltd.

Miller, J. Hillis. 2017. *Reading Conrad*, edited by John G. Peters and Jakob Lothe. Columbus: The Ohio University Press.

Mukherjee, Narugopal. 2017. "Joseph Conrad and E. M. Forster in Search of a Transcultural Space." *Yearbook of Conrad Studies(Poland)* 12: 159–72.

Phillips, Caryl. 2003. "Out of Africa." February 22, 2003. http://www.carylphillips.com/out-of-africa.html. Accessed August 15, 2020.

Raskin, Jonah. 1967. "Imperialism: Conrad's *Heart of Darkness*." *Journal of Contemporary History* 2, no. 2, Literature and Society (April): 113–31. http://www.jstor.org/stable/259954. Accessed October 14, 2020.

Ray, Subhadeep. 2011. "The Paradox of Redemption: A Study of Authority and Responsibility in Joseph Conrad's Novels." PhD Diss. University of Kalyani. http://hdl.handle.net/10603/210891. Accessed October 14, 2020.

Singh, Frances B. 1988. "The Colonialistic Bias of *Heart of Darkness*." In *Heart of Darkness: An Authoritative Text, Backgrounds and Sources, Criticism*, edited by Robert Kimbrough, 268–77. A Norton Critical Edition. Critical Editions Series. New York: Norton.

Srivastava, Anjana. 2014. "A Semiotic Study of the Journey Motif in Conrad's Tales." PhD Diss. Jawaharlal Nehru University. http://hdl.handle.net/10603/20987. Accessed November 10, 2020.

Part 3

Transtextual and Transcultural Politics

12

Transcultural Negotiations:
A Personal Record, "Prince Roman," and "The Warrior's Soul"

Robert Hampson
University of London

In May–June 1885, Conrad spent five days ashore in Cardiff and, having undertaken a commission from another Polish sailor, met the family of Władysław Spiridion Kliszczewski, a watchmaker and jeweler, who was an émigré from the November Uprising, the Polish-Russian War of 1830–1 (Jessie Conrad 1935: 46–7).[1] As Owen Knowles notes, his subsequent correspondence with Kliszczewski's son, Józef Spiridion, represents the earliest surviving examples of Conrad's written English (1989: 10). His responses to the copies of the *Daily Telegraph* and London *Evening Standard*, which Józef Spiridion sent him while he was at sea, have something of the stilted, formal quality of written exercises.[2] Thus, Conrad writes to him on October 3, 1885, from Singapore, expressing a sense of hopelessness about the Polish problem: "We have passed through the gates where '*lasciate ogni speranza*' is written in letters of blood and fire, and nothing remains for us but the darkness of oblivion" (*CL*1 12). In the same letter, he expresses his understanding and acceptance of Spiridion's statement about Britain as "home"—adding, as support: "When speaking, writing or thinking in English, the word 'home' always means for me the hospitable shores of Great Britain." The qualification "in English" is obviously important here, and that word "hospitable" repays attention: it signifies offering a welcome to a guest. The sentence simultaneously claims a sense of "home" and acknowledges the fact of not being at home. In this context, it is significant that, earlier in this paragraph, Conrad made this political observation: "I saw with pleasure the evidence of improved relations with Germany, the only power with whom an anti-Russian alliance would be useful—and even possible—for Great Britain"

(*CL1* 12). In writing about an anti-Russian alliance, it is not Great Britain that he is thinking of, primarily, but rather Poland and that submerged dream of Polish independence.[3] If "home" in English means Great Britain, Conrad and his correspondent are conscious of another language, another homeland, and another belonging. This chapter explores the transcultural negotiations that follow from that situation.

Conrad returned to Cardiff in December 1896, when he and Jessie spent their first married Christmas together as Józef Spiridion Kliszczewski's guests. During this ten-day visit, despite its "typically Polish" hospitality, Conrad got into an argument with his host, which led to a cooling in their relationship. According to Najder, the argument took place at dinner on Christmas Eve, when "the conversation turned to Polish matters" (1983: 203–4). Witold Chwalewik records that "the host addressed the guest, in English for he was not fluent in Polish, expressing his dearest wish, to see Conrad use his talent to glorify Poland's name and to depict in his novels the unhappiness of his native land." Conrad's response was annoyance: "Throwing up his arms he exploded, at first in French: '*Ah, mon ami, que voulez vous?* I would lose my public ….' " Chwalewik explains, or paraphrases Conrad's explanation: "He could not make a living by writing if he were to use it as a tool of propaganda. It would be impossible for him to write about Poland" (qtd. in Najder 1983: 204).[4]

At this point, Conrad had published his first two novels, *Almayer's Folly* and *An Outcast of the Islands*, and was struggling with the third part of this "Lingard Trilogy." He had gained a degree of critical esteem for his annexation of Malaysia for English fiction, a transcultural performance that critics were able to associate with the work of Rudyard Kipling, R. L. Stevenson, and Herman Melville.[5] However, he had not achieved financial success, and, with a new wife and the failure of the investment of his inheritance in South African gold mines in June of that year, Conrad was very conscious of the need to "make a living by writing." In this context, his touchiness on this point is understandable.

His sensitivity was perhaps increased by his consciousness of his failure with *The Sisters* , which he had put aside in March after criticism from Edward Garnett. As the story of a young Ruthenian painter who leaves home and his parents to find "a creed" in Western Europe, *The Sisters* was an attempt to draw directly on some aspects of Conrad's personal past, in particular the landscapes of his childhood (as Conrad's protagonist, Stephen, puts it, "The memory of his land is near the heart of an exile" [Conrad 1968: 43]). In Chwalewik's account, the impossibility of writing about Poland arises in part, Conrad implies, from a sense that his English readership would not be interested in Polish matters. This lack of interest in Poland from English readers contrasts with the readership Marguerita Poradowska found in France for a succession of novels set in Galicia, Podolia, or Ukraine. Indeed, her novel *Demoiselle Micia*, a romance set in a mining community in rural Ruthenian Poland, won a French Academy prize in 1890 (Jones 1999: 94). As for writing propaganda, Conrad makes clear his attitude toward didactic writing in "A Familiar Preface," where he refuses to "reprove mankind for what it is, or praise it for what it is not" (*PR* 14). However, there might also have been other, more personal reasons why writing about Poland was impossible for Conrad at this time.

In August 1908, when he had reached an impasse with *Under Western Eyes* ("I have it all in my head and yet when it comes to writing I simply can't find the words" [*CL4* 113]), Conrad was at last ready to confront his Polish past explicitly in his writing. Indeed, as Keith Carabine suggests, it was necessary for him to do this in order to resolve some of the issues (in particular, issues relating to his parents and their political activities) that he was confronting in writing *Under Western Eyes* (1996: 16, 129). In a letter to Pinker in October, Conrad described a "lucky concourse of circumstances" that would allow him to "make Polish life enter English literature" (*CL4* 138). The "psychological moment" and the publishing opportunity afforded by Ford Madox Ford's "new review" were part of this.[6] But Conrad was also conscious of his own cultural capital: his "literary reputation which seems more clearly defined with every published vol." was such that he now felt he had "enough substance to weigh favourably in the scale for the success of a *personal* book" (*CL4* 138; emphasis in original). What he aimed at was "to reveal a very particular state of society" and to "bring forward individuals with very special traditions" (*CL4* 138). In short, he was ready to place his own transcultural experience directly under the eyes of his British readers.

By the end of the year, he had written the first four chapters of *A Personal Record* and the draft of a story that would become "Prince Roman."[7] To enact the asserted continuity of his life across his different careers and across different geographical spaces, the first chapter of *A Personal Record* moves from writing a chapter of a novel set in Malaysia on board his last ship in Rouen harbor; through starting that first novel in furnished apartments in London and showing the novel in manuscript to his first reader on board the *Torrens en route* to Australia; via his last trip to Poland in 1893, which was also the last time he saw his uncle, Tadeusz Bobrowski; and then to a memory of his mother during their 1863 visit to Nowochwastów—a visit that, he realized retrospectively, was permitted because she was fatally ill. This implicit realization of "the tragic significance of it all" (*PR* 34) is made explicit when Conrad returns to this episode in chapter III, where he details her brutal treatment by the Governor General, who rejected the medical evidence put forward by the family and "signed the order" for her return to exile (*PR* 68). In chapter I, the brief account of his 1863 visit is simply followed by a reference to "the oppressive shadow of the great Russian Empire" (*PR* 34) that hangs over the memory. This first chapter is held together, not by memories of Poland, but rather by the travels of the manuscript of *Almayer's Folly* across numerous borders, which then provides another thread through subsequent chapters. The manuscript containing this transcultural narrative of Dutch, Sulus, and Arabs in Borneo itself becomes a mobile transnational object.[8]

The next two chapters of *A Personal Record* focus on Conrad's great uncle, Nicholas Bobrowski, an admirer of Napoleon Bonaparte, who began his military career as an officer in the French army. Chapter II focuses on his part in Napoleon's 1812 "Russian campaign" (*PR* 42) and the disastrous retreat of the Grande Armée from Moscow. Conrad tells how, "in the depths of the great Lithuanian forest," Nicholas Bobrowski and two fellow officers were so hungry that they ate a dog (*PR* 42). He offers the following summation of the story:

> He had eaten him to appease his hunger, no doubt, but also for the sake of an unappeasable and patriotic desire, in the glow of a great faith that lives still, and in the pursuit of a great illusion kindled like a false beacon by a great man to lead astray the effort of a brave nation. (*PR* 43)

Thus, in this comment on his great uncle, Conrad offers his judgment on Napoleon, on the Russian campaign, and on the hopes that many Poles placed on Napoleon as a potential liberator. At the same time, he also celebrates his great uncle's patriotism ("a great faith that lives still") against which his own career choices seem "a fatuous and extravagant form of self-indulgence" (*PR* 43).

In chapter III, Nicholas Bobrowski becomes the embodiment of loyalty to that faith during a specific period of Polish history:

> The first memories of Mr Nicholas B. might have been shaped by the events of the last partition of Poland, and he lived long enough to suffer from the last armed rising in 1863, an event which affected the future of all my generation and has coloured all my impressions. (*PR* 60)

In this chapter, Conrad recounts how Nicholas Bobrowski, after surviving the French Army's retreat from Moscow, next served in "the army of the newly-constituted Polish kingdom," Congress Poland, created in 1815 by the Congress of Vienna, "under the sceptre of Alexander I, Autocrat of all the Russians" (*PR*

58). However, as Conrad observes, the Polish Army "took no part in the wars of the Russian Empire either against Persia or Turkey": "Its first campaign, against Russia itself, was to be its last" (*PR* 59). This was the November Uprising, the Polish-Russian War of 1830–1. At the first news of the uprising, Bobrowski was arrested and exiled, for the next three years, to Astrakhan. His subsequent life of quiet retirement, first in his brother's house and then as tenant of a friend's estate, was disrupted by the outbreak of the 1863 January Uprising. A squadron of Cossacks invaded the house, which was then ransacked by the local peasantry, who smashed everything (furniture, mirrors, glasses, china) and made a bonfire of the books and papers. His life of faithful service in two armies, which had earned him both the French Legion of Honor and the Polish Cross for Valor, was rewarded also with exile and the destruction of his home.

Conrad ends by recounting his sole meeting with his great uncle, during that 1863 visit to Nowochwastów with his mother: "The little child a few months old he had taken up in his arms on the day of his home-coming after years of war and exile was confessing her faith in national salvation by suffering exile in her turn" (*PR* 65). From his great uncle through to his mother, "faith in national salvation" is repaid with exile and suffering. Nor are Conrad's great uncle and mother exceptional in their commitment to Polish independence: "My paternal grandfather's two sons and his only daughter were all deeply involved in the revolutionary work; he himself was of that type of Polish squire whose only ideal of patriotic action was to 'get into the saddle and drive them out!'" (*PR* 61). In these two chapters, with the foregrounded narrative of his great uncle (and the secondary narrative of his mother), Conrad represents something of "the unhappiness of his native land" as Józef Spiridion Kliszczewski had demanded. At the same time, other details also gesture toward this larger picture: in particular, there is the implied but untold history behind the reference to Tadeusz Bobrowski's role as "guardian of many orphans of land-owning families" since 1860 (*PR* 33).

As noted above, "Prince Roman" was produced from material originally intended for *A Personal Record*, but it was not included in that volume.[9] It was not written until 1910 and not collected in Conrad's lifetime. This, too, is a story marked by the 1830–1 Polish-Russian War. Indeed, it begins with a Polish narrator recalling "the year 1831" as "one of those fatal years" when "we had once more to murmur '*Vae Victis*' and count the cost in sorrow," although he adds, "That's a lesson we could never learn" (*TH* [D] 29). He summons up that history of uprisings and defeats as a result of which "our enemies ... have bestowed upon us the epithet of Incorrigible" (*TH* [D]29), and he describes "Polish nationality" (in the idiom Conrad used for "Autocracy and War") as "that nationality not so much alive as surviving, which persists in thinking, breathing, speaking, hoping, and suffering in its grave, railed in by a million of bayonets and triple-sealed with the seals of three great empires" (*TH* [D] 29).

The story of Prince Roman begins with his marriage, in 1828, when he was an officer in the Russian Imperial Guards. However, his happiness is short-lived: his wife falls ill, and he takes unlimited leave from the Russian Court to move with her back to her "native land" (*TH* [D] 36). After her death, he finds solace in riding through "this countryside where he had been born and had spent his happy boyish years" (*TH* [D] 38). Conrad evokes this countryside—"every slight rise crowned with trees amongst the ploughed fields, every dell concealing a village," and, far away to the north, "the great Lithuanian forest" (*TH* [D]38). The landscape of childhood and the affections attached to it, which had featured in *The Sisters*, become the sensuous basis of, or accompaniment to, Prince Roman's patriotism. At the same time, the portrait of the invalid wife, "thin and pale in the great armchair," and the inconsolable grieving husband inevitably recall Conrad's own childhood, while the Prince's love for "this familiar landscape associated with the days without thought and without sorrow" (*TH* [D] 38) is also reminiscent of Conrad's account, in *A Personal Record*, of his 1893 coach ride across "the Ukrainian plain" and the palimpsestic memories of the travels of his childhood (*PR* 33). The narrator, with his maternal family roots in "the southern provinces" and his memory of "a cold brilliant sun … low above an undulating horizon of great folds of snow in which the villages of Ukrainian peasants remained out of sight" (*TH* [D] 31), literally echoes Conrad's account of his own later coach ride. Like the Bobrowskis and Korzeniowskis, the narrator seems to be from a borderland *szlachta* family.

When Prince Roman encounters a train of carts full of soldiers "under the escort of mounted Cossacks" and then hears from a patriotic Jewish innkeeper that "all the landowners great and small are out in arms and even the common people have risen," he immediately resigns his commission in the Guards and joins the 1831 uprising as a common soldier (*TH* [D] 38, 39). After the defeat of the uprising, when he faces a military commission, the Prince refuses the line of defense offered to him and makes the written testimony, "I joined the national rising from conviction" (*TH* [D] 52).[10] As a result, he is "condemned for life" in the Siberian mines. There are obvious parallels between Prince Roman and Nicholas Bobrowski. However, where Nicholas Bobrowski is, in the words Conrad applied to his father in his final days, "a vanquished man" (*PR* 7), Prince Roman remains unbowed. He survives the death of his wife and what was clearly intended to be "a sentence of deferred death," since "very few survived entombment in these mines for more than three years" (*TH* [D] 53). After three years, he is permitted "to serve as a common soldier in the Caucasus," but with "no civil rights" (*TH* [D] 53). He presumably served in the Caucasian Wars of 1817–64, in which Russia engaged in the invasion and annexation of the North Caucasus.[11] Twenty-five years after his sentence was passed, Prince Roman is allowed to "return to Poland" (*TH* [D] 53), broken in health. However, unlike Nicholas Bobrowski, Prince Roman "did not shut himself up as if his work were done" (*TH* [D] 53). Instead, he devotes himself to "his fellow citizens": "There was hardly anything done in the private and public life of the neighbourhood, in which Prince Roman's advice and assistance were not called upon" (*TH* [D] 54). He becomes an exemplary figure of civic virtue, "always guided by a simple wisdom, a high sense of honour, and the most scrupulous conception of private and public probity" (*TH* [D] 54).

In these contrasting portraits of representatives of an older generation whom he had met briefly as a child, Conrad presents the traditions of the *szlachta*, the class into which he was born, and, in particular, the culture of the borderland *szlachta* between the third partition of Poland in 1795, after the defeat of the Kościuszko Uprising, and the 1863 January Uprising.[12] He presents a culture that placed value on military courage, on civic duty, and on honor in public and private life. It is shown to be a culture that is both patriotic and cosmopolitan. While Conrad foregrounds the patriotic element, it is clear that the three partitions necessitated contact with Russian, Prussian, and Austrian political cultures as a minimum, and Conrad's narratives specifically mention service in the French, Russian, and Austrian armies. Like Conrad's uncle, Stanisław Bobrowski, Prince Roman served in the Russian Imperial Guards, while the account of Nicholas Bobrowski's career mentions "a relative of ours who happened to be an Austrian officer" (*PR* 55). Meanwhile, Nicholas Bobrowski, himself, testifies to the special place of French culture for this class. French is acquired as a second language, and, indeed, the narrative of Nicholas Bobrowski's service in Napoleon's Grande Armée ends with Conrad's own acquisition of French.[13] As he prepares to leave the country estate in Nowochwastów to return to exile with his mother, various relations, friends, and servants gather to say farewell. These include Mlle Durand, the governess: "In three months, simply by playing with us, she had taught me not only to speak French but to read it as well" (*PR* 66). This borderland *szlachta* culture was reinforced for Conrad by his reading of the Polish Romantic poets Adam Mickiewicz, Juliusz Słowacki, and Zygmunt Krasiński during his years of exile with his father.[14] In these two stories of patriots of an older generation, as in *The Sisters* and *Under Western Eyes*, Conrad brought his memories of the

Polish landscape and Polish Romanticism into English literature. In recounting these narratives with their complex transcultural loyalties, Conrad finally made "Polish life enter English literature" (*CL4* 138), matching his own movement across borders.

* * *

Were Conrad's earlier anxieties about losing his public justified? Despite its "fragmentary" and "wilfully discursive" form, the British critics were almost unanimous in their praise of *A Personal Record* (*CR3* 13–70, 27, 34). As Richard Niland notes, the years 1912–17 mark "the zenith" of Conrad's critical and popular appeal in Britain during his lifetime (*CR3* 1). Certainly, the reviews of *A Personal Record* make clear Conrad's recognized position as "one of the best of living novelists and writers of English" (*CR3* 31). They acknowledge the book's "background of Polish patriotism" (*CR3* 25) and respond positively to his picture of "unhappy Poland," commenting not only on "the atmosphere of Russian terror and domestic kindliness in which his childhood was spent" (*CR3* 22), but also on the "stirring scenes of a Poland struggling for freedom" (*CR3* 47). The reviewer in *The Scotsman*, perhaps with another independence struggle in mind, noted Conrad's presentation of "the traditions of a family which had contributed more than one martyr to the cause of Polish nationalism" (*CR3* 54). The popular reception is harder to gauge. As Niland notes, up to this point, Conrad's works had achieved "high esteem" but "low sales" (*CR3* 2). A number of reviewers referred to the general reader. One commented that "Mr Conrad's readers will have formed their own opinion of Mr Conrad long ago," and Conrad's reminiscences would help "make those opinions a little more accurate and complete" (*CR3* 30). Another, however, admonished Conrad for his disregard for narrative in *A Personal Record*, advising that "no writer for the public ... can wisely spurn the humbler rules of composition and arrangement" (*CR3* 25). Richard Curle, in his generally perceptive review for the *Manchester Guardian*, noted that "there will always be people temperamentally incapable of appreciating Mr Conrad" and explained why: "He is queerly unEnglish" (*CR3* 33). The reviewer in the *Glasgow News* took the opportunity of the publication of Conrad's reminiscences and directly addressed the question "why Conrad, although one of the greatest—perhaps the greatest—living writer of English prose, is relatively unpopular" (*CR3* 43). The reviewer clarified what they meant by "relatively unpopular:" "Conrad is still utterly unknown to that public which rejoices in Correlli and Caine ... Yet there is a section of the reading public which long ago recognised with eager delight that a new master had arisen in English literature" (*CR3* 42–3). The reviewer attributes

Conrad's relative unpopularity "in great part to his virtues, to his calm, austere, dignity of attitude, to his restraint of emotion … to the incessant pressure of an intellect which had passed far beyond the commonplaces of average thought" (*CR3* 42–3). As for Conrad's Polishness, this reviewer relates that to Conrad's "pessimism:" "the sober resignation of a man who is profoundly impressed by the futility of most human ambitions" (*CR3* 44). He derives this attitude from Conrad's "tragic remembrance of blighted hopes, of omnipotent oppression, of endless suffering and dumb humiliation" (*CR3* 44–5)—in short, precisely "the unhappiness of his native land." It is necessary to add, in this context, Conrad's own observation: "resignation is not indifference" (*PR* 14).

The reviewer in the *Athenaeum* raises another consideration. They note Conrad's "distinction," but also the absence, in *A Personal Record*, of the "indiscretion which makes for popularity" (*CR3* 33). It is possible to glimpse, in other reviews too, the sense that Conrad did not play the game expected of novelists as public figures. The reviewer in the *Westminster Gazette*, for example, referred to the public's "pardonable curiosity concerning a great writer" (*CR3* 35). Percival Gibbon, in his review for *The Bookman*, more fully invokes the public world touched on here, when he asserts, "No writer has taken the paragraphist less into his confidence, or served so little the purpose of the interviewer and the press photographer" (*CR3* 63). This recalls the new professional world of popular journalism with its paragraphs, interviews, and photographers that Henry James attacks in stories like "The Death of the Lion" and "The Papers," "this age of advertisements and newspaperism, this age of interviewing," in which artists are cultivated for their celebrity, while their art is ignored (Matthiessen and Murdock 1961: 148). By contrast, Gibbon describes *A Personal Record* as "a book which so handsomely makes a guest of the reader who has hitherto been no more than an acquaintance" (*CR3* 63), replacing the contemporary modes of the commodification of literature that James attacks with an older model of hospitality. Interestingly, the Conrad who earlier had presented himself as a guest arriving at "the hospitable shores of Great Britain" has, in *A Personal Record*, become the host through this opening up of his Polish past to his British readers. His own border crossing has been reversed in this invitation to his readers. Indeed, Gibbon had first enjoyed Conrad's hospitality in June 1909, while Conrad was completing *A Personal Record*, and Curle, who had reviewed *A Personal Record* in February 1912, was to begin his friendship with Conrad in November of that year.

"Prince Roman" was collected in the posthumous volume, *Tales of Hearsay*. In his preface, Cunninghame Graham described it as "the only one of all his tales in which he deals directly with the country of his birth" (*TH* [D] x), and, after quoting the opening paragraph, asserted that "in every word there breathes the spirit of the Polish patriot, the burning sense of wrong" (*TH* [D] xi). Many of the reviewers followed this lead, often repeating Cunninghame Graham's words verbatim (*CR4* 418–87).[15] The volume was generally well-received, and "Prince Roman" was much praised: "one of the most august and moving pieces in the great novelist's gallery" (*CR4* 436). The other tale that was regularly praised by these reviewers was "The Warrior's Soul," another story of the Grande Armée's retreat from Moscow: "the finest story in the book" (*CR4* 424); "one of the best things Conrad ever did" (*CR4* 426); one of "the great short stories of the language" (*CR4* 427). Later criticism has been less kind, and the stories in this final volume have been largely neglected. If there was a British readership for these tales in 1928, there has not been one since the Anglo-American academic revival of interest in Conrad after the Second World War.

Together with "Prince Roman," "The Warrior's Soul" was commended for "the rendering of the spirit of one people into the language of another" (*CR4* 454). However, "The Warrior's Soul" is not about Poles and Poland: the narrator and the central figure in "The Warrior's Soul" are both Russians. So far, I have been writing about Conrad's attempt to "make Polish life enter English literature." "The Warrior's Soul" raises a different issue with its sympathetic presentation of its Russian narrator and protagonist. The narrator, an old cavalry officer, describes his part in "the great rout of the Grand Army" (*TH* [D] 3) and then introduces the story of his subaltern, the young Tomassov. Tomassov had been attached to the Russian mission in Paris, where he fell in love with a French lady, whose salon he attended, and was saved from arrest at the outbreak of war between France and Russia by advance warning from an older French officer, de Castel. As Edward Garnett suggests in his review, the contrast between the "brilliant, accomplished man of the world" that Tomassov admires in Paris (*CR4* 451) and the "grotesque horror of rags and dirt" (*TH* [D] 23) whom he takes prisoner is the affective heart of the story. De Castel begs Tomassov to shoot him—and makes his appeal through various transnational bonds: as "a fellow soldier," as "a humane man," and through the code of honor (*TH* [D] 2–3, 25). The "humane Tomassov" (which was the working title for the story) puts the Frenchman out of his misery, is criticized for "the shooting of a prisoner in cold blood," and retires to his home province "where a vague story of some dark deed clung to him for years" (*TH* [D] 26).

Conrad's understandable hostility to Russia is well established. In 1899, for example, when Cunninghame Graham invited Conrad to join him on the platform of a Social Democratic Federation meeting in London, designed to counter the Tzar's call for an international conference of heads of state, he famously turned down the invitation in part because "*Il y aura des Russes*" (*CL2* 158): he would have to share the platform with Russians. Less often remarked is that he did go to the meeting to hear Cunninghame Graham speak. Similarly, in *The Secret Agent*, with its covert tracing of Conrad's own visits to the Russian embassy in Chesham Square for release from his Russian subjecthood, the negative portrayal of Mr. Vladimir, with his "Hyperborean manners" (*SA* 25), is qualified at the end by the revelation of his "inherited weakness" when confronted by the Assistant Commissioner, the product of his descent "from generations victimized by the instruments of an arbitrary power" (*SA* 169). As Arthur Waugh affirms, in his review, there is "a nobler sentiment yet than love of country, and that is love for one's fellow men" (*CR4* 424), and this is what "The Warrior's Soul" asserts. The story was written at the start of 1916. Garnett's review notes that Conrad had been brooding over "war's fatalities" at the time, but that brooding had really started with the mass slaughter of the Russo-Japanese War (cf. Hampson 2014). In his brooding over modern warfare, Conrad could extend his sympathies to this young Russian subaltern and his humane bond with a French officer during the Napoleonic campaign. Where Conrad's Russian narrator feels compassion when he contemplates the "long, long trail of frozen corpses" left by the retreating army ("They were Frenchmen. We didn't hate them; they didn't hate us" [*TH* [D] 20]), in this story, at least, Conrad could consider the humanity of "*Des Russes sauvages*" (*TH* [D] 5), while never surrendering his active promotion, at precisely this period of his life, of an independent Poland. Conrad's engagement in transnational politics, as the active expression of his sustained loyalty to Poland, coincides with his arrival at "that spirit of piety towards all things human" that he had argued, in *A Personal Record*, sanctioned the "imaginative and exact rendering of authentic memories" (*PR* 35).

Notes

1 Jessie gives the sailor's name as Komorowski. Jessie also provides an account of the Christmas Eve argument. I am grateful to Laurence Davies for advice and information about this family.

2 Najder observes that "many sentence fragments" in this letter "suggest that the writer's thoughts ran along the lines of Polish syntax and phraseology" (1983: 86).

3 Compare with "Autocracy and War," where the analysis of international politics again has a concealed Polish center.

4 It is interesting that, on this "typically Polish" occasion, Józef Spiridion Kliszczewski, who was born in Wales and had a Welsh mother, expressed his "dearest wish" in English and that Conrad's immediate emotional response found its voice in French.

5 See the reviews of *Almayer's Folly* in *The Daily News*, *The Spectator*, and *The Bookman* (*CR1* 13, 47, 54).

6 One contributing factor to this psychological moment was the criticism he had received from Robert Lynd, which had described him as a man "without country or language" (*CR2* 446–8). See also Conrad's letters to Edward Garnett (August 21, 1908) and to John Galsworthy (August 23, 1908), in which he repeats this phrase, which had clearly stung him (*CL4* 106–9, 110–11).

7 *A Personal Record* (1923). These essays were first published in England as *Some Reminiscences*. The American title, *A Personal Record*, was used for the collected editions and has become the accepted name for the volume.

8 For a fuller account of this opening chapter of *A Personal Record*, see Robert Hampson (2017–18).

9 It is based on the story of Prince Roman Sanguszko (1800–81), whom Conrad met as a child. Conrad was drawing on Tadeusz Bobrowski's *Memoirs*.

10 Verloc, in *The Secret Agent*, is a double agent working against revolutionaries "from conviction," as is Sevrin in "The Informer" (*SoS* 97). This is the first time in Conrad's works that the phrase is used to justify acting against those in power. Conrad was clearly fascinated, in this period, by those who could act politically "from conviction."

11 Russia was at war with Turkey (1828–9) and with Persia (1826–8); after 1833, Russia renewed military activities in North Caucasus for a further twenty years.

12 For more on Conrad and *szlachta* culture, see G. W. Stephen Brodsky (2013: 19–71).

13 For Conrad, this was probably his third language—after the Ukrainian he probably used to speak with servants (much as Kipling would have used Hindi in his everyday life as a child).

14 There is no space in the present article to consider their presence in "Prince Roman."

15 See, for example, Arthur Waugh's review in the *Daily Telegraph* (*CR4* 423–4).

References

Brodsky, G. W. Stephen. 2013. "The Dispossessed: Joseph Conrad as Borderland Writer." In *From Szlachta Culture to the 21st Century: New Essays on Joseph Conrad's*, edited by Wiesław Krajka, 19–71. Boulder, CO: East European Monographs.

Carabine, Keith. 1996. *The Life and the Art: A Study of Conrad's* Under Western Eyes. Amsterdam: Rodopi.

Conrad, Jessie. 1935. *Joseph Conrad and His Circle*. London: Jarrolds.

Conrad, Joseph. 1968. *The Sisters*. Milan: Mursia.

Hampson, Robert. 2014. "Conrad, the 'Polish Problem' and Transnational Activism." *Conradiana* 46 (Spring/Summer): 21–38.

Hampson, Robert. 2017–18. "'Books may be written in all sorts of places': Conrad's Transnational Beginnings." *L'Epoque Conradienne* 41: 29–40.

Jones, Susan. 1999. *Conrad and Women*. Oxford: Oxford University Press.

Knowles, Owen. 1989. *A Conrad Chronology*. London: Macmillan.

Matthiessen, F. O., and Kenneth B. Murdock, eds. 1961. *The Notebooks of Henry James*. New York: Galaxy Books.

Najder, Zdzisław. 1983. *Joseph Conrad: A Chronicle*. Cambridge: Cambridge University Press.

13

Rereading *Under Western Eyes* from the Polish Perspective

Joanna Skolik
University of Opole

It frequently transpires that, while accepting Joseph Conrad's Polish background and heritage, Western Conradians wonder why Polish researchers still attach such great importance to it. If Conrad's Polish origin is neither rejected nor questioned, what is the reason for repeating the facts and details from his childhood and youth over and over again? Why do Polish scholars endlessly return to "the oppressive shadow of the great Russian Empire" (*PR* 34), identifying it in almost every work of Conrad's, instead of focusing on his artistry and imagery, and why is Conrad's Polishness so important for them when reading his novels and tales? I will endeavor to answer these questions by rereading *Under Western Eyes* along with its various interpretations, focusing on its main protagonist Razumov. I hope I will also be able to show why, in view of Poland's history as well as Conrad's own life story, it is impossible for Polish scholars to accept some Western interpretations of this Conrad novel.[1]

As pointed out by Zdzisław Najder, despite the fact that currently no Western researchers question the role that the Polish tradition and culture had on Conrad, sometimes it is vital "to explain certain cultural and intellectual categories to the English-speaking reader who, while understanding the language, is not always able to grasp the implicit meanings" (2007: ix):

> Still, there are attempts to understand Conrad's behaviour and the opinions he expressed in the same categories that are applied to other English novelists of the late 19th and early 20th century … Sometimes, critics who know something about the existence of the Polish element in the life and work of Conrad, but are only superficially familiar with Polish history, "explain" various mysterious facts according to the Latin formula of translating *obscurum per obscurius*, the

mysterious through the even more mysterious, referring to the "Slavicness" of
the writer. (2006: 9–10; author's own translation)

To understand Conrad's attitude toward Russia and Russian matters, it is
necessary to understand the Polish history of the time. This is why it is important
to remember Najder's words about the role that Polish components played in
Conrad's life and letters: "not as elements of local colour but those that allow
to better understand the writer's life and throw a 'fresh light' on his works …
not marginal or the secret key to it all but a legitimate part of the richness and
complexity of [his] life and oeuvres" (2006: 10; author's own translation).

Poland, known as the Polish-Lithuanian Commonwealth, was once the
largest country in Europe (1569–1795); yet it disappeared from the world's
maps in 1795 (for the next 123 years) with the third partition of Poland, when
the three neighboring countries, Russia, Prussia, and Austria, divided Poland's
territory among themselves. When Conrad was born in 1857, Poland existed
only as a spiritual phenomenon, a phantom, or a memory. On the territories
of the Russian partition, a very restrictive policy of russification had been
introduced, with harsh repressions and persecutions (especially following the
1830 November Uprising) involving forfeiture of property (belonging to the
Polish nobility), banning the Polish language from schools and offices, and
destroying Polish culture and any traces of patriotism.

For the first seventeen years of his life, literally from his very birth, on the
one hand, Conrad experienced his parents' absolute love and support from their
friends and family, and on the other hand, he witnessed the victimization of his
family and his compatriots by the tzarist authorities and went through the fear
and toils of exile. What lay at the core of all Conrad's traumas and torments was
the Russian state's policy and attitude toward anything Polish and all Poles—
namely, "the oppressive shadow of the great Russian Empire."

When Conrad left Poland (or rather its former territory) at the age of
seventeen, his personality, character, and worldview had already been shaped,
and he (as can be seen in his letters, utterances, and works) could not accept
either the Russian Empire or anything connected with Russia. He left his
motherland not only because he wanted to live an adventurous life, or because
he was a nuisance to his grandmother or uncle, but also because, if he had stayed,
as a son of an insurrectionist and Siberian convict, he would have been drafted
into the Russian army for many years. Later, when he started his maritime career
in Marseilles, "the great Russian Empire" again cast its "oppressive shadow" over
his life. As a Russian subject (he was born in the Russian part of the former

Polish-Lithuanian Commonwealth), he had to obtain special permission from the Russian consul to leave the country, for he was still supposed to serve in the Russian army.

Conrad's negative attitude toward Russia (presented throughout all his life in his letters, conversations with his friends and family, or his behavior at various public events), along with the trauma connected with writing *Under Western Eyes* when he was overwhelmed with the memories of the past, show the thin line of the researcher's freedom of interpretation related to that very book (particularly looking from the Polish perspective). Various Western interpretations of *Under Western Eyes* involve numerous aspects of the novel: the psychological insight in presenting the Russian reality, its connections with Dostoevsky's *Crime and Punishment*, the understanding of Conrad's protagonists and their conduct, narrative structure (multiple perspectives, unreliable narrator[s], etc.), irony, Conrad's attitude to women, and so on (cf. Knowles and Moore 2000: 382–6). All these interpretations are accepted as valid and are appreciated by Polish Conradians as long as they align with the writer's values connected with his Polish cultural heritage. If a contradiction occurs, Polish researchers refer to Conrad's Polish legacy, questioning the validity of such interpretations.

It should be remembered that Conrad's reception in Poland has been shaped by the special place that Conrad holds in Polish culture: in Nazi-occupied Poland (1939–45), he became a spiritual guide for the young generation, helping them to survive the horrors of the war and occupation. After the Second World War, Conrad's works were banned by the Polish communist authorities with the aim of committing them to oblivion (his works were perceived as dangerous and subversive because of their moral message of respect for human dignity and individuality). The experience of communism made Polish scholars especially sensitive to Conrad's message expressed in his Author's Note to *Under Western Eyes*: "Those people were unable to see that all they can effect is merely a change of names. The oppressors and the oppressed are all Russians together; and the world is brought once more face to face with the truth of the saying that the tiger cannot change his stripes nor the leopard his spots" (*UWE* 7). Conrad's words also describe the writer's attitude toward "the very soul of things Russian" (*CL2* 695), from which perspective it is hard for Polish researchers to accept one of the interpretations related to the main character of the novel, Kyrilo Sidorovitch Razumov: that is, a perception of his betrayal as "an expression of Conrad's own guilt at having abandoned his native country and language" (Knowles and Moore 2000: 385), an interpretation that has been proposed, for example, by

Gustav Morf (1929) and Keith Carabine (1996), the last of which I would like to discuss here in greater detail.[2]

Similarly to the old language teacher and the narrator of the novel, Razumov has inspired numerous interpretations. As the illegitimate son of Prince K and an archpriest's daughter, he has no other experience of family relationships than the financial support of his father: Razumov is "officially and in fact without a family" (*UWE* 16). Because of his background (and his status of an illegitimate child), he is forced to fight for his position in society. Razumov realizes that only an official certificate can enable him to obtain noble status and thus become a member of the upper class. He thinks that if there is nothing "secret or reserved" in his life (14), he can achieve what he has planned, but he does not reckon with the Russian autocracy. He behaves as if he lived in a state that offers "the prospect of an orderly ascent of the professional ladder" (Berthoud 1978: 171). His life is lived in his imagination. He does not want to admit that Russia is "a country where an opinion may be a legal crime visited by death or sometimes by a fate worse than mere death" (*UWE* 13). He sees himself as a man with a mind—rational and down-to-earth. Just when Razumov assumes that he is able to shape his own life and does not foresee anything unexpected, Victor Haldin appears in his rooms saying, "It was I who removed de P—this morning." Razumov's reaction to this is, "There goes my silver medal!" (20). His imagination starts racing, and he allows it to govern his conduct: "He saw himself deported by an administrative order, his life broken, ruined, and robbed of all hope" (24). He decides to help Haldin because he is terrified. He wants to rid himself of the revolutionary. At the beginning of the novel, "Razumov sincerely and honestly identifies himself with the State"; however, "His sympathy with autocracy is not as definite at this moment as it will be after he meets Ziemianitch" (Hay 1963: 294). When it turns out that Ziemianitch—the only person who could help Haldin—fails, Razumov finds another solution. His "only parentage"—Russia—shows him which direction he ought to take. Razumov decides to betray Haldin, without realizing that he is deluding himself. He convinces himself in his own mind: "Betray. A great word. What is betrayal? They talk of a man betraying his country, his friends, his sweetheart. There must be a moral bond first. All a man can betray is his conscience" (*UWE* 36). He does not realize that Haldin has created a moral bond between them by entrusting him with his own safety. Razumov tries to justify and rationalize his deed. He seeks approval and moral support, which he needs desperately, as "no human being could bear a steady view of moral solitude without going mad" (37). He finds support in the person of Prince K, who tells him that "nobody doubts the moral soundness of your action" (13).

Unlike Conrad's readers, Razumov does not notice the evident ambiguity and irony in General T-'s words when the latter says, "My existence has been built on fidelity. It's a feeling. To defend it I am ready to lay down my life—and even my honour—if that were needed" (*UWE* 46). Razumov follows in General T-'s footsteps by trying to build his existence on his "fidelity" to the state, which has obliged him to betray a man who trusted him. However, Razumov cannot persuade himself that he is not responsible for Haldin's death. After Haldin leaves the room, he tries to work, but he is unable to read, or even think about his essay. The betrayal leads to the disintegration of Razumov's personality and life. He finds that though he tries hard, he cannot get back to his daily routine. The broken watch reminds him that time—the time of his life—has stopped.

> Razumov sets down his creed:
> History not Theory.
> Patriotism not Internationalism.
> Evolution not Revolution.
> Direction not Destruction.
> Unity not Disruption. (*UWE* 57)

He writes down the values to which he decides to remain loyal and that are the opposite of Haldin's ideals. In the reality of Russia, however—and in such circumstances—these words are nothing but a sham. Razumov lists history first, but it is impossible to gain any advantage from history in a country where history is "inconceivable." Describing Russia, the narrator says that "the snow covered the endless forests, the frozen rivers ... levelling everything under its uniform whiteness, like a monstrous blank page awaiting the record of inconceivable history" (*UWE* 33). Moreover, its pages are blank because "the Russian citizen has not been left free to inscribe his action upon it" (Berthoud 1978: 173). History must be created by people who love their country and who are devoted to it—not by people who are threatened or forced to serve. Patriotism—as understood by the state officials—is nothing more than servility to autocratic institutions. No evolution is possible, because even the slightest change is treated as an attack on the edifice of the state. Administration means absolute submission to the state directives and prohibitions. Unity cannot be achieved in a country ruled by fear and terror. Thus Razumov's creed, instead of "proving" his patriotic convictions, is ironic and ambiguous. The reader knows that the creed merely serves to justify Razumov's betrayal and that he writes it in a desperate bid to protect his own self-image. It is nothing more than self-delusion and wishful thinking.

Avram Fleishman argues that Razumov's creed is also Conrad's profession of faith and that it is not only "an anti-revolutionary utterance, but also an anti-individualistic one. The philosophy that stands behind each of its values is that of the organic state, evolution through history in the direction of patriotic unity." Fleishman claims that both men—that is, Conrad and his hero—want "to separate themselves from ... the liberal individualism of the West, which minimizes the communal life of men and from the populist revolutionism of Russia, which pushes the theory of organism into mysticism and terrorism" (1967: 228).

According to Carabine, Razumov's political creed can be read as Conrad's attempt "to balance the competing ideological traditions of his Polish heritage in relation to the painful accusations of betrayal he endured." One might agree with these opinions concerning Razumov's creed, were it not for the fact that it is written just after he has betrayed Haldin—and were it also not for the fact that Razumov does not live in a democratic country—that is, in a country where there is no contradiction between morality and legality and where "political institutions are justified by ethical principles and ethical principles substantiated by political institutions" (Carabine 1996: 122). Neither Fleishman nor Carabine takes into account the circumstances in which the creed is professed. As they stand in the book, Razumov's words appear to be derisive.

Quoting Conrad's words from *A Personal Record*, Carabine reminds us that the author "remains to a certain extent, a figure behind the veil, a suspected rather than seen presence—a movement and a voice behind the draperies of fiction" (Carabine 1996: 12). The critic goes on to explain:

> I attempt to locate the inner story and to disclose the figure behind the veil in Razumov's naming and in all of his various writings—his prize essay, his political confession of faith, his spy report, his final written confession to Natalia, and his personal record—all of which intimately intertwine with Conrad's own life and authorship. (Carabine 1996: 98)

However, the idea that Razumov might be Conrad's surrogate is hardly credible. From a historical point of view, it even appears ridiculous. The affinities between Conrad and Razumov that are described by Carabine appear to be illusory. Indeed, on a closer inspection, the two seem to have nothing in common at all. Carabine says,

> Razumov, like his creator, is an "orphan" who believes his "closest parentage" is "defined" by his nationality: and his conviction that "whatever good he expected

from life, would be given to or withheld from his hopes by that connection alone" … can be read as a secular version of Korzeniowski's messianic definition for his son of what it is to "Be a Pole!" (1996: 100)

There does not seem to be much point in comparing Razumov's and Conrad's heritage or "closest parentage." Razumov is a Russian subject who has to fight for his social position. Conrad was born a Polish nobleman—a *szlachcic*—and his social position was never questioned. To paraphrase Conrad's words, Razumov is born into "a savage, not chivalrous tradition" (*CL2* 289). Tzarist Russia was an absolute monarchy whose subjects owed blind obedience to the state officials. Servility, not service, was what was expected of Russians. In Russia there were only "slaves of the Tsar and slaves of slaves of the Tsar,"[3] whereas the citizens of pre-partition Poland were conscious of their civil rights and liberties. Russia was an Asian autocracy, whereas Poland had always been democratic in its structure, politics, and philosophy. Hence, it is futile to draw similarities between tzarist Russia and partitioned Poland—that is, between the oppressor and the oppressed.

Carabine also claims that "both the national and personal aspects of Razumov's dilemma and his different modes of writing began to refract Conrad's own urgent need to seek 'discourse' with, to be understood by and, perhaps, to exorcize his haunting, inescapable Polish 'shades'" (1996: 99). It seems, though, that what "had long haunted Conrad" was not the "deeply ambivalent relationship to his parents' messianism and militancy" (95) but distant recollections of his childhood: the atmosphere of mourning, the sadness and despair, and the shadow of the omnipotent Russian autocracy, which was the root cause of all family and national disasters. If anything, it was the very name of Russia—associated as it was with secret agents, police, prisons, and death—that constituted Conrad's "Polish shade" in need of exorcizing. There is no need to look for analogies in names or in Razumov's writing, as these elements are not necessarily related to each other. "To capture the very soul of things Russian" was to show the cruelty and autocracy of the Russian empire and the effect that it had on its subjects. Conrad's discourse with his "Polish shades" also takes place elsewhere: in "Prince Roman," "The Crime of Partition," and *A Personal Record*. In *Under Western Eyes*, the writer tries to present the reality of Russia as he sees it. This novel does battle with tzarist Russia.

Furthermore, Zdzisław Najder appears to be right in arguing that "when we read in Bobrowski's memoirs the pages devoted to the time he spent at St. Petersburg, it is impossible not to think about an analogy with another student of the same university—Kirylo Razumov of Conrad's *Under Western Eyes*." As a student, Bobrowski obtained a silver medal for a dissertation. What is more, Razumov's opinion about the irresponsible conspiracy in which his peers were involved echoes Bobrowski's own words: "What Razumov says about Victor Haldin ... sounds similar to what Bobrowski writes about Zygmunt Sierakowski, who was later one of the leaders of the 1863 insurrection" (Najder 1997: 46). The "figure behind the veil" might therefore be not so much Conrad as his uncle Bobrowski.

Thus, being aware of Conrad's attitude to things Russian, Polish scholars always have Polish history at the back of their minds, which results in a "national conviction" they share about perceiving Russia as an autocratic state and Russian secret policy an instrument of brutal terror. Thus, when analyzing *Under Western Eyes*, they invariably take the political context into consideration, never placing Conrad on the side of Russian institutions.

Berthoud claims that Razumov could be seen as the "portrait of the narrator as a young man" and that his creed could be described as "a paradigm of the narrator's convictions" (1978: 170). If Razumov had grown up in the West, he would indeed have been able to live the quiet life of a conscientious student who was totally absorbed in his studies and—like the narrator—could have become a language teacher. In Russia, he became a traitor and a secret agent.

Ultimately, Razumov decides to tell the truth and to expose himself. He cannot live the rest of his life pretending to be someone else. It is because of his love for Natalie that he realizes this. He says: "You were appointed to undo the evil by making me betray myself back into truth and peace ... Your light! Your truth! I felt that I must tell you that I had ended by loving you. And to tell you that I must first confess. Confess, go out—and perish" (*UWE* 272, 274).

Although he ruins his future and his career, he finds peace and tranquility and can now withdraw. Razumov realizes that "a man's real life is that accorded to him in the thoughts of other men by reason of respect or natural love" (*UWE* 19). He yearns for human understanding. His confession not only brings him inner peace and relief, but also restores his personal identity. He is free from falsehood and suspicion. He can feel his moral rebirth. When he gets wet while coming back home, he says: "I am washed clean" (*UWE* 271). Carabine remarks that "from this providential perspective, *Under Western Eyes* is perhaps the most quixotic, enthralling and heroic narrative in modern English fiction" (1996: 251). And, once again, it turns out that the world "rests on a few very simple ideas" (*PR* 17)—that fidelity, honor, and sympathy are universal human values.

To sum up, if we consider the multitude of different interpretations dictated by various critical approaches, as well as various cultural and moral codes, we can but paraphrase the famous words of Marlow as follows: "We read as we live, alone."

Acknowledgments

The reprint of this text, first published as part of the article titled "Lord Jim and Razumov: Interpretations Lost and Found Under Western Eyes" in the *Yearbook of Conrad Studies (Poland)* 6 (2011): 7–22 (16–22), has been made possible courtesy of the Jagiellonian University Publishing House in Kraków, Poland.

Notes

1 The issue of Western misinterpretations of Conrad's novels is also discussed by G. W. Stephen Brodsky in *Joseph Conrad's Polish Soul: Realms of Memory and Self* (2016: 43–77).

2 The interpretation referring to Razumov comes from my article titled "Lord Jim and Razumov: Interpretations Lost and Found Under Western Eyes" (Skolik 2001: 16–22).

3 To paraphrase Speransky's famous dictum,

> I would like someone to show me the difference between the dependence of peasants on landowners and nobility on a ruler; someone to discover whether a ruler has the same right to landowners as owners have to their peasants. So, instead of all the wonderful divisions of the free people of Russia into the most free classes of nobility, merchants, etc., I find two social strata in Russia: the servants of the ruler and the servants of the landowners. The former are called free only in relation to the latter, but there are no really free people in Russia, except beggars and philosophers. (1961: 43)

References

Berthoud, Jacques. 1978. *Joseph Conrad: The Major Phase*. Cambridge: Cambridge University Press.

Brodsky, G. W. Stephen. 2016. *Joseph Conrad's Polish Soul: Realms of Memory and Self*, edited by George Z. Gasyna. Lublin: Maria Curie-Skłodowska University Press.

Carabine, Keith. 1996. *The Life and the Art: A Study of Conrad's* Under Western Eyes. Amsterdam: Rodopi.

Fleishman, Avram. 1967. *Conrad's Politics: Community and Anarchy in the Fiction of Joseph Conrad.* Baltimore, MD: Johns Hopkins Press.

Hay, Eloise Knapp. 1963. *The Political Novels of Joseph Conrad: A Critical Study.* Chicago: University of Chicago Press.

Knowles, Owen, and G. Moore, eds. 2000. *Oxford Reader's Companion to Conrad*, 382–6. Oxford: Oxford University Press.

Morf, Gustav. 1929. *The Polish Heritage of Joseph Conrad.* London: Sampson Low, Marston.

Najder, Zdzisław. 1997. *Conrad in Perspective: Essays on Art and Fidelity.* Cambridge: Cambridge University Press.

Najder, Zdzisław. 2006. *Życie Josepha Conrada-Korzeniowskiego.* Vol. 1. Lublin: Gaudium.

Najder, Zdzisław. 2007. *Joseph Conrad: A Life.* Translated by Halina Najder. Rochester: Camden House.

Skolik, Joanna. 2011. "Lord Jim and Razumov: Interpretations Lost and Found Under Western Eyes." *Yearbook of Conrad Studies (Poland)* 6: 7–22.

Сперанский, М. М. *Проекты и записки*, подготовили к печати А. И. Копаневи, М. В. Кукушкина, под Редакцией С. Я. Валка. Ленинград: Издательство Академии Наук СССР, 1961 [Speransky, M. M. 1961. *Projects and Notes*, prepared for printing by A. I. Kopaneva and M. V. Kukushkin. S. Ya. Valka, ed. Lenigrad: Izdatelstvo of the Academy of Sciences SSSR].

14

The Dangerous Subject Is the Displaced Subject: Conrad's Short Fictions

George Z. Gasyna
University of Illinois at Urbana-Champaign

This amazing tale that was not so much told as suggested to me in desolate exclamations, completed by shrugs, in interrupted phrases, in hints ending in deep sighs.

—Joseph Conrad, "Heart of Darkness" (56)

Through an examination of two of Conrad's best-known shorter fictions, this chapter mobilizes the concept of the "native informant"—after Gayatri Spivak (1999)—to analyze the textual deployment of subaltern, displaced, unbounded, and otherwise dangerous individuals who, by virtue of their speech and/or specific speech acts, radically query or subvert established regimes of truth. In the discussion that follows, the concept of native informing is extended to incorporate the notion of alterity—and more specifically, the special condition of otherness occasioned by emigration and exile[1]—that motivates the speech acts within a broader typology of deterritorialization in the sense proposed by Deleuze and Guattari—that is, always with reference to communities both inside and outside of normative cultural positions and practices.[2] I briefly examine the concept of expatriate displacement and loss, both in the historical Polish (Partitions-era) context of *zsyłka*[3] and later sociopolitical figurations, arguing that the expatriated individual—and, in particular, a displaced person—gains special insight into the goings on in the host culture—a type of naked, shameless honesty that stems from an exilic muteness-become-outrage. Both phenomena figure directly into Conrad's calculus of alterity.

I begin with the allegorical "Amy Foster," wherein the tragic protagonist Yanko speaks haltingly at first, but then in a torrent of "queer" words that broadcast his foreignness and alienness to the hosting culture. My investigation then shifts focus to attend to forms of dangerous enunciation of alterity found in perhaps the most sustained of Conrad's narrative encounters with the phenomenon of outraged speech. In "Heart of Darkness," the danger of language is focalized by the Russian Harlequin—a displaced, othered figure if ever there was one—as a lead-in to a confrontation with a language master (and master over language, thereby also over silence), Kurtz himself. The Harlequin's modalities of perilous speech acts, variously forced or withheld, are fittingly seen by Marlow as nothing less than a life-and-death matter: uttered and heard, mere words may in themselves constitute proof of treachery.[4] As Josef Skvorecky (1984) has shown, the (Russian) Harlequin is a representative of a nation-state that at the time of Conrad's writing held no overseas colonies. While himself a European— from Tambov, south of Moscow—he is nonetheless cast as an Other onto the map of Africa that had been divided up by western European powers (a fact that is symbolically re-presented in the Harlequin's multicolored rags evoking the map of Africa, with yellow "dead in the centre" [HD 13], which Marlow mentions at the beginning of his tale). More than simply a traditional "Russian Fool" (a buffoon or a *durak*)[5]—but rather an obverse and countersign to the hyperrational, progressive, yet still "mad" (HD 54) Kurtz, ready to excuse his master's most contemptible excesses as proof-of-concept of a new community— the "improbable, inexplicable" (HD 54) Harlequin thus emerges as a native informant of a new, *othered* order.

The two textual figures under examination here are marked by their status as presences in-between, operating as they do in the interstice between communal practices of cultures, nations, and languages. As will be shown, they are hopeful speakers or incomprehensible messengers, sometimes attempting to be both at once. More crucial, perhaps, is the motivation for, and anxiety about, their transmission: both address their interlocutors in a mode of compulsion that leads the latter to question their own received ideas (about otherness and difference, for one, but also about more universal human concerns, such as the very possibility of meaningful communication between those whose life experiences are drastically divergent—in brief, those who are not "of our own"). Their speech acts likewise cause the interlocutor, whether Marlow in the Belgian Congo or Doctor Kennedy in Kent, to doubt the sureness of their perceptions, before ultimately retreating in fear at the vision of difference that has presented itself in front of their eyes. That ultimate retreat into a defensive posture of forced "certainty"—an anxious return to prior knowledge—is motivated, I contend, by primal anxiety about difference.

In this way, these characters, in the poetics of their interactions with the interlocutors, render concrete Conrad's own, protracted, now-muted, now-outraged, transnational and transcultural transit as emigrant, laborer, agent of imperial interests, and author. This is a trajectory that took Conrad from nineteenth-century partitioned Poland into exile in the Russian interior and back again to another part of partitioned Poland—exchanging tzarist cultural oppression for Habsburg neglect—thence to Western Europe via southern France, finally to Britain and its far-flung colonies and trade posts, where he eventually domesticated himself as a hybrid subject. Having come to refer to himself as a *homo duplex*, a double man,[6] Conrad felt that he had to take a side and eventually swore loyalty to the Red Ensign of the British Merchant Marine flag. This was to become *a*, or perhaps *the*, crucial symbol of his transformation from avowed "Pole-Catholic"[7] of his early childhood to British subject of his adult years and a kind of scaffolding around which he wove his complex Polish-British-European persona and played his cosmopolitan (as a European) and parochial (as a hyphenated Pole) identity dramas.

Particularly important to the latter were Conrad's pained negotiations of the memory of the Romantic Poland of yore,[8] whose longed-for national restoration, the dream of a *Polonia Restituta* (which would finally come to fruition in the immediate wake of the First World War), had consumed his immediate family forebears, including his father Apollo Korzeniowski, and which was dramatized most intensely in Conrad's 1911 tale "Prince Roman." That quasi-autobiographical story treats the life and tragedies of a landowner, indeed a prince, well acquainted with the Korzeniowski-Bobrowski clans, and his transformation from a "convicted" Romantic martyr to a positivist ("work from the foundations") type of organizer.[9] Here we see reflected some of Conrad's own struggles with properly accounting for his own family's catastrophic fates during the long winter of the Russian, Prussian, and Austrian occupations of Poland and a legacy of cultural oppression—a project that for him took the dimensions of both a kind of history and a concrete task.

* * *

Proceeding from a Foucauldian theorization of a regime of truth and truth-telling as a form of liberation practice, in her seminal work *A Critique of Postcolonial Reason*, Gayatri Chakravorty Spivak employed the sociological concept of the "native informant" to bring into relief the limited access to humanity of the "other as subject" (1999: 5) This figure of the native informant in her reading constitutes a strategic means of undoing a subaltern's status as a presence that remains muted (her term is "co-presence"). In reimagining and rescripting this *de*-territorialized presence, Spivak follows Deleuze when she writes that the "native informant" is a name for "that mark of expulsion from the name of man—a mark crossing out the impossibility of … ethical relation" (4, 6).

Within the continuum of suppressed and, indeed impossible, voices, the figure of the Other becomes subjected to forces of double displacement and, thus, silencing in—and by—the Western imaginary. The first level in this economy of silencing, one recalls, is the criterion of class, given that the subaltern Other putatively belongs to the proletarian biomass. That economic condition is then multiplied by gender.[10] The third element of this process of effective dehumanization is racial or ethnic measure. For a person formalized as different (via racial or gendered markers), there is no position from which to voice the self, she concludes, and consequently, no recipient can receive the speech act (1994: 90–104).

Compelling as the characterization may appear for postcolonial studies of abjection, the figure of the Other, in modernist fiction, as a presence a priori to be treated with suspicion, is silenced or muted further by the problematic status of emigration and exile. The emigrant who, already for Karl Marx, had been connected with the category of rebel, for example in his *Manifesto of the Communist Party*, is structurally a suspect figure to be formally disinherited, if s/he has not been disinherited already, and thus left unvoiced (1983: 227). Spivak's deployment of the term "native informant," which sought to disrupt the self–other binary from the side of a deplorable, and thus suppressed, alterity, delicately captures the dichotomy of the natural and the cultural in the hierarchies of speech. Further, it traces the foreclosure of the natural (agency, voicedness) by the cultural and again by the ideological, the latter understood in terms of access to forums of representation.

Exile and emigration, it has been my view, complicate this opposition significantly, for at least two reasons. First, as a number of theorists of exilic discourse and commentators on the emigrant experience have noted—among them Edward Said (1994), Joseph Brodsky (1994), Czesław Miłosz (1994), Emile Cioran (1994), Clarice Lispector (1988),[11] Witold Gombrowicz (1988), and Joseph Conrad himself (the message resonates especially powerfully in his 1915 reflection essay "Poland Revisited")—the appearance of an exiled person can cause a disruptive shockwave because his or her banishment simultaneously forms an entry into a temporally parallel, Other world, into "another mode of seeing" (Miłosz 1994: 39). Second, detached forcefully and painfully (cf. Said 1994: 137–8) from community and tradition, the exiled individual and emigrants more generally fall a priori into the category of a menacing figure/Other. No matter how liminary his or her actual situatedness, or precarious his or her daily existence, that person is forever imperiling the monolingual message that stems from the center, threatening to be a cultural informant of smuggled, unofficial, transgressive messages that may work to contest or discredit normative truth regimes. The exile/emigrant, in short, is often a dangerous messenger from his/ her native place—but also from the forum of the adoptive one.[12] In his essay "Notes on Exile," for example, Miłosz contends that, from the outside looking in, the experience/subject position of "(e)xile is morally suspect because it breaks one's solidarity with a group, that is, it sets apart an individual who ceases to share the experience of [those] left behind." The process is no less disruptive from the inside looking out, Miłosz claims: "As long as an individual lives in his country, the privileged space ... of one's childhood or native region ... by centrifugally enlarging itself, becomes more or less identified with his country as a whole." Miłosz concludes by pressing on the inexorable disruptiveness of the experience: "Exile displaces that center or rather creates two centers ... This leads him [the exile] to discover how new divisions between men [*sic*] come about" (38–9).

The recuperative strategy of Spivak's specific counter-narrative, represented in the enunciation of the voice of the native (subaltern) informant as a kind of "metropolitan hybrid" (1999: 17), the status of this figure a priori problematic through the conditionality of his or her status as emigrant or exile, is dramatized in several texts of Conrad's in which the speech act can be seen as an avatar for a graphically and conceptually decentering, and hence dangerous, "insurrection of subjugated knowledges" (Foucault 2003: 294). In Conrad, this particular strategy *for* speech—a form of coercion, actually, and indeed a coercion to speak, after Aaron Fogel (1985)—is mobilized in the service of intersubjective confrontation, as part of an idealist regime of claims-testing. Though viewed as menacing to the narrative and cultural authority or hegemon (cf. Said 1979: 5–6), the exiled individual nonetheless desperately looks for a space for himself or herself to speak as a basic prerogative of subject-formation. The danger to the center can sometimes be inadvert, but in other cases, it is intended as an expression of outrage.[13]

In "Amy Foster" (1901), which articulates this theme in a blunt and unadorned manner, chiefly as a text of *unheimlich* cultural terror (cf. Israel 2000) and the transit of bare life through a hostile environment,[14] the transnational subject is axiomatically rendered into a dangerous Other. This fact is narratologically determined precisely as a consequence of his (the protagonist's) apparent inability to speak—or at least to express himself intelligibly (and perhaps no less important, courteously and respectfully) to interlocutors. Shipwrecked, left for dead, and then recaptured by a well-meaning—albeit guarded—member of the local body politic, Yanko the Slavic Highlander, the man who had been sent away from his native realm by the fiat of geopolitics in a banalized form of the Polish *zsyłka*, is activated as an extraterritorial Other on the island of his inadvertent and, by the evidence of the text, also unintended exile. After all, the narrator avows that Yanko's expected itinerary had as its terminus the sylvan hills of America—though it is much more likely he would have been employed at one of its foundries, tanneries, farmsteads, or meat-processing plants. Yet even as a hoped-for economic migrant, Yanko is also a displaced person, expropriated by a partitioning power, the Habsburgs, and tricked into leaving the land and his family homestead (this land had long been part of the Polish state but belonged to the Austro-Hungarian House of Habsburg throughout the nineteenth century, known as the Kingdom of Galicia and Lodomeria, or *Galizien* in its short German form). As the following passage makes clear, the text's embedded narrator is perfectly well aware that Yanko's arrival on the English coast was the result of forced (e-)migration of a type that falls within the categories of the modern experience of exile. Here, it is specifically a consequence of a form of ethnic cleansing:

> He [Yanko] was a mountaineer of the eastern range of the Carpathians, and the vessel sunk the night before in Eastbay was the Hamburg emigrant-ship *Herzogin Sophia-Dorothea*, of appalling memory.
>
> A few months later we could read in the papers the accounts of the bogus "Emigration Agencies" among the Sclavonian peasantry in the more remote provinces of Austria. The object of these scoundrels was to get hold of the poor ignorant people's homesteads, and they were in league with the local usurers. They exported their victims through Hamburg mostly. (AF 161)

Once wrecked off England's coast, and "taken out of his knowledge," as the narrator memorably puts it on two occasions (AF 155, 159), Yanko departs the expected time-space of the transatlantic journey, which would have at least provided a kind of stabilized sojourner identity, as determined by the narratology and mythopoeia of late nineteenth- and early twentieth-century Polish economic migrations.[15] Instead, displaced and deterritorialized into abject isolation, an England that would for him remain for some time an "undiscovered country" (AF 151), he is dehumanized by the text's narrator into merely a "creature," and thus something markedly less than a proper subject who might speak (and whose proclamations might be heard or indeed welcomed).[16]

Indeed Yanko—who had not yet been given a name at this particular point of the account—is seen initially occupying a liminal space between apparition and monster.[17] Approaching farmer Smith while "jabbering in a most discomposing manner," Yanko is next determined to be a "lunatic" possessed of an "insane, disturbing [speaking] noise" when he is heard "crying obstinately through the door" (AF 160). Thereafter, in a final stage of his abjection, Yanko becomes known for what he truly is: neither a "Hindoo" (164) nor a "Basque" (164) nor even a (vaguely European-sounding) "hussar" (168), the embedded narrator reports, but simply a highlander (little John the Goorall in a portmanteau) from the mountains of an unspecified Eastern European hinterland, its contours misty in the mental geography of the Western metropolitan West.[18] No less "outlandish" (167) than his appearance or his behavior, noted ethnographically by the narrator using speech reported from Mr. Smith the farmer, his wife, Dr. Kennedy, and sundry others, is Yanko's own halting, broken, and (likely) hysterical manner of speech. The scene of initial encounter with farmer Smith sets up the paradigm of dangerous and indeed lunatic conspiratorial discourse to be textually exploited later—though even here, in that opening interchange, Smith is unaware, the frame narrator notes wryly, that Yanko has all along been addressing him as "a gracious lord" and begging "in God's name to afford [him] food and shelter" (160). In effect, Yanko is asking for the satisfaction of the most elemental human needs, the granting of which requires only a basic act of empathy; it is the manner of asking—its frenzied desperation—however, that is apparently seen as deficient.

Conrad outlines here a process of otherization, whereby the unintelligible becomes incomprehensible, and then, in consequence, elementally frightening. In this sense, Yanko's very facticity, his deployment as it were, reminds his interlocutors of not only their conscious, but also subconscious fears: his sudden appearance on the coast and his presence (as co-presence, in Spivak's archaeology of otherness) is tangible evidence to them of the topics they are not capable of discussing or willing to entertain, possibly reaching as far back as questions of elemental, "tribal," identity and affiliation (as Britons who *belong* to their place). His appearance, in brief, triggers a message to their buried selves: a message of possible invasion.[19]

Once relocated into something resembling a domestic situation, one homologous to what might be expected at home in the Eastern European mountains, though ultimately unhomely and distressing in its actual context,[20] Yanko begins to speak at last, albeit haltingly, of the state of his emotions and desires. Extending his putatively conspiratorial purview, he now addresses the subject of his affections and the others in the village, and then his child, to whom he hums and sings, though—again—*oddly*. It is in his final act of defiance of local authority, which in this case coincides with his ultimate stage of exilic subject-formation (as, ultimately, an Other), that Yanko explodes in a torrent of noises and incomprehensible ("queer") words that both mesmerize and terrorize his interlocutor:

> He was very feverish, and kept on muttering to himself. She [Amy] sat on a chair and looked at him fixedly across the table ... Towards the night his fever increased ...
>
> He tossed, moaned, and now and then muttered a complaint. And she sat with the table between her and the couch, watching every movement and every sound, with the terror, the unreasonable terror of that man she could not understand creeping over her ... I believe he spoke to her for a long time, entreating, wondering, pleading, ordering, I suppose. And then a gust of rage came over him. He sat up and called out terribly one word—some word. She heard him call her twice after her down the road in a terrible voice—and fled ... Ah! (AF 173–4)[21]

In this final tableau, in which Yanko's wife Amy decides to escape their shared home with their child (his ostensible possession, and the thing connecting them culturally and potentially allowing him to assimilate as a local), Yanko, the exilic man, might in effect be cursing, welcoming, praying: indeed, who knows? While his aim is most emphatically to inform of his humanity and thus the links that connect him and them, there is no true transmission, only entrenchment in prior knowledge, and thus only prejudice. One—or at the very least, Conrad's local Englishman narrator, the stand-in for the *us*—cannot know for sure; one may only "suppose."

In this manner, the narrator of "Amy Foster" echoes and amplifies (one wishes to say, brings to the level of locality) the structuring logic of the narrative we move to next, a text set in as foreign a land as any in Conrad. In "Heart of Darkness," Marlow's quizzical wonderment is a form of capitulation of his knowledge when faced with the enunciations of dangerous, informing, extraterritorial Others whom he encountered on his upriver voyage in the Belgian Congo—not only the most loquacious of the lot, the Russian Harlequin at the terminus, but also the deformed, "empty" European agents chanced upon along the way.[22] In "Amy Foster," an *étude* of difference that brings home a sense of wilderness of another kind, including mental, Yanko Goorall's words are likewise uttered into a void of misprision where they are left to linger, his speech manifestly perilous to him—the *he that dares to speak*—but initially they do not threaten in an existential way the general body politic of the gathered community, the ordinary folk of southern England's coastal and farming villages. While characters in Conrad frequently struggle to speak, as a general principle that both sanctions and extends their alterity, the speech act that proved dangerous for Yanko in the relatively familiar coast of England becomes voluble beyond the point of endurance in the significantly more "foreign" Congo, which is the setting of the final clash between truth regimes in "Heart of Darkness." Here, the Russian Harlequin—a geographically and, more to the point, ideologically and ethically displaced person—comes to embody the native informer. An adventurer-turned-desperate-foreigner, asked to serve as envoy of and interpreter for a murderous para-state, a dystopia in miniature, the Harlequin is a mysterious co-presence from the very moment he opens his mouth. He is a character who, when encountered by Marlow, has clearly been longing for an affirmative audience—perhaps even more desperately than Yanko himself, who at the beginning simply needed to be fed—and hoping to find this affinity in Marlow. He is a native informant who has come from Kurtz's forest realm and boarded a river steamer full of emissaries of progress and order. His fevered enunciations fill the entire bandwidth of the jungle, while his exhortations and blinded praise of his master-subject Kurtz betray a desperate necessity to justify and to *inform*. This need proves contagious. Indeed, even from the retrospective view of the text's framed discourse, Marlow, as he shares his tale with the men on the *Nellie*, can still only *report* the Harlequin's speech and try to *order* it, without pretending to understand (or interpret) fully either the speech or the aleatory displaced speaker he is ultimately describing. Nor, indeed, does he comprehend the full sense of cultural horror hiding behind his interlocutor's wall of assurances, proclamations, hesitations, and sudden silences.

As the Harlequin increasingly permits himself to voice his inner experience during his encounter with Marlow, the tenor of his "intercourse" (HD 55) shifts, too. In terms of voiced subjectivity, both the speech act and the agent who speaks become transformed from the level of "one of us" to the level of the native informant, while the tone of enunciation moves in the course of the long passage of reported speech from basic recognition of common humanity and consanguinity (in the shape of core European values as expressed by the Scramble for Africa and the business opportunity it initially presented) to submission to forces of otherness, the latter being partly, but *only* partly, of an economic nature, of mammon allaying men's greed by slaying his better angels, the agent of death being of course Kurtz himself, the agent plenipotentiary and extraordinary:

> The man filled his [the Harlequin's] life, occupied his thoughts, swayed his emotions. "What can you expect?" he burst out; "he came to them with thunder and lightning, you know—and they had never seen anything like it—and very terrible. He could be very terrible. You can't judge Mr. Kurtz as you would an ordinary man. No, no, no! Now—just to give you an idea—I don't mind telling you, he wanted to shoot me, too, one day—but I don't judge him." "Shoot you!" I cried "What for?" "Well, I had a small lot of ivory the chief of that village near my house gave me. You see I used to shoot game for them. Well, he wanted it, and wouldn't hear reason. He declared he would shoot me unless I gave him the ivory and then cleared out of the country, because he could do so, and had a fancy for it, and there was nothing on earth to prevent him killing whom he jolly well pleased. And it was true, too. I gave him the ivory ... When he came down to the river, sometimes he would take to me, and sometimes it was better for me to be careful. This man suffered too much. He hated all this, and somehow he couldn't get away. When I had a chance I begged him to try and leave while there was time; I offered to go back with him. And he would say yes, and then he would remain; go off on another ivory hunt; disappear for weeks; forget himself amongst these people—forget himself—you know." "Why! he's mad," I said. He protested indignantly. (HD 56)

The confession, which adopts the trope of *consolatio*, never seems to come to a terminus, the Harlequin (and consequently Marlow, who has tasked himself with this protracted memory work) finding new and progressively more novel ways of articulating his one impression of sublime vision and exculpatory affect:

> The Russian tapped me on the shoulder. I heard him mumbling and stammering something about "brother seaman—couldn't conceal—knowledge of matters that would affect Mr. Kurtz's reputation." I waited. For him evidently Mr. Kurtz was not in his grave; I suspect that for him Mr. Kurtz was one of the immortals ... "Ah! I'll never, never meet such a man again. You ought to have heard him recite poetry—his own, too, it was, he told me. Poetry!" He rolled his eyes at the recollection of these delights. "Oh, he enlarged my mind!" (HD 61, 63)[23]

Once released from the silence of his radical yet perplexing solipsism, the Harlequin cannot stop himself from reporting and indeed informing; he needs to be unburdened of the fundamental truth—a legacy of Kurtzian new order—that weighs heavily on him. These secrets,[24] half whispered and half shouted, combine into a series of self-revelations effected in the present, but for the future benefit of the other, the interlocutor (at that point in their encounter, Marlow has still not yet seen Kurtz in person and is becoming increasingly agitated, but also feels increasingly compelled to hear more; the Harlequin is thereby both gatekeeper and intermediary to the universe of alternate fact that Kurtz had manufactured in his realm). The interchange between the ambivalent messenger of European polity, dispatched in a steamer to bring order to the Company's account, and the envoy of the Sovereign in the heart of the jungle, who has created his own mandate to rule over—and, if necessary, "exterminate"—the "brutes" (HD 50), relies initially on a shared phantasmagoria that makes communication smoother to the extent that it is improbably detached from reality. The Harlequin's epiphany, which he is all too eager to disclose, is encapsulated in his famous dictum, "This man has enlarged my mind" (54). But what of the effects on Marlow's mind? Had he really seen and spoken with this man, this "phenomenon" (63), Marlow wonders to himself, even if the two of them had once—long ago, it seems—been "of the same profession" (62), so that the Harlequin too would at one point have reflexively understood "the code" of "the sea" and thus been reterritorialized as one of the community, "one of us."[25] And Marlow implies as much when his language reveals that this Other, his informant, is asking for empathy based on the residual worth of the sailor's creed as compass and azimuth, a putative bond between men who between them have witnessed too much bare reality (and notably, Marlow plays along and obliges the Harlequin in all of his requests, which he claims were made due to the latter's state of agitated "despondency" [55]). This scene of conspiratorial whisperings, allusions, and alliances between representatives of formerly aligned orders of values—but now inhabiting two entirely different universes and systems of knowledge—shifts again, now to assume a radically re-embodied form. It is marked, at the conclusion of the passage, by physical urgency:

> He informed me, lowering his voice, that it was Kurtz who had ordered the attack to be made on the steamer. "He hated sometimes the idea of being taken away … But I don't understand these matters. I am a simple man … But quiet-eh?" he urged anxiously. "It would be awful for his reputation if anybody here—" I promised a complete discretion with great gravity. "I have a canoe and three black fellows waiting not very far. I am off" … He helped himself, with a wink at me, to a handful of my tobacco. "Between sailors—you know—good English tobacco." At the door of the pilot-house he turned round—"I say, haven't you a pair of shoes you could spare?" (HD 63)

The Other, exiled from history and moved to an ex-centric orbit of existence, thus appears as a complete disruption of the former order and former hierarchies of knowledge, whether domestic and thus "natural" or, ultimately, as both texts show, Western—that is, "our own." The Other who *dares to/must* speak is more than a sum of its parts for Conrad. In "Heart of Darkness," this figure, the native informant, is more than a foreign mass, a "phenomenon" who embarked on the steamer in full view of other mates of the ship (though they were not privy to his speeches); in "Amy Foster," he is something more than a dehumanized animal "creature" encountered along a country road, whose "unhomeliness" as a survivor of a storm and yet a reject from his own purported history (of emigration) was legitimated and substantiated by accounts of others—most vividly, the eponymous Amy herself. The Other slips in like a phantom and departs in the same manner with all his/her differences ultimately intact, leaving the narrator's world and system of knowledge, however, traumatically altered in the process. The Other, in short, as a native informant, recurs like a returned repressed through the pressure of speech, a kind of conscience awakened through affiliative empathy, and as a symbol and talisman of all the "others" who refuse or cannot bear to remain silent. Inverting the final image of the passage above, the native informants in Conrad's work are inviting the reader to walk in *their* shoes, and see what they have seen—no matter how "discomposing" (AF 160) this might feel.

Notes

1 See Edward Said's late 1980s essay "Reflections on Exile," where the experience/ experiencing of exile is likened to an illness, a "condition" (1994: 147).
2 See Gilles Deleuze and Felix Guattari (1986), especially the first three chapters.
3 The Polish term *zsyłka*, adapted from the Russian *ssylka*, refers to the banishment of Poles to tzarist Russia and—after the fall of the Russian Empire—to the hinterland of the Soviet Empire, usually Siberia (see Korzeniowski 1983: 83; Grudzińska-Gross and Gross 2008: 395–414 and *passim*).
4 At one moment during their protracted exchanges, the Harlequin informs Marlow that he managed to persuade Kurtz to spare the lives of Marlow and his search party. Similarly, during their final conversation, Marlow reminds the Harlequin that "the manager thinks you [Harlequin] ought to be hanged" (HD 62).
5 Josef Skvorecky, "Why the Harlequin? (On Conrad's *Heart of Darkness*)."
6 Conrad first defines himself in this manner in the December 5, 1903, letter to Kazimierz Waliszewski (*CL* 3: xxiii; 88–90).

7 A reproduction of a photograph on the back of which Conrad, then not quite five, articulates these two elements of his identity, can be found in Zdzisław Najder (2007: plates 11, 12).

8 See, for example, Joseph Conrad, "Confidence" (*NLL*).

9 Stephen Brodsky devotes a chapter to the inaccuracies and inventions found in the story, before concluding that the work, nonetheless, belongs to the realm of autobiography—since autobiography is an immanently fictionalizing genre (2016). For further discussion on the obliqueness—as "emotional" not physical record of traces—of Conrad's autobiographical writings, see for example Leo Robson (2017).

10 In Spivak's (1994) archaeology of difference elaborated in "Can the Subaltern Speak?" the silenced figure is already always an Other biologically, as female.

11 I am referring here to Lispector's exilic feminist classic, *The Passion According to GH*, originally published in Brazilian Portuguese in 1964.

12 As is frequently noted in analyses of exilic discourse, this position—and the potential transgressive freedom that it can enable—is rarely if ever exploited "in real life." See Cioran (1994: 151–3) and Gombrowicz (1988: 66–9), in particular.

13 There are many types of exile, beyond the bluntly political one-way passport scenarios of Cold War expulsions and medieval-era city-state banishment of popular imagination, or the original expulsion of humankind from Paradise as a kind of cultural urtext (though partitioned Poland certainly was no paradise). In the nineteenth and twentieth centuries, in particular—the century of migrants and refugees made to inhabit "mixed population zones," as Hannah Arendt so memorably put it—migration and exile became closely interlinked, and still remain inextricably coupled, as sociopolitical phenomena. For further discussion of the taxonomy and ontology of exile—as well as related phenomena, such as emigration and forced migration due to ethnic strife or territorial conflict as they bear on the poetics of modernist fiction—see my earlier *Polish, Hybrid, and Otherwise: Exilic Discourse in Joseph Conrad and Witold Gombrowicz* (Gasyna 2011/2013), especially the first two chapters.

14 The phrase is Giorgio Agamben's (1998), extended here to its properly biopolitical component, already prefigured in Agamben's theorization (though there it is deployed always with reference to a Sovereign who rules over the logic of exception, governing docile bodies and rebellious truth-tellers alike).

15 Polish historiography refers to this phenomenon as *emigracja za chlebem* [emigration for bread]. Znaniecki and Thomas (1996), especially in the Introduction and Chapter 1, but indeed throughout the first volume of their classic study, provide dozens of detailed reports by and about migrants of this kind, typically those who resettled and found gainful (if mostly lowly) employment in the American Midwest and the Great Lakes region around the time that "Amy Foster" is set.

16 Edward Said invokes Yanko's isolation to make a very similar point in a discussion of the autobiographical echoes of Conrad—especially the notion of loneliness of the foreigner—within his own life (1998).

17 It does not help matters that Conrad has exoticized his Carpathian highlander mercilessly, rendering him into a near caricature of the total abject Other; it is also notable that Yanko the highlander's outlandishness and foreignness do not wither over time, even once he has been relatively accepted as a familiar sight among the villagers—though, obviously, not as one of them. This, however, is perhaps the price that must be paid by Yanko (and in a pedagogical extension, by other would-be emigrants) for his daring and transgressive miscegenation—specifically his wooing (such as it was), marriage, and sexual life with a local woman.

18 Ironically, the coastal and inland farming villages of the south of England (Brenzet is in Kent, approximately twenty-five miles west of Dover) where these events are said to occur are also indubitably provincial—and in the mixture of superstition and common prejudice on the part of the local inhabitants, depicted thus by Conrad's narratorial voice—if not entirely marginal.

19 A connection to other texts of potential invasion, such as the roughly contemporary *Dracula* by Bram Stoker (which appeared four years prior to the publication of "Amy Foster") is made tangible here, though Conrad's irony ensures that the "invader" in question here is a pathetic creature, mostly incapable of causing harm.

20 Cf. Israel (2000: 33–5).

21 The configuration of words on the page shows eloquently the breakdown of language between these two protagonists, and—what follows—the broader failure of signification.

22 As is the man with "no entrails" (HD 22), the unnamed Manager of Central Station, whom Marlow encounters on the early part of his journey toward Kurtz and who seems to relish his own banal emptiness.

23 The reference to the cranial enlargement occurs twice in the text within a space of eight pages and in several conversations dutifully reported by Marlow.

24 Indeed, one of the "excellent" fellows listening to Marlow spin his yarn about "one of [his] inconclusive experiences" chides him for supposedly having revealed "trade secrets" (whether explicitly or through the effect that the Harlequin's self-reflexive loquacity may have had on his way of relating the story of the encounter). Marlow denies the charge (HD 5, 7, 57).

25 The reference is to the frame narrator's declaration that, of the gathered company of men about to share a story on the *Nellie*, Marlow is the only one who "still followed the sea" (HD 5).

References

Agamben, Giorgio. 1998. *Homo Sacer: Sovereign Power and Bare Life*. Translated by Daniel Heller-Roazen. Stanford, CA: Stanford University Press.

Brodsky, Joseph. 1994. "The Condition We Call Exile: An Address." In *Altogether Elsewhere: Writers on Exile*, edited by Marc Robinson, 3–11. Boston: Faber and Faber.

Brodsky, Stephen. 2016. *Joseph Conrad's Polish Soul: Realms of Memory and Self*, edited by George Gasyna. Lublin: Marie Curie-Skłodowska University Press.

Cioran, E. M. 1994. "Advantages of Exile." In *Altogether Elsewhere: Writers on Exile*, edited by Marc Robinson, 150–3. Boston: Faber and Faber.

Deleuze, Gilles, and Felix Guattari. [1975] 1986. *Kafka: Toward a Minor Literature*. Minneapolis: University of Minnesota Press.

Fogel, Aaron. 1985. *Coercion to Speak: Conrad's Poetics of Dialogue*. Cambridge, MA: Harvard University Press.

Foucault, Michel. [1976] 2003. "Society Must be Defended." In *The Essential Foucault*, edited by Paul Rabinow and Nikolas Rose, 294–9. New York: New Press. https://monoskop.org/images/9/99/Foucault_Michel_Il_faut_defendre_la_societe.pdf. Accessed February 7, 2022.

Gasyna, George. 2011. *Polish, Hybrid, and Otherwise: Exilic Discourse in Joseph Conrad and Witold Gombrowicz*. London: Bloomsbury.

Gombrowicz, Witold. 1988. *Diary Volume 1*. Translated and edited by Lillian Vallee. Evanston, IL: Northwestern University Press.

Grudzińska-Gross, Irena, and Jan Tomasz Gross, eds. 2008. *W czterdziestym nas Matko na Sibir zesłali … : Polska a Rosja 1939–1942*. Kraków: Znak.

Israel, Nico. 2000. *Outlandish: Writing Between Exile and Diaspora*. Stanford, CA: Stanford University Press.

Korzeniowski, Apollo. [1864] 1983. "Poland and Muscovy." In *Conrad Under Familial Eyes*, edited by Zdzisław Najder, 75–87. Cambridge: Cambridge University Press.

Lispector, Clarice. 1988. *The Passion According to GH*. New York: New Directions.

Marx, Karl. 1983. "The Manifesto of the Communist Party." In *The Portable Karl Marx*, edited by Eugene Kamenka, 203–41. London: Penguin Classics.

Miłosz, Czesław. 1994. "Notes on Exile." In *Altogether Elsewhere: Writers on Exile*, edited by Marc Robinson, 36–40. Boston: Faber and Faber.

Najder, Zdzisław. 2007. *Joseph Conrad: A Life*. Rochester, NY: Camden House.

Robson, Leo. 2017. "Joseph Conrad's Journey: Was the Novelist Right to Think Everyone Was Getting Him Wrong?" *The New Yorker*, November 20, 2017. https://www.newyorker.com/magazine/2017/11/20/joseph-conrads-journey. Accessed February 7, 2022.

Said, Edward. 1979. *Orientalism*. New York: Vintage.

Said, Edward. 1994. "Reflections on Exile." In *Altogether Elsewhere: Writers on Exile*, edited by Marc Robinson, 137–49. Boston: Faber and Faber.

Said, Edward. 1998. "Between Worlds: Edward Said Makes Sense of His Life." *London Review of Books* 20, no. 9 (May 7): 3–7.

Skvorecky, Josef. 1984. "Why the Harlequin? (On Conrad's *Heart of Darkness*)." *Cross Currents* 3: 259–64.

Spivak, Gayatri Chakravorty. 1994. "Can the Subaltern Speak?" In *Colonial Discourse and Post-Colonial Theory: A Reader*, edited and introduced by Patrick Williams and Laura Chrisman, 66–111. New York: Columbia University Press.

Spivak, Gayatri Chakravorty. 1999. *A Critique of Postcolonial Reason: Toward a History of the Vanishing Present*. Cambridge, MA: Harvard University Press.

Znaniecki, Florian, and William I. Thomas. [1918] 1996. *The Polish Peasant in Europe and America*. Chicago: University of Illinois Press.

15

"I Must Live Till I Die—Mustn't I?": The Hybrid Art of Joseph Conrad and Salman Rushdie

G. W. Stephen Brodsky
Royal Roads Military College (Retired)

James Wait and Joseph Anton

In Joseph Conrad's *The Nigger of the "Narcissus"* (1897), when James Wait tells Mr. Baker he is dying, the mate demands, "Then why did you ship aboard here?" Wait replies, "I must live till I die—mustn't I?" (*NN* 39). Nearly a century later, after Salman Rushdie's *The Satanic Verses* (1988) appeared, the Iranian Ayatollah Ruhollah Khomeini issued his infamous *fatwa* (1989); in fear for his life, novel fiction's consummate postcolonial writer went into hiding. In his essay "Influence," Rushdie summons Conrad's Wait, "who insisted that he must live until he died" (2002a: 67); and in *Joseph Anton: A Memoir* (2012), he wrote in his pseudonymous third-person identity, "It was Conrad who gave him the motto to which he clung as if to a lifeline … 'Joseph Anton,' he told himself, 'you must live until you die,'" (165; cf. Robben 2013: 1), reject despair, and get on with writing. So Conrad saved Rushdie and *in toto* shaped his post-*fatwa* oeuvre. Rushdie's metafictional no-man's land of realist fantasy is objectively correlative with Wait's words as its central trope resonating through time and space across the cultures of East and West.

Double Irony

When Conrad left the sea in 1894, among the sailors' lore he brought with him would have been a couple of rollicking sea shanties with the refrain, "We will live till we die."[1] Wait means merely that he needs a berth. No devil-may-care dash.

Only desperation. "Superb, towering" at first sight (*NN* 20), he is the European ideal of the noble savage; but he is an "impostor" (*NN* 130; cf. "To my Readers in America"; *NN* 130–1). Out of his natural element, he is merely "our nigger" (32), sickly and unable to work, his condescension reduced to a whine of fearful denial. Both impressions accord with European colonialism's West Indian–African stereotype.

Wait's reply, then, is Conradian irony, the device by which Rushdie both memorializes Conrad and subtly reveals late colonialism's fault lines extending into postcolonialism's hybrid cultures. So, while Conrad's monocultural portrayal of Wait as the Other is symptomatic of the Colonialist years, his canon, molded by his own exilic anxieties, anticipates the cultural hybridity of Rushdie and other Postcolonial writers. Somewhat bitter triumphalism marks Rushdie's 1983 prophecy, "Commonwealth [vs. English] literature was invented to delay the day when we rough beasts actually slouch into Bethlehem" (Rushdie 1991: 70).

Rushdie's reappropriation of Wait's words, restoring their traditional devil-may-care sea shanty timbre as a sustaining apothegm, compounds that irony. Until the "distorted, ugly" reception of *The Satanic Verses* (1988), to "stop writing, to become something else, *not a writer*," had never occurred to Rushdie (2012: 165); but his talent was crippled by this new dread. At first, he tried to "stave off such thoughts" by writing reviews (166); but that was merely avoidance. Whereas Wait, both dreading and denying his imminent death, is the plaintive object of the crew's pity, Joseph Anton, inspired by his wishfully perverse reading of Wait's surly despair, rallies as subject of courageous self-regard and gets on with Being. Rushdie's recontextualizing of Wait's words as his motto became the fulcrum of his art[2] until overborne by a modern American outrage, prompting his polemical satire, *The Golden House* (2017).

Disorientation and Hybridity

In *A Personal Record* when asked his birth year by his maritime examiner, Conrad replies, "I am of the year 1857." The examiner comments, "the mutiny year" (105–6), a reference to the Sepoy Mutiny, implying a slight to Conrad's Polishness. In Rushdie's *The Moor's Last Sigh* (2002b), the narrator Moraes "the Moor" Zogoiby (Bad Luck)—his "Pass the pepper" (2002b: 3) a homage to Marlow's "pass the bottle" (Y 13, 17)[3]—is born in 1957, the centenary of both the mutiny year and Conrad's birth. Moraes describes how in 1961 (incidentally the centenary of Conrad's father Apollo's arrest), the Indian Army entered and occupied Moraes's island home state of Goa (2002b: 155). Moraes's self-destructive sister Ina, although born in India's Independence year 1947, rejects the influence of her Indian mother Aurora (light), adopts the Portuguese-Jewish paternal family name Gama, and becomes a celebrity, soon to die of cancer. These dates alone nod at Rushdie's literary and moral debt to Conrad (Rushdie himself was born that year); together Moraes and Ina symbolize Rushdie's own Indo-European identity reifying the post-imperial East-West encounter, heir and successor to Conrad's insistently Western Anglo-Polonism.

In *Lord Jim*, Marlow ponders whether Jim, after his maritime board trial, an outcast and no longer "one of us" (*LJ* 6), "felt the ground cut from under his feet" (67); and in *Nostromo*, Emilia, Charles Gould's marriage proposal facing her with the prospect of becoming the *doyenne* of Sulaco's Europeans, has "the physical experience of the earth falling away from under her" ([D] 63). Conrad and Rushdie are analogues of this vertiginous spatiality. Conrad, born to *szlachta* parents in Russian Ukraine, left Poland for France, then Britain, and Rushdie, of Kashmiri Muslim parentage and raised in Bombay, lives in England and America; both authors are perforce self-exiled. In *The Ground Beneath Her Feet* (Rushdie 1999), Vina Apsara speaks of earthquakes, "Two worlds in collision" (326, 469),[4] the symbolism of Himalayan tectonic subduction embracing the cultural war of East and West.[5]

Ground's narrator Rai muses on the claustrophobic prison of culturally imposed tyranny, yet paradoxically also its agoraphobic destruction of meridional norms. Rushdie's trauma is expressed in terms of the Conradian *Mirror of the Sea* metaphor:

> Disorientation is loss of the East. Ask any navigator: the east is what you sail by. Lose the east and you lose your bearings, your certainties, your knowledge of what is and what may be, perhaps even your life. But let's just suppose … that it's only when you dare to let go that your real life begins? When … you cut your ropes, slip your chain … Suppose you've got to go through the feeling of being lost … the wild panic of losing your moorings. (Rushdie 1999: 177)

Swine and Slaves

"Sometimes it is necessary to touch bottom in order to know which way is up," Rai says of Ormus Cama; "to go a long distance down the wrong road before you know the right way" (Rushdie 1999: 193). The anonymous "we" of *The Nigger of the "Narcissus,"* a perceptively retrospective voice for a crew on a false tack, describes Wait in colonialism's terms as an aberrational inversion of the natural order of authority and subordination: a "sick tyrant overawing a crowd of abject but untrustworthy slaves" (*NN* 32). The maudlin Belfast "scratch[es] the ear of his favourite pig" (41)[6] with the same sorrow at its sure fate that compels him to assuage his own empathetic pain by overweening service to Wait. The crew's thralldom to its guilt-fraught pity, making them mutinously delinquent, is different merely in kind from Wait's slavery to dread.

Ground's Persis is named for the mother of the Odyssean Circe (Rushdie 1999: 172) who turned men into swine. Joseph Anton, virtually in protective custody and self-admittedly querulous, initially is like Wait, but restive in longing for freedom. Their and the "*Narcissus*" crew's passivity before their existential pain inheres in the proleptic image in Conrad's "The Idiots" of a "helpless pig, with tied legs, grunted a melancholy sigh at every rut" being brought to market for sale and slaughter (*TU* 51). The crew finds respite from projected anguish in "meditative languor" induced by routine work, "the problem of life abandoned … to the sea … the realm of safety and peace beyond the frontiers of sorrow and fear" (*NN* 104)—and beyond thought. Rushdie's whimsical mythopoesis makes similar demands; *Moor*'s Moraes learns, "Either, like a bullying tyrant, [fear] rules your life … or else you overthrow it" (2002b: 164), also by unreflective acceptance.

Thought, Despair, and Regret

Upon leaving his past life behind at Cracow and arriving in Marseilles, Conrad "left off being thoughtful." With "no ghosts of the past and no visions of the future … [he] walked down to the quay of the *vieux port* to join the pilot boat" (*PR* 113). But at age twenty, ill-fortune had him thinking again, desperate enough for suicide (or a faked attempt; Najder 1983: 53). It may have been that nadir which resigned him to the dubious "privilege of thought," the "chain and ball" of self (July 20, 1894, *CL4* 473), and resolved him never again to lose "possession of (him)self" (*PR* 15); defiance of despair and suicide became morbidly obsessive preoccupations (Cox 1973: 288). The *noms de guerre et de plume* of both authors mark these epiphanies; Józef Korzeniowski chose his third forename (anglicized) on joining the *Mont Blanc*, and Rushdie in hiding chose Conrad's and Chekhov's forenames (Rushdie 2012: 165).

By contrast, James Wait's "steadfastness to his untruthful attitude in the face of the inevitable truth," "his obstinate non-recognition of the only certitude" (*NN*

104) is despairing self-delusion. When Donkin goads Wait with the prospect of his imminent death, Wait calls him a "cadging, stinking liar" (112), and plagued by Podmore's prayers, he cries, "Keep him away from me" (90). In death, even, Wait "yet seem[s] to cling to the ship with the grip of an undying fear" (119). The vehemence of Wait's denials is affirmation; he does not know what he knows, life and death asserting conflicting claims. However, as Conrad wrote in "Heart of Darkness," "One can't live with one's finger everlastingly on one's pulse" (86).

Soon after the *fatwa*, Rushdie's writing of *Moor*, begun in 1988 (2012: 107), became a nostalgic shrug of *carpe diem* acceptance of a lost past and foreboding future—a decadal forerunner of *Joseph Anton*. Wait's dread is echoed by Moraes "with death at [his] heels" (2002b: 3): "I did indeed grow up good-looking, but for a long time that crippled right hand made me unable to see anything but ugliness in myself" (162). The Moor's clubhand is an objective correlative of Rushdie's inability to write, his inspiration and talent disfigured when he was reborn into fear, until he saw that he "must live until he dies," the motto that Rushdie used for the first time in *Moor* (2002b: 164), the novel a memorial to its author's decision to face down dread and live in the moment.

Death by Water

In a letter to John Galsworthy, Conrad described his own neurasthenia and crippling gout as a struggle to stay afloat: "I am trying to keep despair under … nevertheless I feel myself losing footing in deep waters" (November 30, 1903; *CL3* 84). His Jim dodges fear of drowning by jumping from the *Patna*, and Captain Montagu Brierly dodges Jim's cowardice as a mirror on his own moral frailty by drowning. Both leaps proceed from failure to withstand the blessed curse of consciousness. Conrad's Geoffrey Renouard in "The Planter of Malata," rejected and humiliated by Felicia Moorsom, "set[s] out calmly to swim beyond the confines of life" (73),[7] and Moraes's grandfather Francisco da Gama, suffocating in his own debauchery and his wife Epifania's contempt, "dived off the island [Cabral] and swam away; perhaps he was trying to find some air beyond the island's enchanted rim" (2002b: 24). Moraes's grandfather and father are reduced to self-knowing despair like Brierly's. "Water claims us," Moraes sighs. "They dove into the black night-harbour and swam out to the mother-ocean" (67).

In *Ground*, Vina Apsara's lover Ormus Cama (Kama: the god of love; Rushdie 1999: 148) writes a song, "The Swimmer": "The best in our natures is drowning in the worst" (130). The narrator Rai is of sterner stuff: "I was, I remain, a strong swimmer. Even my nine-year-old self would strike boldly out beyond my depth, heedless of danger" (59). *Lord Jim*'s Stein tells Marlow, "A man that is born ... is like a man who falls into the sea. If he tries to climb out into the air ... he drowns ... The way is to the destructive element submit yourself, and with the exertions of your hands and feet in the water make the deep, deep sea keep you up" (*LJ* 162–3).

Nostalgia—the Lost Ages of Islam and Sail

Physical and moral survival therefore demands a paradox: immersion in Being while staying afloat on the surfaces of thought, accepting the past that birthed the dreaded future. The history of asthmatic Moraes, his family, and his forebears, is a synecdochical metaphor for the nostalgic resignation to the decline of Muslim hegemony and culture. The historical backdrop to *Moor* is the *fin de siècle* of Moorish Spain in 1492, when the last Moorish stronghold Al-Andalus fell and Boabdil of Granada, the last Moorish sultan, fled into exile. Moraes's father Abraham sighs his last "thinking on Boabdil's end": "Breath left his body with a whine, and the next breath was a gasp ... Those eyes hot with ancient grief" (Rushdie 2002b: 80). This sorrow of dispossession and exile is a sentiment Rushdie shares with Conrad. Abraham's end echoes Wait's, berating the crew "with gasps between the words" (*NN* 32).

Moor's heroin addict Vasco Miranda's palimpsest compounds the symbolism: the original canvas, a painting of Aurora, is covered by Vasco's "equestrian [self]-portrait of the artist in Arab attire ... weeping on a great white horse" (Rushdie 2002b: 159), an allusion to Boabdil in Francisco Pradilla's painting *La rendición de Granada* [The Capitulation of Granada]. It resembles Joseph Anton Koch's (note his forenames) *Der Tyroler Landsturm Anno 1809*, depicting the leader of the failed 1809 Tyrolean rebellion. Vasco tells the contemptuous Aurora, "I have called it *The Artist as Boabdil, the Unlucky (el-Zogoybi), Last Sultan of Granada, Seen Departing from Alhambra ... Or The Moor's Last Sigh*" (2002b: 160). The visual and onomastic symbolism renders Vasco a pseudonymous post-figuration of Boabdil.[8] Like Moraes, Vasco is analogically and anagogically a Rushdie persona, a fictional revenant of Wait's creator Conrad.

Boabdil has as literary descendant not only Abraham Zogoiby, but Conrad's Singleton, a relic of sail's nova, of a generation of "men who knew how to exist," knowing "neither doubt nor hopes" (*NN* 31). Unthinking, he knows "how to be." His craft ethos from sail's halcyon days had by Conrad's reckoning sickened, like the intellectual malaise succeeding the culture of Ibn Rushd (1126–98): "Their successors are the grown-up children of a discontented earth … [T]hey have … learned how to whine" (*NN* 25). Superficially, Wait's and Abraham's dying gasps and Donkin's "whines" differ, the former symbolizing loss and regret, the latter an abject plaint. Yet, a nineteenth-century fictional malingering malcontent and a twentieth-century Iranian Imam are symptomatic paradigms of *fins de siècle* when the "air" of moral ethos has grown thin. Like Donkin's feeding on the near-carrion Wait, for Rushdie, Khomeini's stifling *fatwa* is symptomatic of the withering of Islam's erstwhile vibrant intellectualism, leaving only its sere husk.

The Tyranny of Time

From birth, Moraes has suffered accelerated growth and premature aging, a condition he associates with his congenital asthma, a lack of air symbolically to exhale as art: "In my family we've always found the world's air hard to breathe; we arrive hoping for somewhere better" (Rushdie 2002b: 53–4). Like Rushdie, Moraes is sentenced to an early death. The thin air of hope threatens suffocation in despair, "but I surmount it …" Moraes says. "I awake gasping and, sleep-heavy, grab fistfuls of air … Still, it is easier to breathe in than out" (53–4).

The air Moraes breathes is his every experience, even the natal sentence of early death. But only in his "breathing out," the *doing* of his art, giving written form to what he has taken in, does his being have meaning: "At such times I become my breathing … I am what breathes. It is not thinking that makes us so, but air … A sigh isn't just a sigh. We inhale the world and breathe out meaning" (Rushdie 2002b: 53–4). Joseph Anton's antetype Moraes is rescued by his Conradian apothegm; and Conrad's own "doing," his exhalation, was his work as sailor and writer. By contrast, *Lord Jim*'s Jones describes Brierly's last moments: "Captain Brierly … says with a little sigh: I am going aft" (*LJ* 51) and is gone. No "breathing out," no meaning to his life or death. Beyond the "dying whisper … " as Moraes says, only "the airless, silent void" (Rushdie 2002b: 54).

Vasco tells the child Moraes that a needle left in his, Vasco's, gut could kill him at any time: "Until the needle I have much to do … Live until you die. That is my creed. I'm like you … I'm also short of time" (Rushdie 2002b: 154). The white lie contains not only a sustaining truth, but also an uglier one; for unlike James Wait, whose denial is no lenitive for dread, Vasco is resigned to impending opiate death. Yet he both desires and runs from Moraes's mother Aurora Zagoiby, the "Snow Queen" (155). A "super-power" (3) modeled on Boabdil's domineering wife Ayxa la Horra, she is a modern version also of Doña Erminia in Conrad's "Gaspar Ruiz," presumably inspired by Simón Bolivar's Manuela Sáenz. Conrad, apostle of disinterested resignation, created Gaspar Ruiz as a simple-minded, yet inspirational, hero with the "lungs of giants" ([D] 29), whose "indifference to his fate was genuine" (21); yet it is to the indomitable Erminia that Gaspar Ruiz "exhale[s] the plaint of his wounded soul" (30).

The "splinter of bitterness in her blood" (Rushdie 2002b: 155), the figurative fairy-tale ice splinter, brings art to life and death to the artist: "Perhaps the needle, if indeed it really was in there … was in truth the source of his whole self—perhaps it was his soul. To lose it would be to lose his life at once, or at least its meaning. He preferred to work, and wait" (155), investing his life with the meaning of his art.

Do or Die

The "work and wait" wordplay on James Wait (who does not work) amounts to "Do or die" (*NN* 72), found on the stern of the doomed *Judea* in "Youth"; even in the ship's last hours, the mad Captain Beard insists on trimming the yards and winding the chronometers (26, 29). Willful illusion that denies futility gives life. As with *Nostromo*'s Charles Gould, "Action is consolatory. It is the enemy of thought … Only in the conduct of our actions can we find the sense of mastery over the fates" ([D] 66). To do or die is to accept the inevitable and get on with life, the alternative living death—to do or not to do, thus to be or not to be.

Moraes's version of Descartes's Ontological Argument is "*Suspiro ergo sum*. In the beginning and unto the end is the lung" (Rushdie 2002b: 53). Moraes's play on "*cogito*" is its converse: thought is the undoing of Being. Conrad, whose father Apollo translated *Hamlet*, perhaps would have seen in Joseph Anton, before his succor by Wait's workless words, resolution sicklied over with the pale cast of thought by the oppressor's wrong; he cannot write, his creative currents stilled, losing the name of action.

So Rushdie conflates both Vasco and Moraes with himself, coping with the prospect of early death. Aurora, symbol of Rushdie's enduring muse, continues to "do," painting Moraes posed nude "into immortality, giving [him] the gift of being part of what would persist of her" (Rushdie 2002b: 221). Moraes recalls, "I needed consolations and was happy to take whatever was on offer" (220). The painting's worth is symbolically the measure of Rushdie's own literary art shorn of artifice and stripped for action: "Tragedy disguised as fantasy and rendered in the most beautiful, most heightened colour and light she could create: it was a mythomaniac gem. She called it *A Light to Lighten the Darkness*" (220). That passage is the self-appraisal of a captive in safe houses liberated by his pen, who embraces the prospect of dying. A different order entirely from "thought."

Transcending Tyrannies of Time

Time is in short supply for Wait in *The Nigger of the "Narcissus"* and in Rushdie's post-*fatwa* novels. When *Moor*'s Aurora takes Moraes, aged five but physically aged ten, to Lord Khusro Bhagwan, the "mahaguru,"[9] his counsel is like Stein's " 'how to be': … 'In the destructive element you must immerse' " (*LJ*: 162–3). Khusro emptily intones, "Embrace your fate … turn and run towards it … Only by becoming your misfortune can you transcend it" (Rushdie 2002b: 163). Moraes profits by Khusro's canned wisdom: "By embracing the inescapable, I lost my fear of it … because, if my time on earth was limited, I didn't have seconds to spare for funk. Lord Khusro's injunction echoed Vasco Miranda's motto, another version of which I found, years later, in a story by J. Conrad. *I must live until I die*" (2002b: 164; emphasis in original).

Moraes lives an eremitic existence, the promise of an early end made real when his first lover Uma makes him hear "Death's lightning footsteps as they ran towards me; then, O then, I heard each lethal scything of his blade" (Rushdie 2002b: 192). He makes his clubhand infirmity into a strength when his mentor Lambajan teaches him to box (146, 195). Living in the moment, he collects "priceless nuggets" (240), symbolically the myth, history, culture, and literature Rushdie arranged in kaleidoscopic holograms of whimsical wit both risible and sad—a sigh for a lost time and time lost.

In Aurora's oil self-portrait with him, Moraes's "stunted hand had become a glowing light, the only light-source in the picture" (Rushdie 2002b: 220); in Aurora's painting, *The Early Moors*, the clubhand is "transformed into a series of miracles" (224) symbolic of Rushdie's art when he concludes that he "must live" and resumes writing. Moraes exults, "As I grew older, so my weapon increased in might" (195)—as did his creator Rushdie's inspiration.[10] Beneath the hard lambent surfaces of Rushdie's wit are abysses of time, like Conrad's unfathomable depths. In *Ground*, with its literal and symbolic earthquakes and abysses, Boonyi and her voluptuary husband Max Ophuls are immured like James Wait in a dreadful present. Like them, Joseph Anton is suspended in an abyss between a lost past and a dreaded future.

In *Ground*, Ormus's "lassitudinous inertia" (Rushdie 1999: 193) can end only with a letting go of futurity, in the nature of the symbolism of Conrad's Jim ascending the Patusan River with an unloaded revolver: "Nothing could have been more prosaic and more unsafe, more extravagantly casual, more lonely" (*LJ* 174). The unloaded pistol is Jim's letting go, stripped for action and no longer in fearful fancied readiness for any of the dreaded eventualities he has imagined, when really some ineffable fate may blindside him yet again. This time, shed of his brittle inner armaments of thought and romantic illusion, he is resigned to an inscrutable future.

Like Jim overcoming regret, Rushdie defeated dread. In *Luka and the Fire of Life* (Rushdie 2010), Luka is yet another Rushdie persona. Like Haroun in *Haroun and the Sea of Stories* (Rushdie 1990), he lives in the city of Kahani, "meaning 'story'" (209): "I have a little house and I live alone. It has no doors or windows, and I must break through the wall" (54). Like Wait's confining quarters and Joseph Anton's safe houses, Luka's walls are symbolic. He defeats the riddling Old Man of the River of Time with his *ecce homo* answer to the question of self, an epiphany revealing a story-telling strength given him by his father Rashid that he did not know he had (158), until Time's eventual triumph (54–6). He concludes: "There are those of us who learn to live *completely* in the moment" (160).

Indifference, the Counterfeit of Courage

In *Shalimar the Clown* (Rushdie 2005), Olga Simeonova muses that she lives "between yesterday and tomorrow in the country of lost happiness and peace, the place of mislaid calm … I now don't feel. Consequently, however, I have no fear of death" (Rushdie 2005: 9). Narcotics symbolize the sleep of reason, surcease from imaginative thought. The epigraph to Conrad's *An Outcast of the Islands* is a line from Pedro Calderón de la Barca's *La vida es sueño* (Life Is a Dream);[11] like a corollary proposition, the epigraph of *Two Years Eight Months and Twenty-Eight Nights* (Rushdie 2015), *El sueño de la razón produce monstruos*[12] elucidates *Shalimar*'s threat of a frenzied society (rather than personal death). *Shalimar*'s India (or Kashmira) Ophuls "remember[s] the drugs, the hallucinogens … bringing forth monsters" (350). The *fatwa* was born of Persian Islam's sleep of reason after the age of Ibn Rushd, breeding monstrous passions like the "*Narcissus*" crew's, capable of being stirred to violence.

The assassin Shalimar understands that "my life was going to be one thing, but death turned it into another" (Rushdie 2005: 83–4). His self-knowing creator Rushdie, changed by the threat of death, had to quell monsters of the mind. A *khwaja* (Islamic teacher) counsels Shalimar's father Abdullah on the death of his wife: "The question of death is also a question of life, panditji, and the question of how to live … [has] no answer except in the going on" (83–4). Faced with encroaching Pathan hordes in Kashmir (85–9),[13] Abdullah rallies to his duty as Sarpanch of Pachigam with the same courageous resignation with which Lord Jim presents himself before Doramin to face inscrutable fate (*LJ* 312–13).

Against a background of Kashmir's descent into murder and violence, Boonyi, who has cuckolded Shalimar, has inner writhings that Rushdie must have felt. Declared dead by Pachigam's *Panchayat* (council) and living in solitary exile, she dreads Shalimar's return: "All that remained between them was death" (Rushdie 2005: 263). Like Conrad's Brierly, who "perceived the gates of the other world flung open wide for his reception" (*LJ* 50), she asks "the gates of hell to open, but no cavity yawned. She was already in hell" (Rushdie 2005: 263–4). Unlike either Wait's denial or Joseph Anton's resignation, Boonyi's response to dread is the counterfeit courage of despairing indifference: "I am just a thing that lives and breathes and if I stopped breathing and living it would make no difference except to him … Come if you want. I'm waiting. I no longer care" (Rushdie 2005: 298).

* * *

Throughout Rushdie's oeuvre, the tropes and leitmotifs always have the same subtext: a longing for freedom—a young woman's longing for a world of infinite possibility untrammeled by her sex, a boy on a tightrope striving to escape gravity (Rushdie 2005: 55–6), Joseph Anton liberated by his art. Rushdie's dread had its origins, not simply in the *fatwa*, but the prior conditions of his life, which inspired *The Satanic Verses*. A function of "outsideness" is that "in every quarter there are a few souls, call them lucky or cursed who are simply born *not belonging*" (Rushdie 1999: 72).

Although differing in kind and degree from Rushdie's, that was Conrad's acquired condition; but the writer in exile from an idealized past and imprisoned in the present always lays claim to freedom and selfhood in a better time and place. The question of freedom, linked to the question of "how to be," is answered in consolatory action: the act of art. Joseph Anton learns what Conrad's Stein knows: He finds his strength and freedom in resignation to James Wait's "I must live till I die—mustn't I?"

In *Fury* (Rushdie 2001), another memoir thinly disguised as fiction, Rushdie's persona Milo Mila "had a bad heart, he knew he was never going to be an old man ... but he had made a decision about his life. You know, like in *The Nigger of the 'Narcissus.'* I must live until I die. And that's what he did, he did great work" (113). With what Captain Alistoun calls the "grit to face what's coming to us all" (*NN* 127), Conrad, apostle of modernism's fixed codes and hierarchies, wrote of the "aim accomplished," that "all the truth of life is there: a moment of vision, a sigh, a smile—and return to eternal rest" (*NN* 9). His life done at sixty-six years and five months with work on *Suspense* in *media res*, Conrad left Rushdie his life and literature's legacy. Postcolonialism's Rushdie amid the urgencies of modernity's rapidly shifting intercultural relativities, having turned Conrad's James Wait to good account, works and waits, living by his persona Geronimo's advice: "Do what you have to do, tell your story, live your life, get out quickly, *spit spot*" (Rushdie 2015: 218).

Notes

1 See, e.g., Cooper 1874: 116; Dibdin 1840: 97; Dent 1984: 480, entries 356, 385, 413; query note by "Pearmain" November 5 (*Bye-gones* 1889–90, New Series I: 169), and reply by "W. O." September 16 (*Bye-gones* 1891–2, New Series II: 503); Jefferies 1887: 157; Garner 2004: 140.

2 The phrase appears as in *The Moor's Last Sigh* (2001), *Fury* (2001), *Step Cross This Line* (2002), and *Shalimar the Clown* (2005).

3 *The Moor's Last Sigh*, its title derived from *Puerto del Suspiro del Moro*, the pass where Boabdil allegedly wept.

4 Reference to literal Himalayan subduction (Rushdie 1999: 60, 210, 216).

5 This is also an over-arching trope in *The Enchantress of Florence* (Rushdie 2008).

6 "We haven't kept pigs together" (*NN* 41) is a Polish idiom: "*świń z tobą nie pas(a)łem*." See Frajzyngier (1985: 143–4).

7 Derived from the Moorsom System for calculating a ship's tonnage capacity, the name has no onomastic significance for the Moor.

8 For Boabdil see Lowry (2016: 1–2). Visual sources in oils for Vasco Miranda's self-portrayal (2002b: 159) are: Koch, *Tyroler Volksaufstand* [Tyrolean Rebellion] (1819); *Der Tyroler Landsturm Anno 1809* [The Tyrolean Militia 1809]; and Francisco Pradilla y Ortiz, *La rendición de Granada* [The Capitulation of Granada] (1882).

9 Khusro (a.k.a. Cyrus Cama) reappears in *The Ground Beneath Her Feet*.

10 From the *fatwa* eight novels (excluding *The Golden House*, 2017, and three collections of essays). The *fatwa* is no longer active (*The Guardian*, September 25, 1998).

11 *Pues el delito mayor del hombre es haber nacito* (Man's greatest crime is to have been born)."

12 Title of a Goya etching, c. 1797–9.

13 Since Independence August 15, 1947, the state has been divided between Pakistan's Azad Kashmir and India's Jammu and Kashmir.

References

Bye-gones: Relating to Wales and the Border Counties. 1889–90. New Series I. Ostwestry: The National Library of Wales. https://babel.hathitrust.org/cgi/pt?id=hvd32044094421139. Accessed May 10, 2022.

Bye-gones: Relating to Wales and the Border Counties. 1891–2. New Series II. Ostwestry: The National Library of Wales. https://babel.hathitrust.org/cgi/pt?id=hvd32044094421229. Accessed May 10, 2022.

Cooper, Thomas. 1874. "The Last Days of an Old Sailor; or 'Butter Your Shirt! Sing Tantra Bobus, Make Shift!'" In *Old Fashioned Stories*, 111–23. London: Hodder and Stoughton.

Cox, C. B. 1973. "Joseph Conrad and the Question of Suicide." *Bulletin of the John Rylands University Library* 55, no. 2: 285–99.

Dent, R. W. 1984. *Proverbial Language in English Drama Exclusive of Shakespeare, 1495–1616: An Index.* Los Angeles: University of California Press.

Dibdin, Charles. 1840. *Songs Naval and National, of the Late Charles Dibdin with a Memoir and Addenda.* London: Murray. https://archive.org/details/songsnavalandna00cruigoog. Accessed May 10, 2022.

Frajzyngier, Zygmunt. 1985. "James Wait's Polish Idiom." *Conradiana* 17, no. 2: 143–2.

Garner, Alan. 2004. *Thursbitch.* London: Vintage.

Jefferies, John Richard. 1887. The "Country Sunday." *Longman's Magazine* 30 (May–October): 146–63. https://archive.org/details/sim_longmans-may-october-1887_30_index. Accessed May 10, 2022.

Koch, Joseph Anton. 1809. *Tiroler Landsturm* [Tyrolean Militia]. Innsbruck: Landesmuseum Ferdinandeum. https://www.alamy.com/tiroler-/landsturm-tyrolean-militia-1809-image387195887.html. Accessed May 10, 2022.

Koch, Joseph Anton. 1819. *Tyroler Volksaufstand* [Tyrolean Rebellion]. *Wikipedia.* Wikimedia Corp 1–4. https://en.wikipedia.org/wiki/Tyrolean_Rebellion. Accessed May 10, 2022.

Lowry, Robina Lambert, and Fiona Flores Watson. 2016. "Boabdil: The Moors in Andalucia, Moorish History in Andalucia, Spain, History of Southern Spain." http://www.andalucia.com/history/spainsmoorishhistory.htm. Accessed May 10, 2022.

Najder, Zdzisław. 1983. *Joseph Conrad: A Chronicle*. New Brunswick, NJ: Rutgers University Press.

Pradilla y Ortiz, Francisco. 1882. *La rendición de Granada* [The Capitulation of Granada]. *El arte en el Senado* 1, 2. Fondo histórico, Senado de España. https://commons.wikimedia.org/wiki/Category:La_Rendición_de_Granada,_de_Francisco_Pradilla_(Palacio_de_Senado_de_España. Accessed May 10, 2022.

Robben, Bernhard. 2013. "Salman Rushdie: The Satanic Consequences," interview by *ExBerliner*, November 8. http://www.exberliner.com./berlin/salman-rushdie-i-must-live-until-i-die/. Accessed May 10, 2022.

Rushdie, Salman. 1990. *Haroun and the Sea of Stories*. Toronto: Alfred A. Knopf.

Rushdie, Salman. 1991. "'Commonwealth Literature' does not exist." In *Imaginary Homelands: Essays and Criticism 1981–1991*, 61–70. London: Granta.

Rushdie, Salman. 1999. *The Ground Beneath Her Feet*. London: Vintage.

Rushdie, Salman. 2001. *Fury*. Toronto: Alfred A. Knopf.

Rushdie, Salman. 2002a. "Influence." In *Step Across this Line: Collected Nonfiction 1992–2002*, 62–9. Toronto: Alfred A. Knopf.

Rushdie, Salman. 2002b. *The Moor's Last Sigh*. Toronto: Alfred A. Knopf.

Rushdie, Salman. 2005. *Shalimar the Clown*. Toronto: Alfred A. Knopf.

Rushdie, Salman. 2008. *The Enchantress of Florence*. Toronto: Alfred A. Knopf.

Rushdie, Salman. 2010. *Luka and the Fire of Life*. Toronto: Alfred A. Knopf.

Rushdie, Salman. 2012. *Joseph Anton: A Memoir*. Toronto: Alfred A. Knopf.

Rushdie, Salman. 2015. *Two Years Eight Months and Twenty-Eight Nights*. Toronto: Alfred A. Knopf.

Rushdie, Salman. 2017. *The Golden House*. Toronto: Alfred A. Knopf.

"The Rushdie Fatwa." 1998. *The Guardian*. September 25. https://www.the guardian.com/world/rushdie-fatwa. Accessed May 10, 2022.

16

Metropolitan Terror in *The Secret Agent*: Truth and Fiction in a Surreal Drama

Gerard Kilroy
Jesuit University Ignatianum, Kraków

My love of this Polish master of English prose was inspired by two monks, from two different Benedictine monasteries. Dom Paul Ziegler of Quarr Abbey, on the Isle of Wight, first introduced me to *Victory*, while Dom Illtyd Trethowan, of Downside Abbey, introduced me to *The Secret Agent*. Since then, I have read, studied, and taught both novels as often as I can. Dom Illtyd also introduced me to the compelling mystery of "The Secret Sharer," with its investigation of the relations between the human person and possibility. Both of these men were mystics—one a poet, the other a theologian. I have never, for this reason, been able to miss the profound moral and metaphysical dimension in Conrad's portrayal of our world.

I should like you to allow me to bring to *The Secret Agent* this metaphysical perspective and to suggest that this novel—obviously not "A Simple Tale" as Conrad ironically suggests in his subtitle—so transforms the conventions of the novel that it deserves to be treated as a genre of its own. I shall leave to the discussion at the end how to situate *The Secret Agent* and first attempt a brief analysis of its very unusual structure and a more detailed one of its wholly original use of language and imagery to create a world that owes more to the modes and patterns of poetry than to the conventional novel. It is no surprise that T. S. Eliot wished to place an epigraph from Conrad at the beginning of *The Waste Land*, one of the greatest poems of the twentieth century. In his patterns of language and imagery, Conrad is surely closer to Eliot than to Dickens, Hardy, or Tolstoy. In *The Secret Agent* as in *Victory*, the shining exception to this imagistic writing is the idealized tragic heroine, who seems to take control of the "plot" in the second half of the novel, as Lena does in *Victory*. As she drives a knife into the idle bulk of her recumbent husband, Winnie shares much with Lena, even if her husband has none of Heyst's idealism; indeed, Verloc shares a great deal with that other "monster" (*SA* 208), Mister Kurtz, in "Heart of Darkness." While Kurtz lies "in an impenetrable darkness," with a terrifying perception of "The horror! The horror!" (HD 117) of his life and deeds, Verloc, on his back, is still unable to grasp the moral depths of what he has done. As he calls "Winnie" to come to him in what Conrad calls his "note of wooing," still imposing his own "leisurely" mode of being on the narrative, he has just time to see the shadow of the carving knife as it "flickered up and down" (*SA* 197).

In a novel full of idle, fat, narcissistic, and parasitical men, who live off "the social mechanism" in the darkened shadows of a "town of marvels and mud" (*SA* 203) and a secret agent who does nothing and works with the anarchists, the Russian embassy, *and* the police, an economically dependent woman is the only person who *does* anything. Of course, in several ways, she demands comparison with Hardy's wronged heroine in *Tess of the d'Urbervilles*: Tess also kills an unfeeling man, but Alec's blood, dripping from the ceiling is much closer to Victorian melodrama, and Tess's murder seems to be attacking the whole patriarchal society that condemned her to shame and left Alec untouched. In Conrad's novel, which affects to be a *roman policier*, where the reader normally enjoys the satisfaction of seeing the police or the law carry out justice, Conrad chooses a heroine able to drive a knife into the breast not just of a monstrous, inert husband, but into the heart of the "social mechanism" that is sustained in delicate and hypocritical balance between the Houses of Parliament, British society hostesses, the police, the Russian embassy, and absolutely idle and grotesque anarchists. One distinctively Polish element in the novel is that the real villain is a Russian, the oily society favorite, Mr. Vladimir.

If Conrad's novel is poetic, indeed surreal, it also reflects the real world of his time. Between 1823 and 1906, no one was refused entry into England, and the result was that by 1880, London was full of anarchists. These fell into three main groups: the Russian *Narodnaya Volya*, usually known as "nihilists"; Irish-American Fenians; and pan-European anarchists. From London, they plotted outrages in Continental capitals, and it was the Russian nihilists who first adopted the term "terrorist" in 1879: their aim, they said, was "terrorist revolution." It is significant that, with one notable exception, they organized no explosions in London; the exception was the explosion in Greenwich Park in 1894, where a bomb appears to have exploded accidentally in the hands of a French tailor well known in anarchist circles, Martial Bourdin. This is often cited in introductions to *The Secret Agent*, as if this is enough to explain Conrad's conception, and yet what is more significant is what Conrad does *not* include: the one group that did terrorize London in this period, the Irish Fenians. Between 1881 and 1885, they carried out thirteen successful plots: bombs exploded "in the City of London, under London Bridge, in the railway stations' left luggage rooms, and the tunnels of the underground" (Short 1979: 1).

As Michael Frank notes, "The sustained campaign (the first of its kind in the history of terrorism) culminated on January 24, 1885, with near-simultaneous explosions at the Tower of London, Westminster Hall, and the Houses of Parliament" (2012: 48). Conrad's omission of the real threat London faced at the time clarifies and makes precise Conrad's philosophical interest. While the Fenians had a political purpose that could be rationally understood, the Russian nihilists did not. Conrad's portrayal of the whole of the social order and those pretending to subvert it—government, police, law, terrorists, anarchists, *agents provocateurs*—as a vast mechanism collaborating to maintain their own interests in the status quo required that the anarchists and Russian *agents provocateurs* should be portrayed as *absurd*. Even if the Clan na Gael and the Skirmishers (the two Irish groups responsible for the outrages) used dynamite, their targets were not the public at large and their aims made political sense. Only the anarchists deliberately staged indiscriminate outrages. In 1892, they blew up a restaurant in Paris, killing two people in the Boulevard de Magenta; in 1893, a Spanish anarchist threw a bomb into the Lyceu Opera House in Barcelona, killing more than twenty. In 1894, Emile Henry threw a bomb into the Café Terminus near Gare Saint Lazare in Paris, injuring more than twenty and killing one. Taken together, these attacks marked the arrival of indiscriminate and destructive terrorism as we know it today. Even if, by 1906, it had not reached London, it must have seemed merely a matter of time before it did.

A portrayal of Irish Fenians as nihilists did get into the earliest literary response to the Fenian campaign: *The Dynamiter* by Fanny Stevenson, the wife of Robert Louis Stevenson, who tried to keep her husband amused as he started losing his sight by reading him terrorist stories. They were published under the title *More New Arabian Nights*, in 1885. The bomb builder in this story, named Zero, who speaks with a foreign accent, has a vision of "the fall of England, the massacre of thousands, the yell of fear and execration" (Stevenson 1924: 118). The targets of Irish Fenians are selected in order to cause the greatest possible public outcry. Zero's companion, Patrick M'Guire, on his way to an abortive attempt to blow up a statue of Shakespeare, reflects with shocking callousness:

> As M'Guire drew near, his heart was inflamed by the most noble sentiment of triumph. Never had he seen the garden so crowded; children, still stumbling in the impotence of youth, ran to and fro, shouting and playing round the pedestal; an old, sick pensioner sat upon the nearest bench, a medal on his breast, a stick with which he walked (for he was disabled by wounds) reclining on his knee. Guilty England would thus be stabbed in the most delicate quarters; the moment had, indeed, been well selected. (Stevenson 1924: 121–2)

Zero has so many failures with his bombs (giving his name an ironic meaning) that he decides to retire, but before he can do so, his bag knocks against a bookstall, the bomb goes off, and he is "expunged" (Stevenson 1924: 201). Even if not technically a nihilist, with his name and methods, which are closer to theirs than to the Fenians', Zero could have provided Conrad with a hint as to how to subject anarchists to a frontal assault by the full force of irony.

One of the most ironic things in *The Secret Agent* is the structure. For the first seven of thirteen chapters, neither anarchists nor police, neither *agents provocateurs* nor Russian embassy officials *do* anything except talk. The only event that reaches the reader, through the newspapers, is the news that a man has been blown to bits in Greenwich Park. As we discover, the only event in the novel until the murder at the end, is an accident whose immediate cause is Verloc and whose ultimate cause is "the favourite of intelligent society women" (*SA* 31), Mr. Vladimir, at the Russian embassy. Vladimir sponges off the very society for which he expresses the deepest contempt. He despises the British veneration for liberty, as he explains to Verloc: "This country is absurd with its sentimental regard for individual liberty. It's intolerable to think that all your friends have got only to come over to—" (*SA* 28). Verloc interrupts him to give exactly the same justification of his "inaction" as Chief Inspector Heat later: "In that way I have them all under my eye" (*SA* 28). In his idle surveillance, Verloc contrasts with the man nicknamed "the Professor," the only radical terrorist in the novel, who says, "Nothing would please me more than to see Inspector Heat and his likes take to shooting us down in broad daylight with the approval of the public. Half our battle would be won then; the disintegration of the old morality would have set in in its very temple" (*SA* 60).

The Professor's reasoning shows Conrad's defense of the British respect for legality, contrasting it with the situation in "the States," where, as the Professor argues, "they don't stand on ceremony with their institutions" and "the collective temperament is lawless" (*SA* 60); so from a revolutionist's point of view, "America is all right. It is this country [England] that is dangerous, with her idealistic conception of legality. The social spirit of this people is wrapped up in scrupulous prejudices and that is fatal to our work" (*SA* 60). What is remarkable about Conrad's portrayal of terrorism and the State is that from the start he portrays them in terms of an elaborate game of point and counterpoint. An additional element of the author's irony is that Mr. Vladimir, who contemptuously expresses a wish for "England to be brought into line. The imbecile bourgeoisie of this country make themselves the accomplices of the very people whose aim is to drive them out of their houses to starve in ditches" (*SA* 28) has exactly the same opinions and desires as the most extreme revolutionary in the book. This "favourite in the very highest society" (*SA* 24), Mr. Vladimir, wishes to blow it to pieces in order for it to abandon its scrupulous adherence to liberty and law, a view identical with the Professor's. In a long conversation with another idle anarchist, Ossipon, the Professor expounds his destructive philosophy and his contempt for "revolutionists": "You revolutionists are the slaves of the social convention, which is afraid of you; slaves of it as much as the very police that stands up in the defense of that convention" (*SA* 57–8). In contrast, the Professor argues that he is superior to them: "They depend on life ... whereas I depend on death, which knows no restraint and cannot be attacked" (*SA* 57).

Sounding like Callicles (a thin disguise for Alcibiades) in Plato's *Gorgias*, the Professor is chosen by Conrad to end the novel with a defense of *force*. The word is repeated, as if force were an abstract concept, five times in these last two pages: four times by the Professor and once in the very last paragraph, as Conrad describes, in a devastating coda, the living embodiment of the intellectual absurdity and metaphysical despair at the heart of terrorism:

> And the incorruptible Professor walked, too, averting his eyes from the odious multitude of mankind. He had no future. He disdained it. He was a force. His thoughts caressed the images of ruin and destruction. He walked frail, insignificant, shabby, miserable—and terrible in the simplicity of his idea calling madness and despair to the regeneration of the world. Nobody looked at him. He passed on unexpected and deadly, like a pest in the street full of men. (*SA* 231)

If Conrad allows us to see the true human tragedy that is at the heart of the novel, he is as withering in his analysis of the intellectual emptiness of force as is Simone Weil, who, in the essay she wrote in December 1940, when France faced the full horror of four years of Nazi occupation, argues that force reduces men to things: both victims of force and those who practice it: "Such is the nature of force. Its power of converting a man into a thing is a double one, and in its application double-edged. To the same degree, though in different fashions, those who use it and those who endure it are turned to stone" (Weil 1965: 23). Conrad seems to have reached the same conclusion, and it is significant that he uses the word *force* when describing the police constable who vanishes without trace, even as "the assistant commissioner, as though he were a member of the criminal classes, lingered out of sight, awaiting his return. But this constable seemed for ever to be lost to the *force*" (*SA* 116; emphasis added). Although it is a common ellipsis for the full title, *police force*, Conrad has chosen the word carefully to emphasize that the assistant commissioner and the terrorist are two sides of the same coin of Death, and that the chief inspector represents the "forces of law, property, oppression and injustice" (*SA* 75). As the Professor contemptuously argues, "The terrorist and the policeman both come from the same basket. Revolution, legality—counter moves in the same game; forms of idleness at bottom identical" (*SA* 58). No wonder that Conrad makes the main cast of policemen and anarchists less alive than the objects around them. As the Professor and Comrade Ossipon, who has just led Winnie Verloc to her suicide, leave the beer hall, "The mechanical piano near the door played through a valse cheekily, then fell silent all at once, as if gone grumpy" (*SA* 231). When Verloc, "tired" by his "labours" (persuading his simple-minded brother-in-law to carry the bomb and blow himself to bits), collapses "heavily" on the sofa, he is described as "disregarding as usual the fate of his hat, which, as if accustomed to take care of itself, made for a safe shelter under the table" (*SA* 194–5). When the Great Personage, Sir Ethelred, interviews the assistant commissioner, he stares at "the ponderous marble timepiece with the sly, feeble tick. The gilt hands had taken the opportunity to steal through no less than five and twenty minutes behind his back" (*SA* 111).

Conrad devotes the first seven chapters to an analysis of the absurdity of the "hate and despair" that characterize the nihilist and anarchist, and of their symbiotic relationship with the police and government. Even as Chief Inspector Heat reflects on "the absurdity of things human" and the fact that police and thieves "understand each other" and are indeed "products of the same machine" (*SA* 74), he regrets that "the anarchist nicknamed the Professor" is not, like them, "free from all taint of hate and despair" (*SA* 75). Nevertheless, Heat and the Professor delicately circle round each other, playing a complex "game" (*SA* 76), and Heat will not arrest him, any more than he will arrest Verloc, "on account of the rules of the game" (*SA* 95); instead, he will "get hold of him" later (Conrad repeats this key phrase) "according to the rules of the game" (*SA* 96). So Heat's relationship with the anarchists, even with one as dangerous as the Professor, is as symbiotic as his superior's. According to the assistant commissioner, Heat is keen to protect Verloc, who works both for him and the embassy, being a useful agent for both. But the assistant commissioner himself is keen to protect Michaelis because "the lady patroness" whose "drawing-room" he frequents, who is not "an exploiting capitalist," as Conrad explains, but "above the play of economic conditions" (*SA* 85), thinks that the "ticket-of-leave" apostle has "the temperament of a saint" (*SA* 86). Conrad is devastating in his analysis of the political naivete of some members of the English aristocracy, another view that was to prove prophetic in the late 1930s, with Diana Mitford and the Duke of Windsor, for example.

What Conrad does show in this elaborate "game" is that those tasked with law and order are very far from pursuing shared goals. Chief Inspector Heat, the unnamed assistant commissioner, and the Great Personage all have their own interests at the front of their minds. Indeed, when the assistant commissioner challenges his subordinate on his use of Verloc, Heat defends his position on the technicality that Verloc is not "in his pay," but "in the pay of a foreign government," and keeps Heat informed of the arrival of any new anarchists (*SA* 103). When Heat maintains his right to preserve his own secrets, "There are things not fit for everybody to know," the assistant commissioner replies, "Your idea of secrecy seems to consist in keeping the chief of your department in the dark" (*SA* 103).

The assistant commissioner is compromised even more, since he is not only anxious to preserve his place in the drawing room of the Lady Patroness by protecting the obese Michaelis from arrest, but he also goes to the same club as Mr. Vladimir, the man behind the whole dastardly plot. When the assistant commissioner tells the "apprentice statesman," the unpaid private secretary of the Great Personage, Toodles, that Vladimir is an honorary member of the Explorers Club, Toodles says, "That's the beastliest thing I've ever heard in my life" (*SA* 164), a verdict that seems ironically contrasted with Stevie's more passionate and precise use of the word "beastly" (*SA* 132) to describe the treatment of the poor. Conrad uses the word once more to describe Ossipon's vision of Verloc's blood: "a beastly pool of it all round the hat" (*SA* 215). Conrad's sharpened awareness of the ironic space behind common idiomatic expressions is unrivaled.

The author's poetic satire of the English system of clubs reaches its peak when Vladimir and the assistant commissioner stand together outside the Explorers Club. When Vladimir hails a hansom cab, the assistant commissioner remarks: "You're not going in here" (*SA* 172). It is a statement, not a question, and seems to be the ultimate verdict passed on Vladimir: "The thought passed through his mind that Mr Vladimir, honorary member, would not be seen very often there in the future" (*SA* 173). This is all Vladimir can expect from the English establishment, as always, keen not to make a fuss, to do anything showy. As we have seen, both the Russian embassy and the radical anarchist agree in wishing the police to use more violent methods. In fact, Vladimir uses the same language of destruction as the Professor: "A bomb outrage to have any influence on public opinion now must go beyond the intention of vengeance or terrorism. It must be purely destructive" (*SA* 30). For all his irony at the expense of the English class system and English clubs, Conrad's admiration for the value the country puts on law and liberty seems touchingly idealistic. By contrast, he is prophetic in warning of where the real danger lies: not in the agitators for Home Rule, but in the "madness and despair" of both Russian anarchists and the Russian state. Sir Robert Anderson (1841–1918) portrayed himself as a successful spymaster and detective in his self-aggrandizing *Sidelights on the Home-Rule Movement*, published on May 12, 1906, after Conrad had written 14,000 words, roughly the first three chapters of his novel (Porter 2004). Conrad takes many details from Anderson, particularly in his running of the Fenian double agent, Henri le Carron (Thomas Beach), for his portrait of the assistant commissioner, but the focus is shifted from the Fenians to the Russian state and idle anarchists. While Special Branch was still focusing on the Fenian threat, Vladimir Lenin (1870–1924) was steering the Bolsheviks to victory in the second congress in London in July 1903. By 1907, when more than 366 delegates came to London for the fifth congress of the Russian Social and Democratic Labor Party, from May 13 to June 1, Special Branch began a close watch. During June and July 1907, Conrad was writing the last (third) part of the book (*SA* xviii).

So if the first half of the book is an almost static analysis of the elaborate game played by the anarchists, the Russian government, the police, and Parliament, the real action takes place with all the drama of Aeschylus's *Agamemnon* in the second part of the novel, Chapters 8 to 13. Winnie drives her knife into the recumbent form of the idle agent with a stronger sense of justice than Clytemnestra, whose purity of revenge for her daughter is qualified by her adultery with Aegisthus. Winnie's revenge for the murder of a boy who is almost the embodiment of innocence not only expresses the desire of the reader for justice, but also acts as a contrast to the inadequacies of the English judicial system. Verloc expects only a short prison sentence for his actions, since technically, he has been only an accessory to terrorism or an accident. The fact that Winnie expects to hang for her murder, and that she flings herself on the dreadful Ossipon to avoid that fate, only heightens the reader's identification with Stevie's view of the world: "Bad!

Bad!" (*SA* 132). The focus of the first half of the book is on the dubious, entirely masculine world of idle anarchists, whose parasitic impotence is suggested by their gross weight and the brown paper packages in Verloc's shady shop and vividly exemplified in Comrade Ossipon's failure to rescue a damsel in distress; instead, he robs her of her money and leaves her to drown. The transition to a world dominated by a feminine sense of justice occurs when the assistant commissioner visits what Conrad ironically calls "the humble abode of Mr Verloc's domestic happiness" (*SA* 117). At this point, Conrad defies chronology and takes us back in time to explain how his domestic arrangements have come about, with Winnie marrying him so she could find a good arrangement for her mother and Stevie. The climactic center of the novel comes in the wonderfully surreal cab journey in Chapter 8, the turning point, when Stevie's simple view of the police contrasts vividly with all we have learnt in the first part of the novel. As Stevie hears how badly the cabbie is treated, he concludes it is a "bad world for poor people" (132) and assumes that the police are there to sort this injustice out. When Winnie tells him that "they are not for that," he replies, amazed, "Not for that? ... Not for that? He had formed for himself an ideal conception of the metropolitan police as a sort of benevolent institution for the suppression of evil" (*SA* 132–3). Conrad is not content to leave this irony there, as Winnie offers a rather Dickensian ex cathedra answer to Stevie's anxieties: "Don't you know what the police are for Stevie? They are there so that them as have nothing shouldn't take anything away from them who have" (*SA* 133). This is entirely in line with Conrad's portrayal of the "game," an elaborate equilibrium between "the force" and anarchists, between embassy and senior policemen, in which the real threat to society, the Professor, whose evil presence Conrad highlights in the last line of the novel, remains untouched: "Nobody looked at him. He passed on unsuspected and deadly, like a pest in the street full of men" (*SA* 231).

Yet, even in this unusual bomb outrage—unusual because Stevie was not "known to the police" like the other anarchists—the police are not as impotent as the anarchists and apparently crack the case in twelve hours, as the assistant commissioner points out to Vladimir (*SA* 172). The praise of the police force seems mainly directed at Vladimir, whose Russian contempt for the English police he is compelled to revise: "But in his heart he was almost awed by the miraculous cleverness of the English police" (*SA* 171). For at the heart of the novel, the point where in an ordinary crime novel, the perceptive detective sees in a blinding flash the significance of some trivial piece of evidence, the roles are reversed. Chief Inspector Heat, anything but hot on the trail of Verloc, shows Winnie Verloc the label Stevie has been wearing. What Aristotle calls the *anagnorisis*, the recognition scene, is Winnie's not Heat's, though Heat realizes immediately what the significance of her recognition is. When Verloc invites Heat into the back room and tells him the whole grisly truth—"Blown to bits: limbs, gravel, clothing, bones, splinters—all mixed up together. I tell you they had to fetch a shovel to gather him up with" (*SA* 159)—Winnie overhears, and "her contract with existence," as Conrad describes it, "was at an end" (*SA* 189). From now on to the end, where a normal detective novel would show the police closing in on the criminal in some climactic duel, the reader is transfixed by Winnie closing in on the man she now believes to be "a monster" (*SA* 193). The novel ends not with a coda describing the sad satisfaction of Inspector Morse or Kurt Wallander, but with the sinister figure of the Professor.

This is anything but "a simple tale," and Conrad's analysis of the relationship between terror and a society committed to law and liberty (a liberal democracy in the current jargon) reveals the hidden dangers exploited by both foreign governments and the most extreme death-driven nihilist in the book. Both desperately (the right word here) desire the government to abandon the protection of law and order and resort to "force." Then force could meet force on equal terms, and society would no longer enjoy any moral superiority. What I think makes Conrad's novel remarkable is the way he balances this ironic and surreal portrayal of anarchists in London at the turn of the century with a profoundly moving human story. That the marital devotion of Winnie, which was her way of ensuring the safety of her "simple" brother, has been thrown away like "some splendid treasure of jewels, dropped in a dust-bin" (*SA* 161), arouses the reader's intense and passionate indignation in what might otherwise have remained a rather poetic, detached, and ironic (even if accurate) portrayal of society and its enemies. On the contrary, Conrad's description of Winnie's murder of her monstrous husband is more intensely moving than Hardy's account of the after-effects of Tess's murder of Alec. It is so, partly because Conrad makes us share the appalling insensitivity (the word itself seems inadequate) of Verloc's reaction to Stevie's murder and his complete failure even to contemplate its possible effects on Winnie: these allow the reader to build up almost as much anger as Winnie. His single "wooing" word, "Winnie," allows him to misinterpret her movement toward him as part of her "unbroken contract" (*SA* 197); her "leisurely" movements (the word is repeated six times) make it plausible that he can see what is coming to him without "stirring a limb" (*SA* 197), so his idleness finally receives its just deserts. The reader is able to enjoy a full sense of this justice before Winnie commits suicide rather than face the fourteen-foot drop she so vividly imagines: Verloc has got what he deserves, and Ossipon's philandering has been ended, although the assistant commissioner argues that "all that's wanted now is to do away with the agent provocateur to make everything safe" (*SA* 172).

Conrad's novel ends with the greater solitary menace of absolute nihilists. At the end of the novel, the Professor still stalks the streets, where "his thoughts caressed the images of ruin and destruction" (*SA* 231). The word "images" alerts us to the prescience of Conrad's analysis, where terrorists trade not just in blood and limbs but in images of horror; their currency is in images able to produce fear, and the arrival of the internet has enabled them to broadcast these worldwide. The primary targets of this *"act of madness and despair"* (*SA* 231; emphasis added) remain completely innocent victims, chosen because they attract the largest outcry. The blatant nature of the Salisbury attack on Sergei Skripal, like the Litvinenko attack in 2006, reminds us that the Russian government is still more interested in the destabilizing effect than in the poison, whether with polonium or A-234. In the Salisbury attack, as in Conrad's fiction, a completely innocent, and very vulnerable, person died. The poison had been thrown away in a dustbin, and a man believing it to be perfume gave it to his partner: both were living in a drugs hostel.

But I wish to end with what perfectly expresses Conrad's surreal purpose: the two great cab journeys in the streets of London—the assistant commissioner's and Stevie's. In the former case,

> His descent into the street was like the descent into a slimy aquarium from which the water had been run off. A murky, gloomy dampness enveloped him. The walls of the houses were wet, the mud of the roadway glistened with an effect of phosphorescence, and when he emerged into the Strand out of a narrow street by the side of Charing Cross Station, the genius of the locality assimilated him. He might have been but one more of the queer foreign fish that can be seen of an evening about there, flitting round the dark corners. (*SA* 124)

In this subaqueous inferno, the assistant commissioner becomes "a fare" when he boards a hansom cab and slips away "leaving an effect of uncanny, eccentric ghostliness upon the driver's mind" (*SA* 124). Conrad's portrayal of the last journey of Stevie in a cab with his sister talks of the vehicle as "the perfection of grotesque misery and weirdness of macabre detail, as if it were the Cab of Death itself" (*SA* 131). It is in this cab that Stevie enunciates his ideal conception of the police.

Conrad's portrait of an infernal London of ghostly shadows and macabre cabs is the surreal setting for his metaphysical analysis of the relation between society and its enemies (some of whom are officially its friends), an analysis that could seem despairing about human beings if it were not for Winnie and Stevie, who redeem nature from the general curse: society and its institutions turn human beings into things, more like automata than the mechanical piano that plays out the pest-Professor and Comrade Ossipon, whose "brain is pulsating wrongfully to the rhythm of journalistic phrases '... *Will hang for ever over this act ...* ' It [his "revolutionary career"] was inclining towards the gutter. ' ... of *madness or despair*'" (*SA* 231; emphasis added). Ossipon with the "embassy's secret service money (inherited from Mr Verloc) in his pocket" ends the novel "marching in the gutter" and the Professor, "like a pest in the street full of men" (*SA* 231). If Conrad's perception of anarchism, nihilism, and revolutionaries as pestilential parasites, no better than rats in the gutter, seems harsh, it reflects the metaphysical preoccupation at the heart of this novel: the portrayal of evil as negation, not being, the absence of good—"Why this is hell, nor am I out of it," says Mephistopheles in *Doctor Faustus* (Marlowe 1994: III, 74). Conrad's image of London is of a damp, watery hell, where the police keep the anarchists in symbiotic play and fail to recognize how "terrible" the Professor is, "in the simplicity of his idea calling madness and despair to the regeneration of the world" (*SA* 231). By contrast with this death-driven ideology, Winnie's plunge into the icy waters of the Channel, as Ossipon recognizes, comes from "a vigour of vitality, a love of life" in a woman driven by "the fear, the blind, mad fear of the gallows" (*SA* 229), which enables her to escape the structures of a "beastly" society that has failed to protect her and the helpless Stevie.

Acknowledgments

The reprint of this article, first published in the *Yearbook of Conrad Studies (Poland)* 13 (2018): 55–64 under the title "*The Secret Agent*: A Far From Simple Tale," has been made possible courtesy of the Jagiellonian University Publishing House in Kraków, Poland.

References

Frank, Michael C. 2012. "Plots on London: Terrorism in Turn-of-the-Century British Fiction." In *Literature in Terrorism: Comparative Perspectives*, edited by Michael C. Frank and Eva Gruber, 41–65. Amsterdam: Rodopi.

Marlowe, Christopher. [1589–92] 1994. *Doctor Faustus*. Dover Thrift Editions. Mineola, NY: Dover Publications.

Porter, Bernard. 2004. "Sir Robert Anderson (1841–1918)." *Oxford Dictionary of National Biography*. Oxford: Oxford University Press.

Short, K. R. M. 1979. *The Dynamite War: Irish-American Bombers in Victorian Britain*. Dublin: Gill and Macmillan.

Stevenson, Robert Louis, and Fanny Van de Grift Stevenson. [1885] 1924. *More New Arabian Nights: The Dynamiter*. In *The Works of Robert Louis Stevenson*, edited by Tusitala, 2nd imp., vol. 5. London: Heinemann.

Weil, Simone. 1965. "The Iliad or the Poem of Force." Translated by Mary McCarthy. *Chicago Review* 18, no. 2: 5–30.

Notes on Contributors

Agnieszka Adamowicz-Pośpiech is Associate Professor at the University of Silesia, Poland, and vice president of the Joseph Conrad Society, Poland. Her books on modernism and translation studies include *Joseph Conrad: Biographical Debates* (2003), *Lord Jim: Interpretations* (2007), *Retranslations: Polish Variants of Conrad's Prose* (2013), *Travels with Conrad* (2016), and *Adaptations of Conrad's Life and Work in Contemporary Culture* (2022) as well as over ninety articles on Conrad, Harold Pinter, William Golding, Jatinder Verma, G. B. Shaw, and T. S. Eliot. She is on the editorial boards of *The Conradian* and the *Yearbook of Conrad Studies (Poland)*.

Grażyna M. T. Branny is Associate Professor at the Jesuit University Ignatianum in Kraków, Poland. Her books include *A Conflict of Values: Alienation and Commitment in the Novels of Joseph Conrad and William Faulkner* (1997); *Fictions and Metafictions of Evil* (co-edited with Gill J. Holland, 2013); and *Intertextualizing Collective American Memory* (forthcoming). She has published extensively on Conrad, Faulkner, Toni Morrison, Louise Erdrich, and Cormac McCarthy and is currently preparing a book on Conrad's short fiction. She reviews for the *Journal of Literature and Art Studies* (US) and is on the editorial boards of *Journal of Interdisciplinary Philology* (Slovakia) and the *Yearbook of Conrad Studies (Poland)*.

G. W. Stephen Brodsky is Special Lecturer (retired) of Royal Roads Military College, Victoria, Canada. His publications include *Joseph Conrad's Polish Soul* (2017) as well as articles and reviews on Conrad in numerous journals: *Conradiana*, *The Conradian*, *Modern Fiction Studies*, and *The Polish Review*. He has written chapters for two Conrad series: *Conrad: Eastern and Western Perspectives* edited by Wiesław Krajka and *Zwischen Ost und West: Joseph Conrad in Europäischen Gespräch* edited by Elmar Schenkel and Hans-Christian Trepte. His other main interest, the literature of war, is best reflected by his book *Gentleman of the Blade: A Social and Literary History of the British Army since 1960* (1989).

Laurence Davies is Visiting Senior Research Fellow at King's College London, President of the Joseph Conrad Society (UK), and general editor of *The*

Collected Letters of Joseph Conrad. His interests include comparative literature, speculative fiction, and literature and science. He is co-author with Cedric Watts of *Cunninghame Graham: A Critical Biography* (1979) and is currently working on the Oxford Edition of Ford Madox Ford. He has written on Hawthorne, Poe, Kipling, Stevenson, Ford Madox Ford, Gothic hostelries, Guillermo del Toro, Katherine Burdekin, and James Baldwin, his latest contribution being to *Migration, Modernity and Transnationalism in the Work of Joseph Conrad* (2021).

Kazumichi Enokida is Associate Professor at the Institute for Foreign Language Research at Hiroshima University. His research interests are in the fields of transcultural literature, applied linguistics, and media studies. His articles on Conrad have appeared in journals such as *The Conradian* and *Hiroshima Studies in Language and Language Education*.

George Z. Gasyna is Associate Professor of Slavic Languages and Literatures and Comparative and World Literature at the University of Illinois at Urbana-Champaign. He is the author of *Polish, Hybrid, and Otherwise: Exilic Discourse in Joseph Conrad and Witold Gombrowicz* (2011) and editor of *Joseph Conrad's Polish Soul: Realms of Memory and Self* (2016). His articles have appeared in such journals as *Slavic Review*, *The Polish Review*, and *Russian Literature*.

Robert Hampson is Research Fellow at the Institute for English Studies, University of London. He was formerly Professor of Modern Literature at Royal Holloway, University of London. He is the author of *Joseph Conrad: Betrayal and Identity* (1992), *Cross-Cultural Encounters in Conrad's Malay Fiction* (2000), *Conrad's Secrets* (2012), and the critical biography *Joseph Conrad* (2020). His co-edited collections include *Conrad and Theory* (1998), *Conrad and Language* (2016), and *The European Reception of Joseph Conrad* (forthcoming). He is Chair of the Joseph Conrad Society (UK) and is a co-editor of *The Conradian*.

Pei-Wen Clio Kao is Assistant Professor at the Department of Foreign Languages and Literature of National Ilan University, Taiwan. Her research interests relate to Conrad studies, Faulkner studies, and literary modernism. She obtained her PhD from National Chengchi University, Taiwan, in 2015, and was recently a visiting scholar at the Center for Faulkner Studies (at Southeast Missouri State University). She also studied at the University of Connecticut as an exchange student during her PhD program. She has published articles and book chapters on Conrad, William Faulkner, and Virginia Woolf.

Brendan Kavanagh is an interdisciplinary researcher in the fields of modernist literature, environmental humanities, media archaeology, and transcultural literature. He recently obtained his PhD from the University of Cambridge, where he wrote his dissertation on the mediation of ecological consciousness in Conrad, Woolf, and Joyce. He also recently finished research scholarships funded by the Polish-US Fulbright Commission and the Kosciuszko Foundation. His publications include essays on Conrad, Joyce, and Shakespeare.

Gerard Kilroy is Professor of English Literature at the Jesuit University Ignatianum in Kraków, Poland, and Senior Research Fellow of Campion Hall, University of Oxford. His books include *Edmund Campion: Memory and Transcription* (2005), *The Epigrams of Sir John Harington* (2009), and *Edmund Campion: A Scholarly Life* (2015). His edition of Evelyn Waugh's *Edmund Campion* will be published next year.

Ewa Kujawska-Lis is Professor at the Institute of Literary Studies of the University of Warmia and Mazury (Olsztyn, Poland). She specializes in Victorian fiction. Her current interest in theoretical and empirical research on literary translation focuses on early translations of the works of Dickens and Conrad and their contemporary retranslations and refractions. She has published in *The Dickensian, Dickens Quarterly, The Conradian*, and *Conradiana*. Her monograph *Marlow pod polską banderą* [Marlow under the Polish Flag] (2011) is a study of Polish translations featuring Charles Marlow. Her interests also include Conrad's multilingualism and its linguistic effects and thematic representations in his fiction.

Gloria Kwok Kan Lee is Lecturer in East Asian Translation Studies at the School of Oriental and African Studies, University of London. She served as the editor of *New Voices in Translation Studies* and research associate of ARTIS initiatives, and has been a co-organizer of the East Asian Translation Studies conferences since 2014. She has published articles and book chapters on literary translation in modern China and collaborative translation. Her research interests focus on translation discourse and agency in translation practice.

Jakob Lothe is Professor of English Literature at the University of Oslo. His books include *Conrad's Narrative Method* (1989) and *Narrative in Fiction and Film* (2000). He has edited a number of volumes, including *Narrative Ethics* (with Jeremy Hawthorn, 2013), *The Future of Literary Studies* (2017), and *Research and Human Rights* (2020). He is now writing a book titled *Memory and Narrative Ethics: Holocaust Testimony, Fiction, and Film*.

Anne Luyat is Professeur Agrege, Docteur d'Etat at Université d'Avignon. She has also taught at Université de Grenoble and the University of Mumbai. Her books include *Joseph Conrad and the West*, a translation of Jacques Darras's *Les Signes de l'empire* (1982), and *Flight from Certainty: The Dilemma of Identity and*

Exile in the English Speaking World (co-edited with Francine Tolron, 2001). She has contributed chapters to *The Reception of Joseph Conrad in France* (ed. Josiane Paccaud, 2006) and *Early Critical Reception of Joseph Conrad* (ed. Zdzisław Najder, 2008) and published widely on Conrad, Faulkner, Pinter, Maupassant, Wallace Stevens, and Wajdi Mouavad.

Narugopal Mukherjee is Associate Professor of English Literature at Bankura Christian College, Bankura University, West Bengal, India. Outside of Conrad studies, his research areas include post-1950s British literature, American literature, Shakespeare studies, applied linguistics, and gender studies. He has reviewed for a number of leading journals and supervised and reviewed PhD dissertations in India. His articles and book chapters have appeared in internationally renowned journals and presses.

Karol Samsel is Associate Professor at the Chair of Literature of Romanticism of the Faculty of Polish Studies at the University of Warsaw. He works on the issue of Conrad and Polish Romanticism. He is the author of *Norwid—Conrad. Epika w perspektywie modernizmu* [*Norwid—Conrad: Epics in the Modern Perspective*] (2015), *Inwalida intencji. Studia o Norwidzie* [*Paralysis of Intention: Studies in Norwid*] (2017), and *Norwid Gomulickich* [*The Norwid of the Gomulickis*] (2021) and has numerous publications in the *Yearbook of Conrad Studies (Poland)*.

Joanna Skolik is Associate Professor at the University of Opole, Poland. Her research focuses on the Polish reception of Conrad, Conrad's ethics, and the cultural significance of the Polish Borderlands. Together with Zdzisław Najder, she edited the two-volume collection *Polskie zaplecze Josepha Conrada-Korzeniowskiego* [Joseph Conrad-Korzeniowski's Polish Background] (2006). In addition to numerous articles on Conrad, her other publications include *The Ideal of Fidelity in Conrad's Works* (2009).

Index

Page numbers in **bold** indicate main discussions of Conrad's texts in the book.

Lightning Source UK Ltd.
Milton Keynes UK
UKHW020151050123
414861UK00003B/67